OVERWATCH®

TRACER—LONDON CALLING

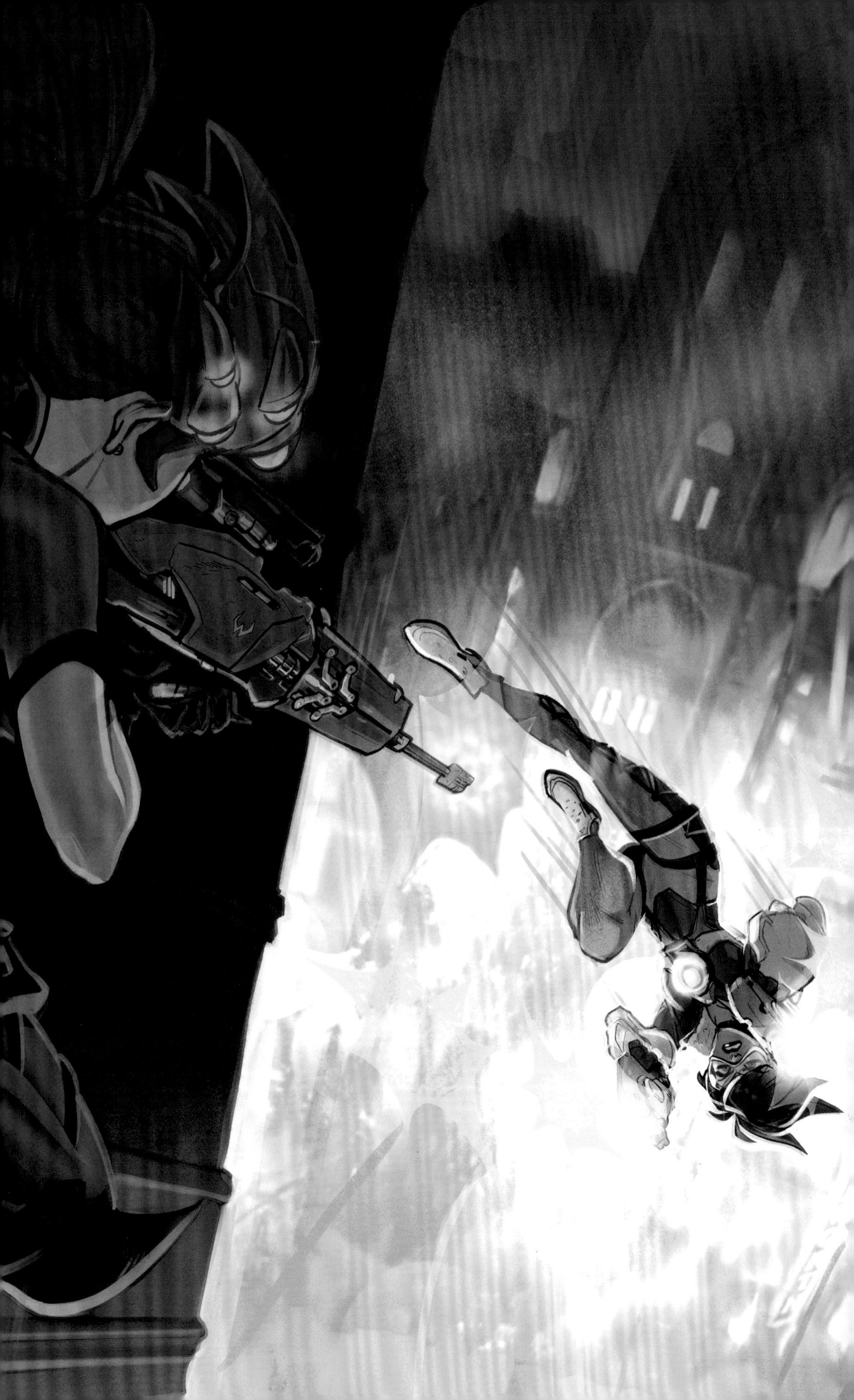

OVERWATCH®

TRACER–LONDON CALLING

WRITER *MARIKO TAMAKI*

ARTIST *BABS TARR*

DRAWING ASSISTANT *HEATHER DANFORTH*

LAYOUT ARTIST *HUNTER CLARK*

COLORIST *RACHAEL COHEN*

LETTERER *DERON BENNETT*

COVER ARTIST *BENGAL*

DARK HORSE BOOKS

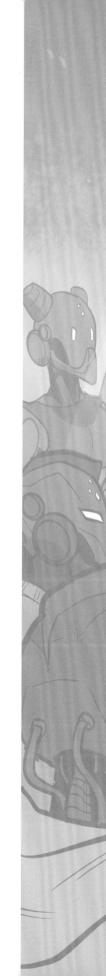

DARK HORSE COMICS

PRESIDENT AND PUBLISHER
MIKE RICHARDSON

SENIOR EDITOR
PHILIP R. SIMON

ASSOCIATE EDITOR
JUDY KHUU

ASSISTANT EDITOR
ROSE WEITZ

DESIGNER
PATRICK SATTERFIELD

DIGITAL ART TECHNICIAN
ALLYSON HALLER

BLIZZARD ENTERTAINMENT EDITORIAL TEAM

LEAD EDITORS
CHLOE FRABONI, PAUL MORRISSEY

PRODUCTION
FELICE HUANG, BRIANNE MESSINA, DEREK ROSENBERG

DIRECTOR, CONSUMER PRODUCTS
BYRON PARNELL

BOOK ART & DESIGN MANAGER
BETSY PETERSCHMIDT

CREATIVE CONSULTATION
JEFF KAPLAN, MICHAEL CHU, JEFF CHAMBERLAIN, ARNOLD TSANG, GEORGE KRSTIC, ALYSSA WONG, SEAN COPELAND, MADI BUCKINGHAM

SPECIAL THANKS TO
DAVID SEEHOLZER

OVERWATCH: TRACER—LONDON CALLING

OVERWATCH® © 2021 Blizzard Entertainment, Inc. All rights reserved. Overwatch is a trademark and Blizzard Entertainment is a trademark and/or registered trademark of Blizzard Entertainment, Inc., in the U.S. and/or other countries. Dark Horse Books® and the Dark Horse logo are trademarks of Dark Horse Comics LLC, registered in various categories and countries. All rights reserved. No portion of this publication may be reproduced or transmitted, in any form or by any means, without the express written permission of Dark Horse Comics LLC. Names, characters, places, and incidents featured in this publication either are the product of the author's imagination or are used fictitiously. Any resemblance to actual persons (living or dead), events, institutions, or locales, without satiric intent, is coincidental.

This volume collects issues #1 through #5 of the Dark Horse Comics series *Overwatch: Tracer—London Calling*, which was initially published digitally from September 2020 to February 2021.

Published by
DARK HORSE BOOKS
A division of Dark Horse Comics LLC
10956 SE Main Street
Milwaukie, OR 97222

To find a comics shop in your area, visit comicshoplocator.com

First edition: September 2021
Ebook ISBN: 978-1-50671-710-4
ISBN: 978-1-50671-709-8

10 9 8 7 6 5 4 3 2 1
Printed in China

Library of Congress Cataloging-in-Publication Data

Names: Tamaki, Mariko, writer. | Tarr, Babs, artist. | Cohen, Rachael, colourist. | Bennett, Deron, letterer.
Title: Overwatch : Tracer--London calling / writer, Mariko Tamaki ; artist, Babs Tarr ; colors, Rachael Cohen ; letters, Deron Bennett ; cover art, Bengal.
Description: First edition. | Milwaukie, OR : Dark Horse Books, 2021. | "This volume collects issues #1-#5 of the Dark Horse comic book series Overwatch: Tracer--London Calling, published December 20202-April 2021." | Summary: "Retired Overwatch hero Tracer tries to ease tensions between humans and omnics surrounding the assassination of a public figure.""-- Provided by publisher.
Identifiers: LCCN 2021009046 | ISBN 9781506717098 (trade paperback)
Subjects: LCSH: Comic books, strips, etc.
Classification: LCC PN6728.0936 T36 2021 | DDC 741.5/973--dc23
LC record available at https://lccn.loc.gov/2021009046

 Blizzard.com

DarkHorse.com   Facebook.com/DarkHorseComics   Twitter.com/DarkHorseComics

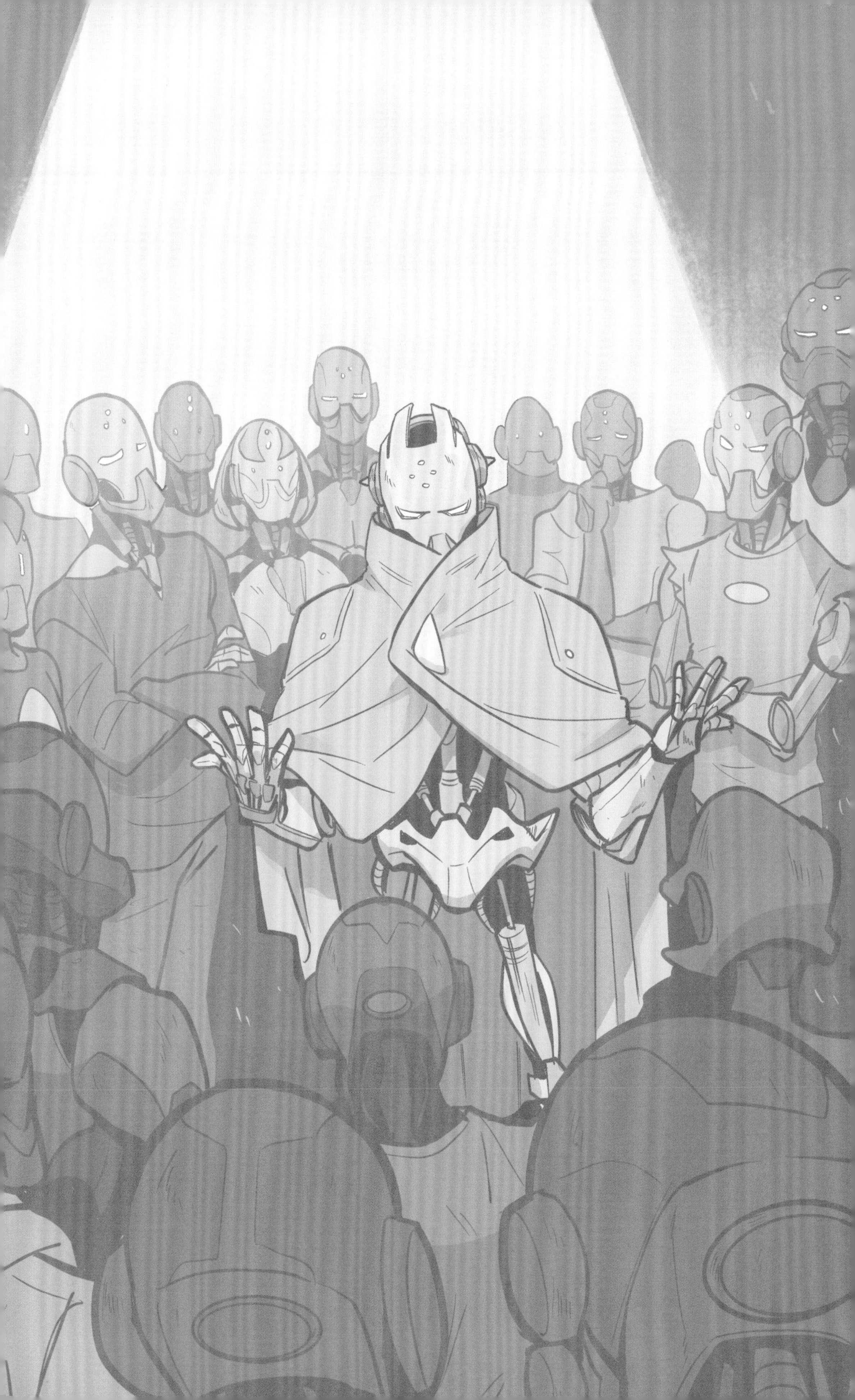

Years after Overwatch has been disbanded, the world finds itself beset by injustice, and vulnerable to self-interested powers. Sentient, intelligent robots called omnics still struggle in the decades since the Omnic Crisis, demanding equality and an end to discrimination against their kind. The world needs heroes again, and heroes often come from unexpected places . . .

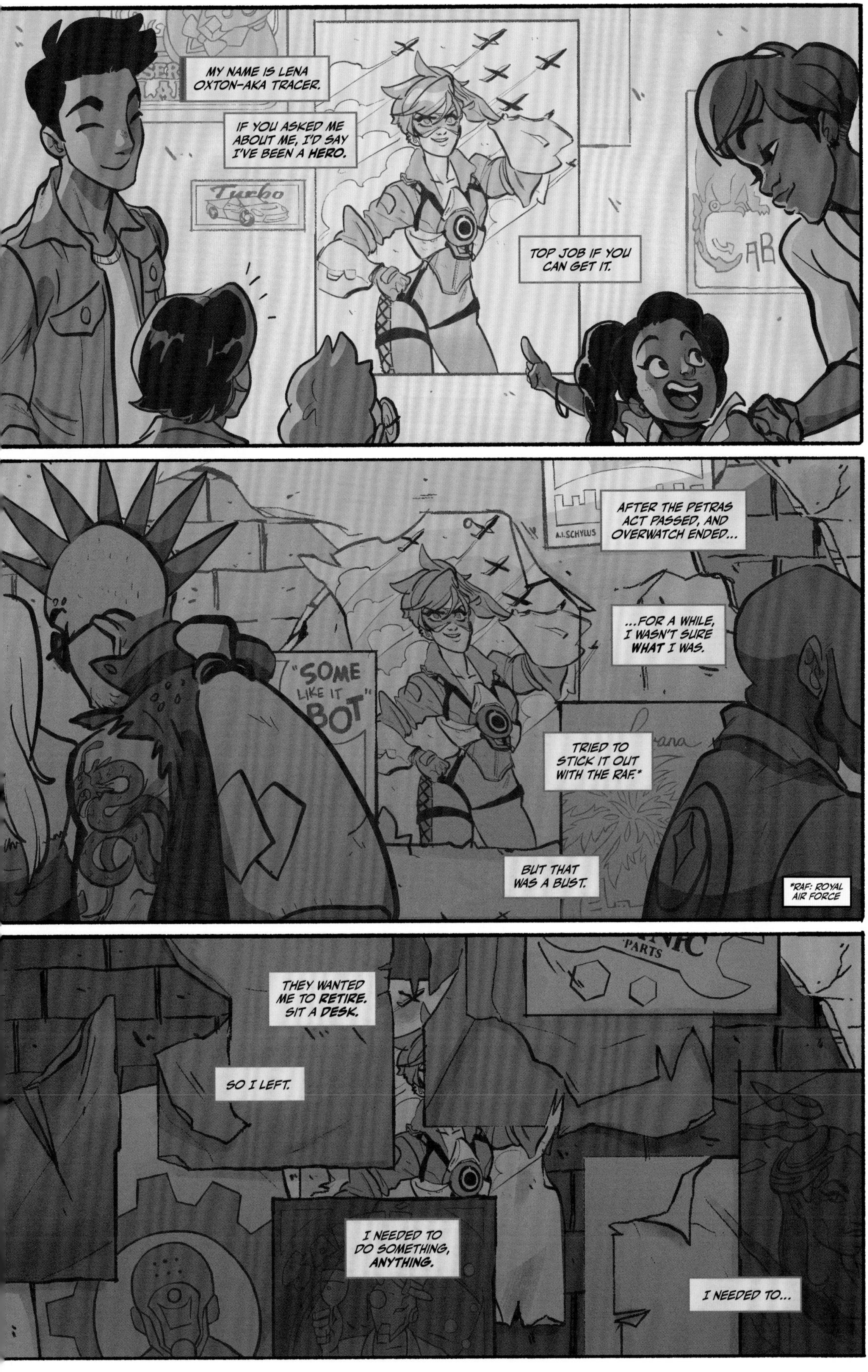
MY NAME IS LENA OXTON—AKA TRACER.
IF YOU ASKED ME ABOUT ME, I'D SAY I'VE BEEN A HERO.
Turbo
TOP JOB IF YOU CAN GET IT.
AFTER THE PETRAS ACT PASSED, AND OVERWATCH ENDED...
A.I. SCHYLUS
...FOR A WHILE, I WASN'T SURE WHAT I WAS.
"SOME LIKE IT BOT"
TRIED TO STICK IT OUT WITH THE RAF.*
BUT THAT WAS A BUST.
*RAF: ROYAL AIR FORCE
PARTS
THEY WANTED ME TO RETIRE. SIT A DESK.
SO I LEFT.
I NEEDED TO DO SOMETHING, ANYTHING.
I NEEDED TO...

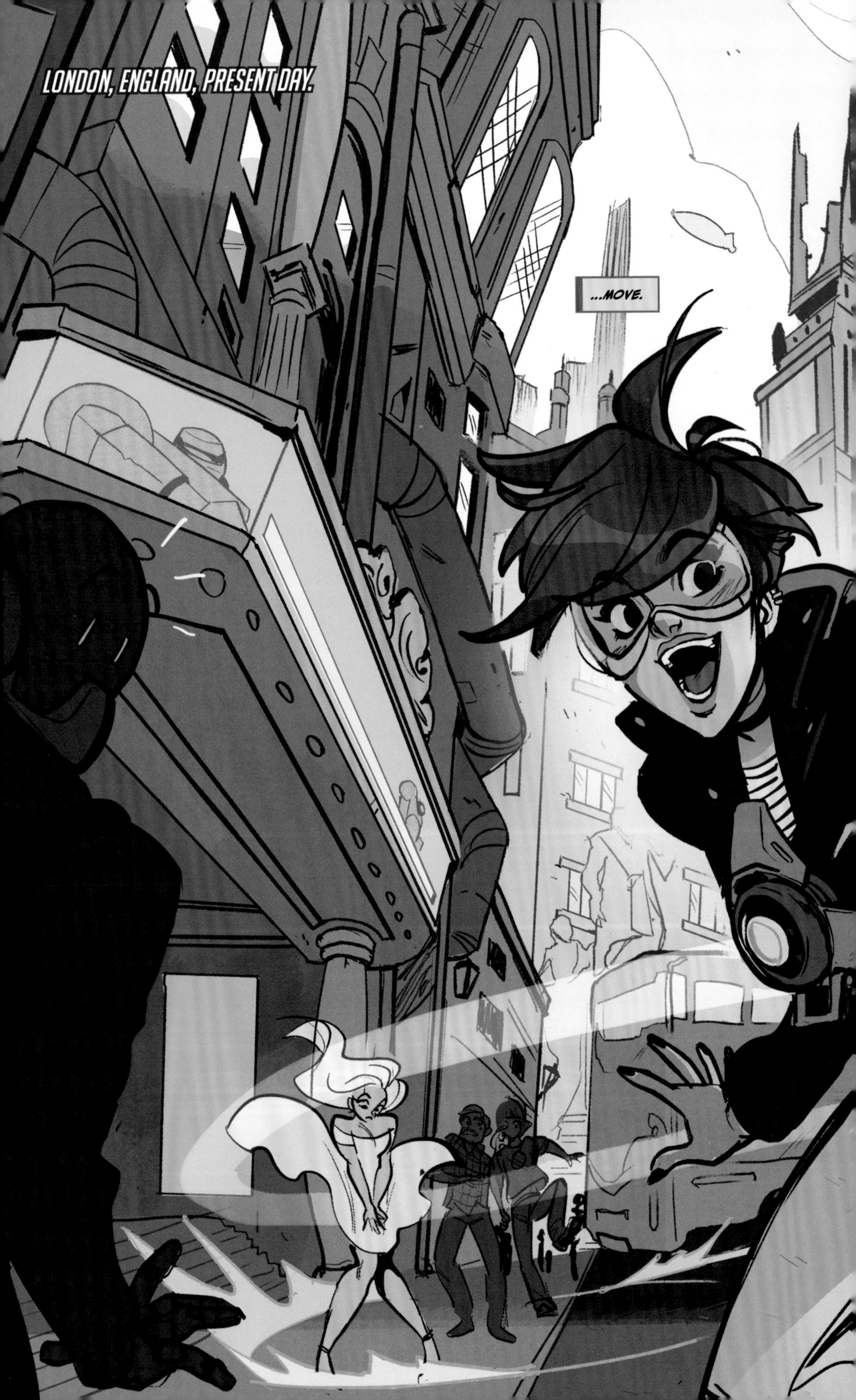
LONDON, ENGLAND, PRESENT DAY.
...MOVE.

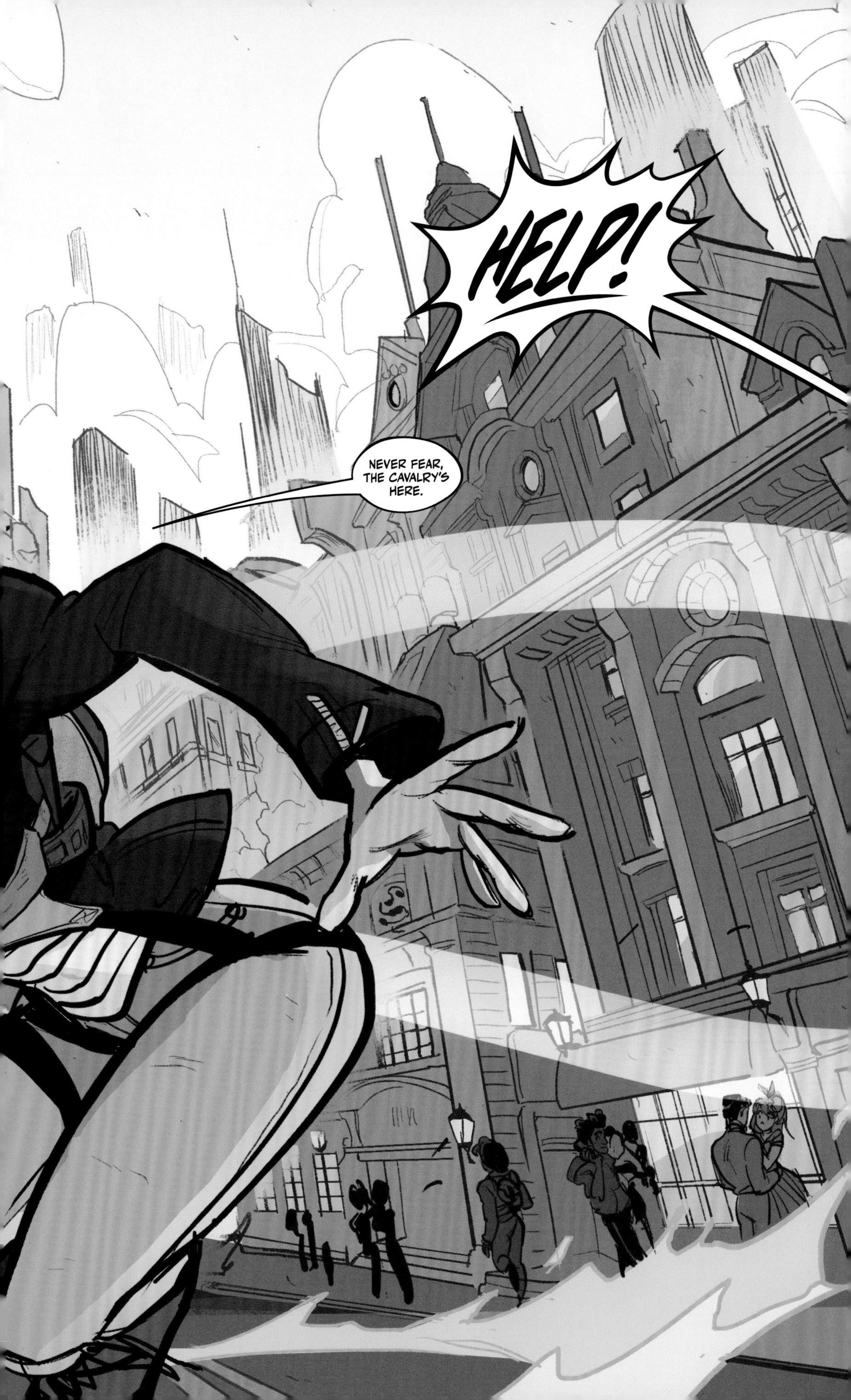
HELP!
NEVER FEAR, THE CAVALRY'S HERE.

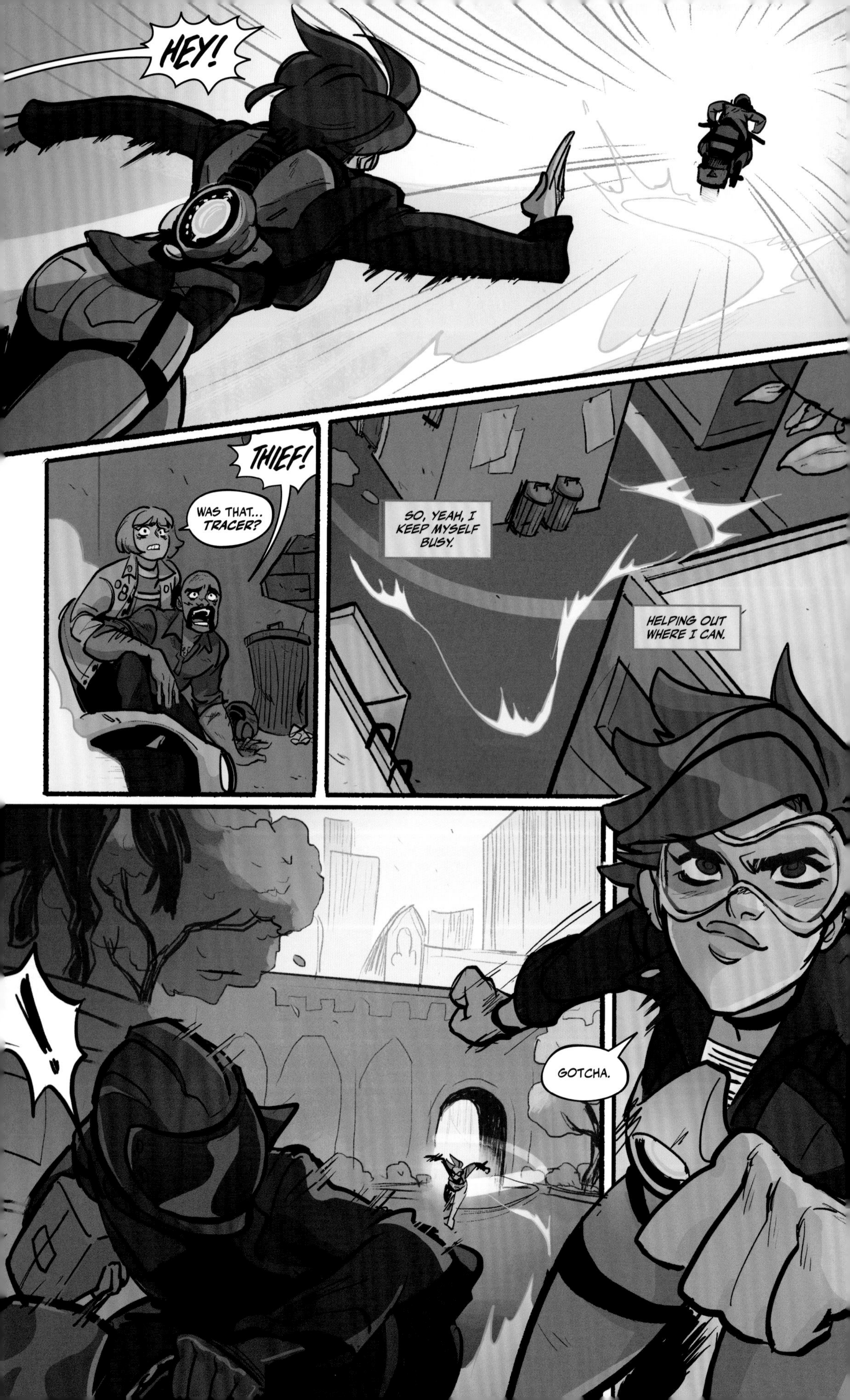
HEY!
THIEF!
WAS THAT... TRACER?
SO, YEAH, I KEEP MYSELF BUSY.
HELPING OUT WHERE I CAN.
!
GOTCHA.

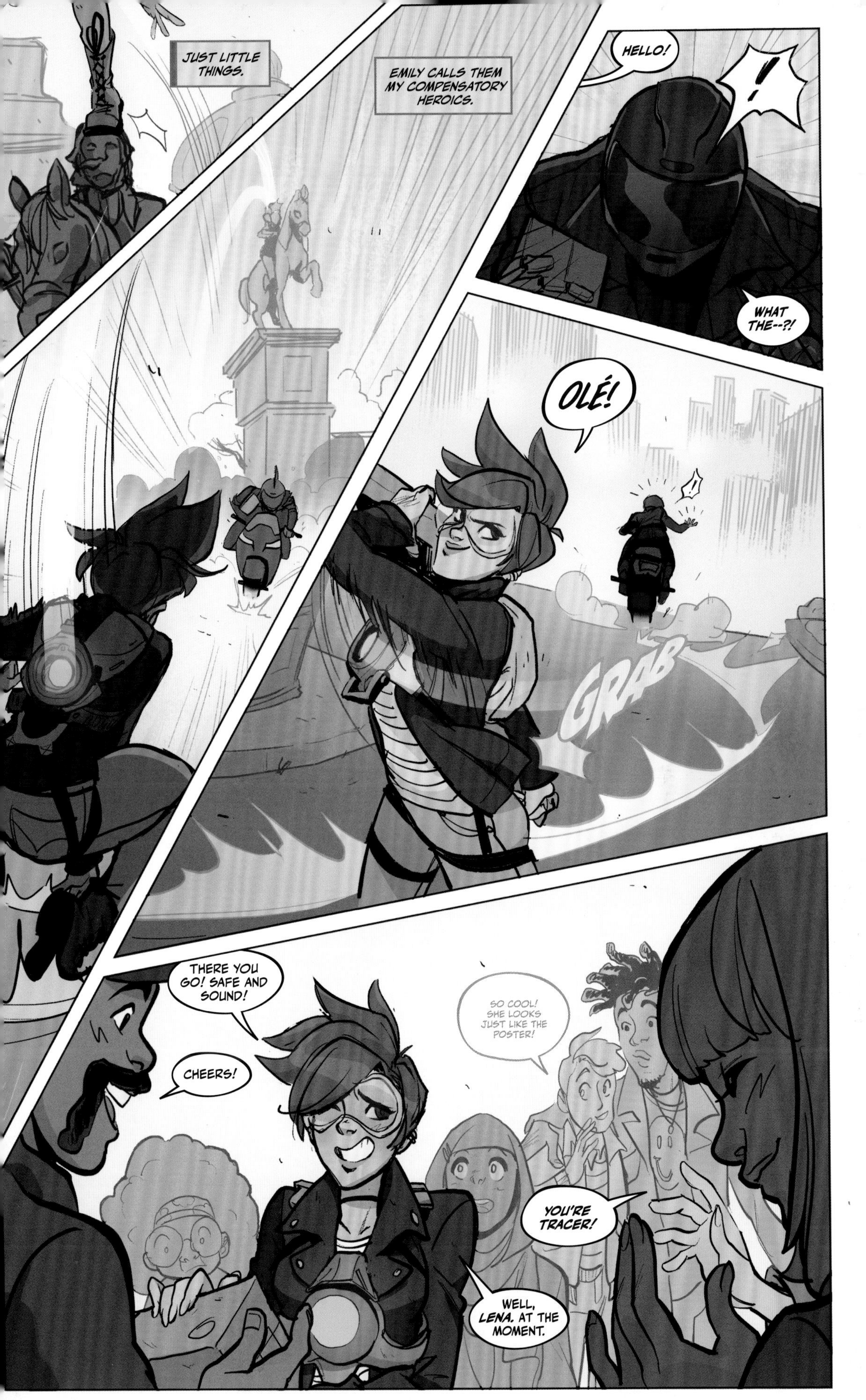
JUST LITTLE THINGS.
EMILY CALLS THEM MY COMPENSATORY HEROICS.
HELLO!
!
WHAT THE--?!
OLÉ!
!
GRAB
THERE YOU GO! SAFE AND SOUND!
CHEERS!
SO COOL! SHE LOOKS JUST LIKE THE POSTER!
YOU'RE TRACER!
WELL, LENA, AT THE MOMENT.

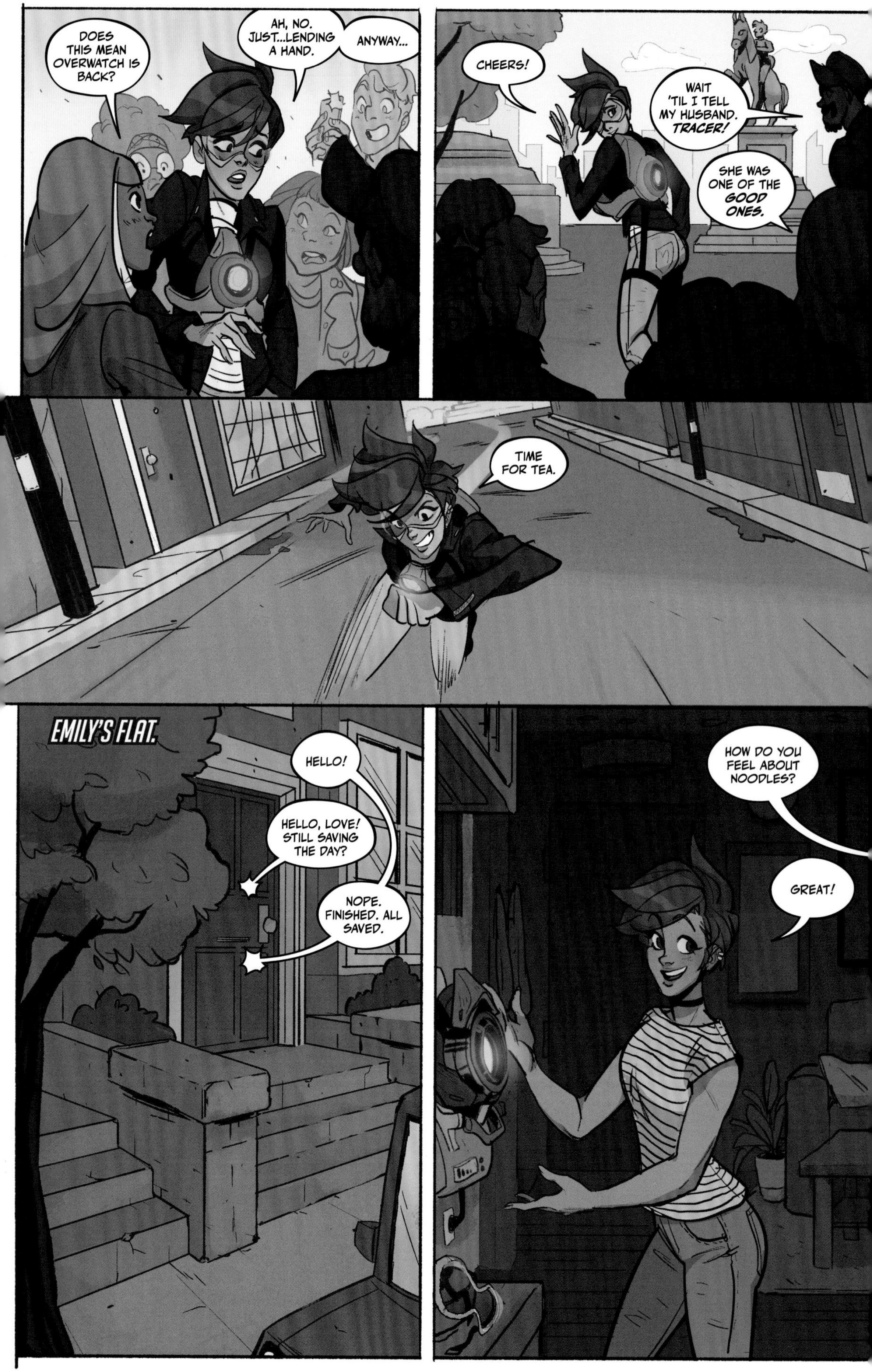
DOES THIS MEAN OVERWATCH IS BACK?
AH, NO. JUST...LENDING A HAND.
ANYWAY...
CHEERS!
WAIT 'TIL I TELL MY HUSBAND. TRACER!
SHE WAS ONE OF THE GOOD ONES.
TIME FOR TEA.
EMILY'S FLAT.
HELLO!
HELLO, LOVE! STILL SAVING THE DAY?
NOPE. FINISHED. ALL SAVED.
HOW DO YOU FEEL ABOUT NOODLES?
GREAT!

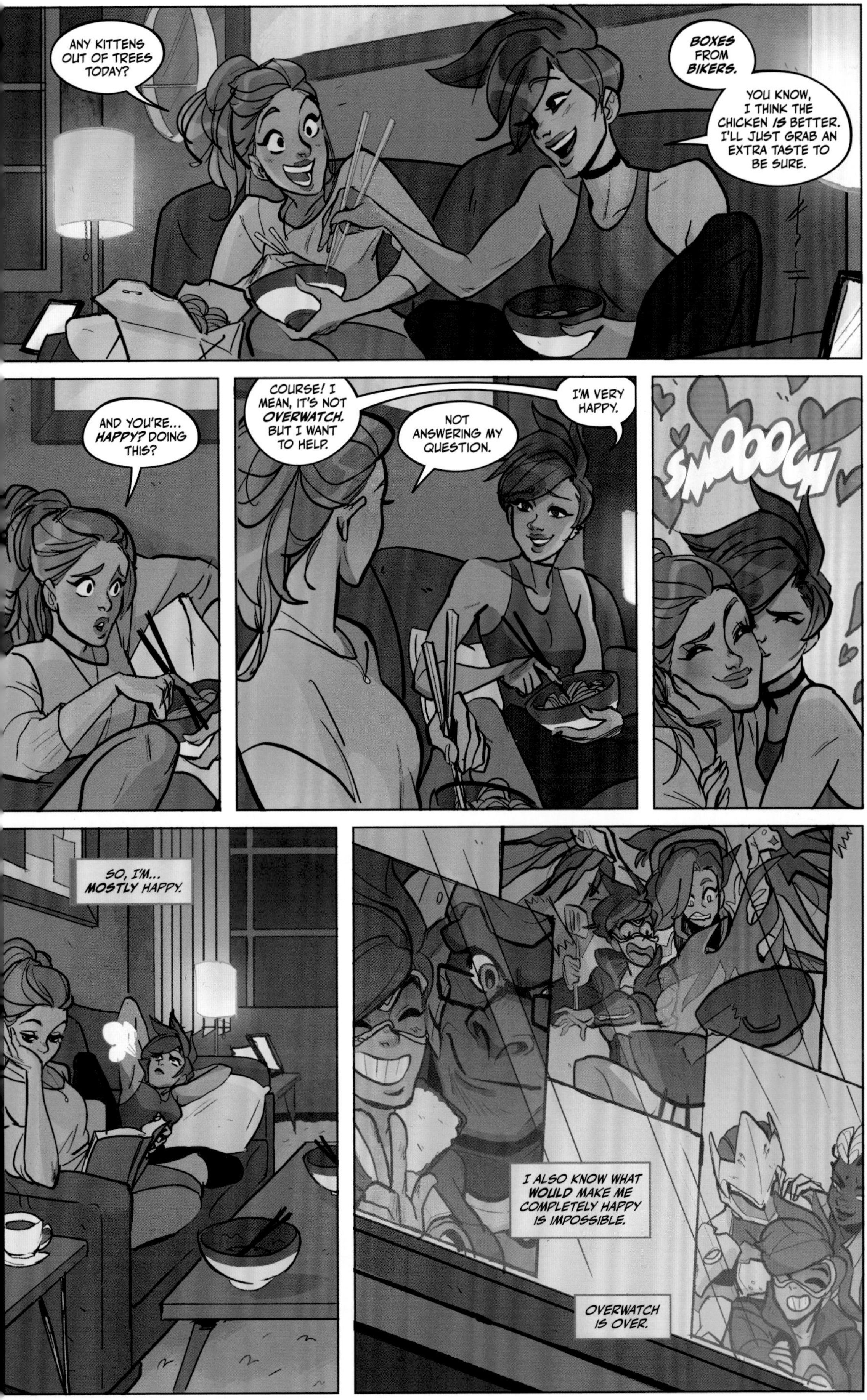
ANY KITTENS OUT OF TREES TODAY?
BOXES FROM BIKERS.
YOU KNOW, I THINK THE CHICKEN IS BETTER. I'LL JUST GRAB AN EXTRA TASTE TO BE SURE.
AND YOU'RE... HAPPY? DOING THIS?
COURSE! I MEAN, IT'S NOT OVERWATCH. BUT I WANT TO HELP.
NOT ANSWERING MY QUESTION.
I'M VERY HAPPY.
SMOOOCH
SO, I'M... MOSTLY HAPPY.
I ALSO KNOW WHAT WOULD MAKE ME COMPLETELY HAPPY IS IMPOSSIBLE.
OVERWATCH IS OVER.

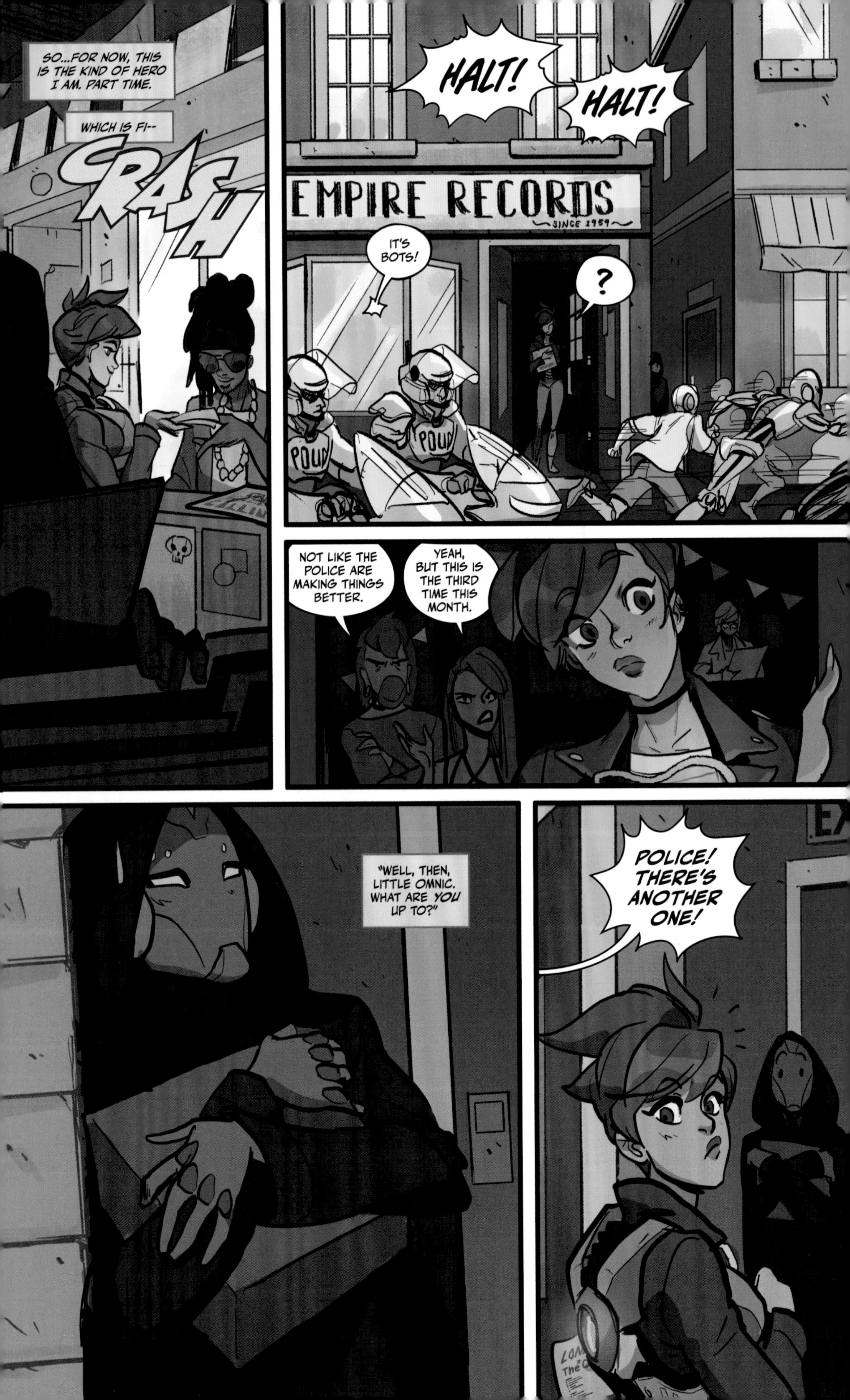
SO...FOR NOW, THIS IS THE KIND OF HERO I AM. PART TIME.
WHICH IS FI--
CRASH
HALT!
HALT!
EMPIRE RECORDS
SINCE 1959
IT'S BOTS!
?
POLICE
POLICE
NOT LIKE THE POLICE ARE MAKING THINGS BETTER.
YEAH, BUT THIS IS THE THIRD TIME THIS MONTH.
"WELL, THEN, LITTLE OMNIC. WHAT ARE *YOU* UP TO?"
POLICE! THERE'S ANOTHER ONE!

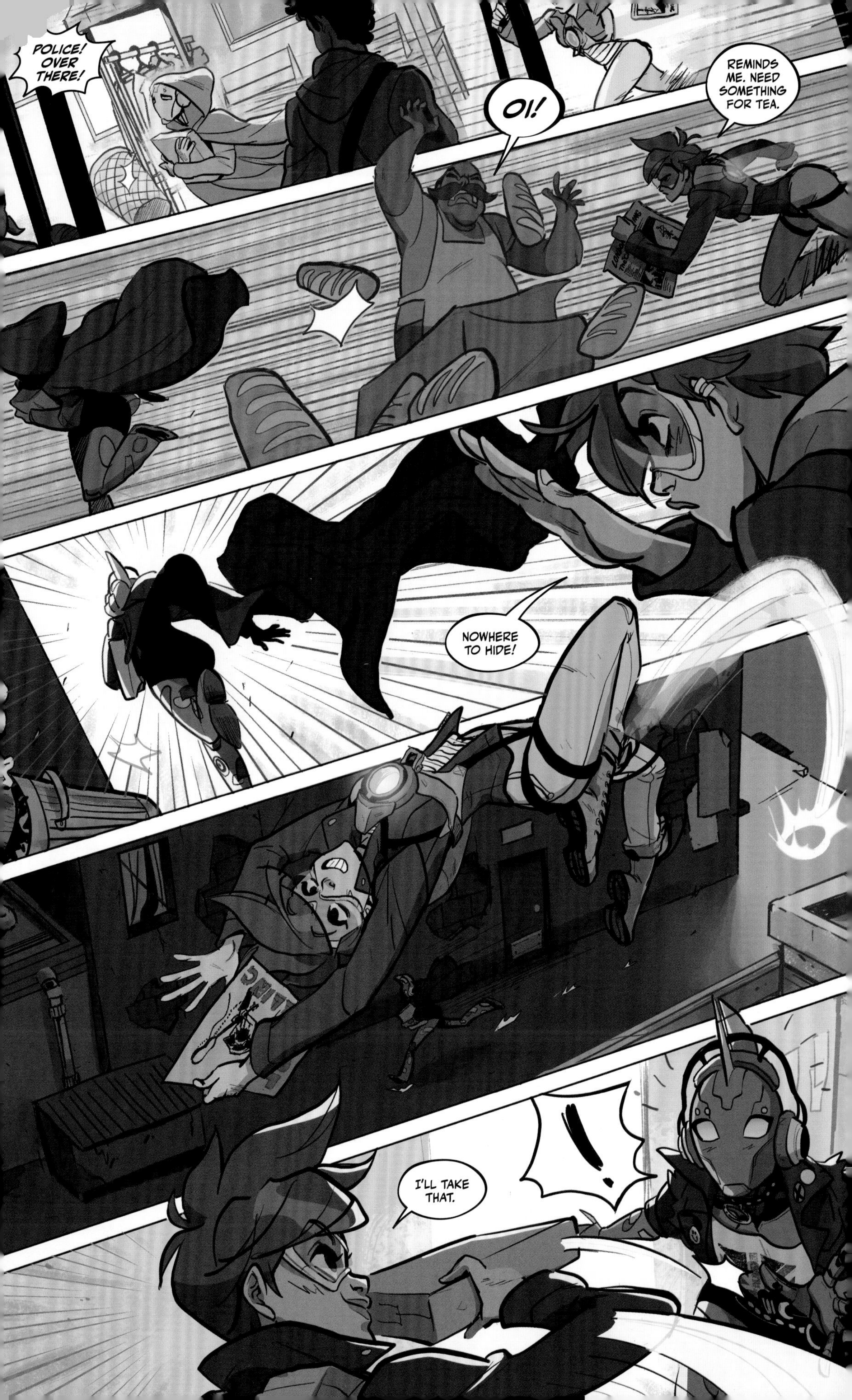
POLICE! OVER THERE!
OI!
REMINDS ME. NEED SOMETHING FOR TEA.
NOWHERE TO HIDE!
!
I'LL TAKE THAT.

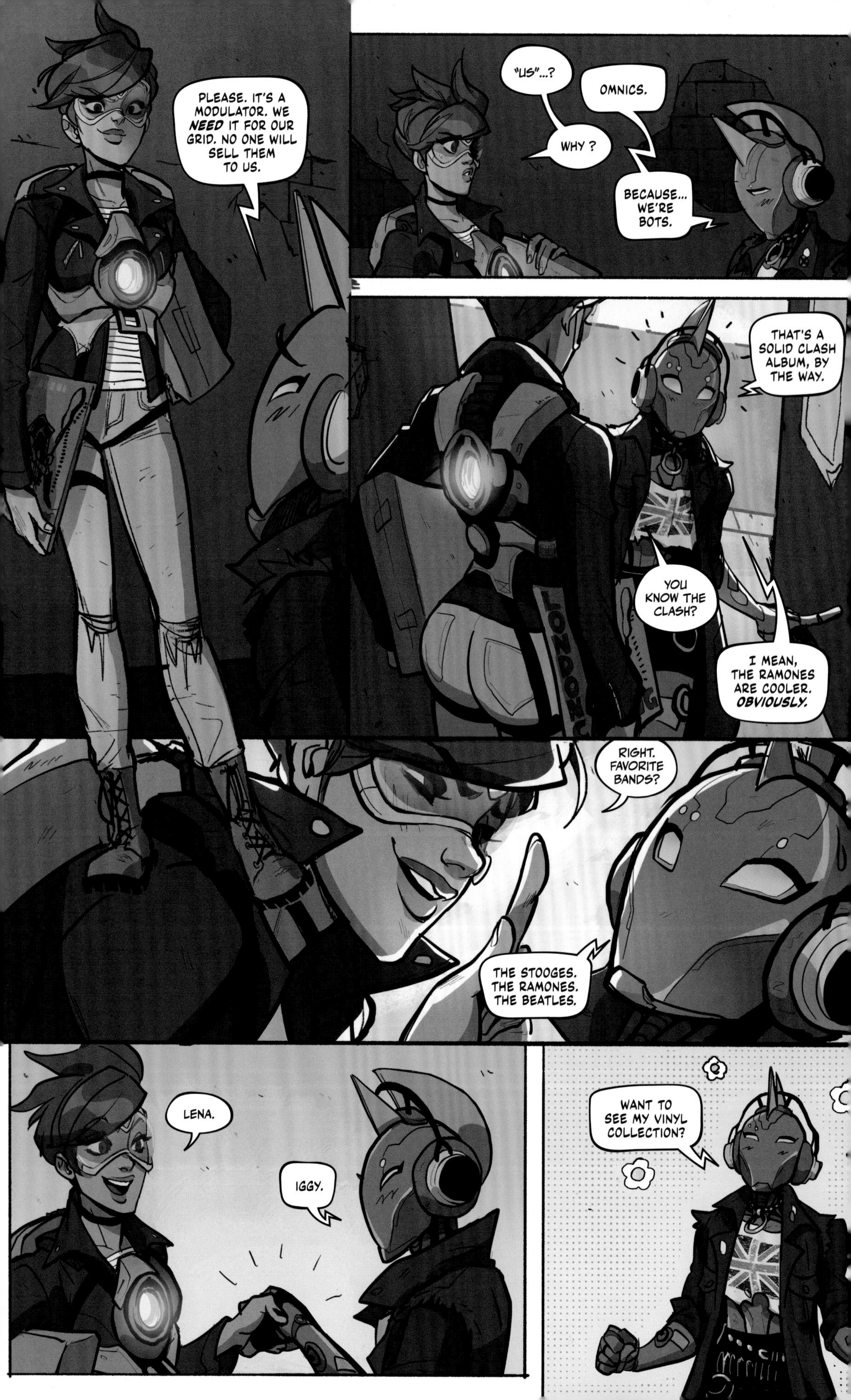
PLEASE. IT'S A MODULATOR. WE *NEED* IT FOR OUR GRID. NO ONE WILL SELL THEM TO US.
"US"...?
OMNICS.
WHY ?
BECAUSE... WE'RE BOTS.
THAT'S A SOLID CLASH ALBUM, BY THE WAY.
YOU KNOW THE CLASH?
I MEAN, THE RAMONES ARE COOLER. *OBVIOUSLY.*
RIGHT. FAVORITE BANDS?
THE STOOGES. THE RAMONES. THE BEATLES.
LENA.
IGGY.
WANT TO SEE MY VINYL COLLECTION?
LONDON

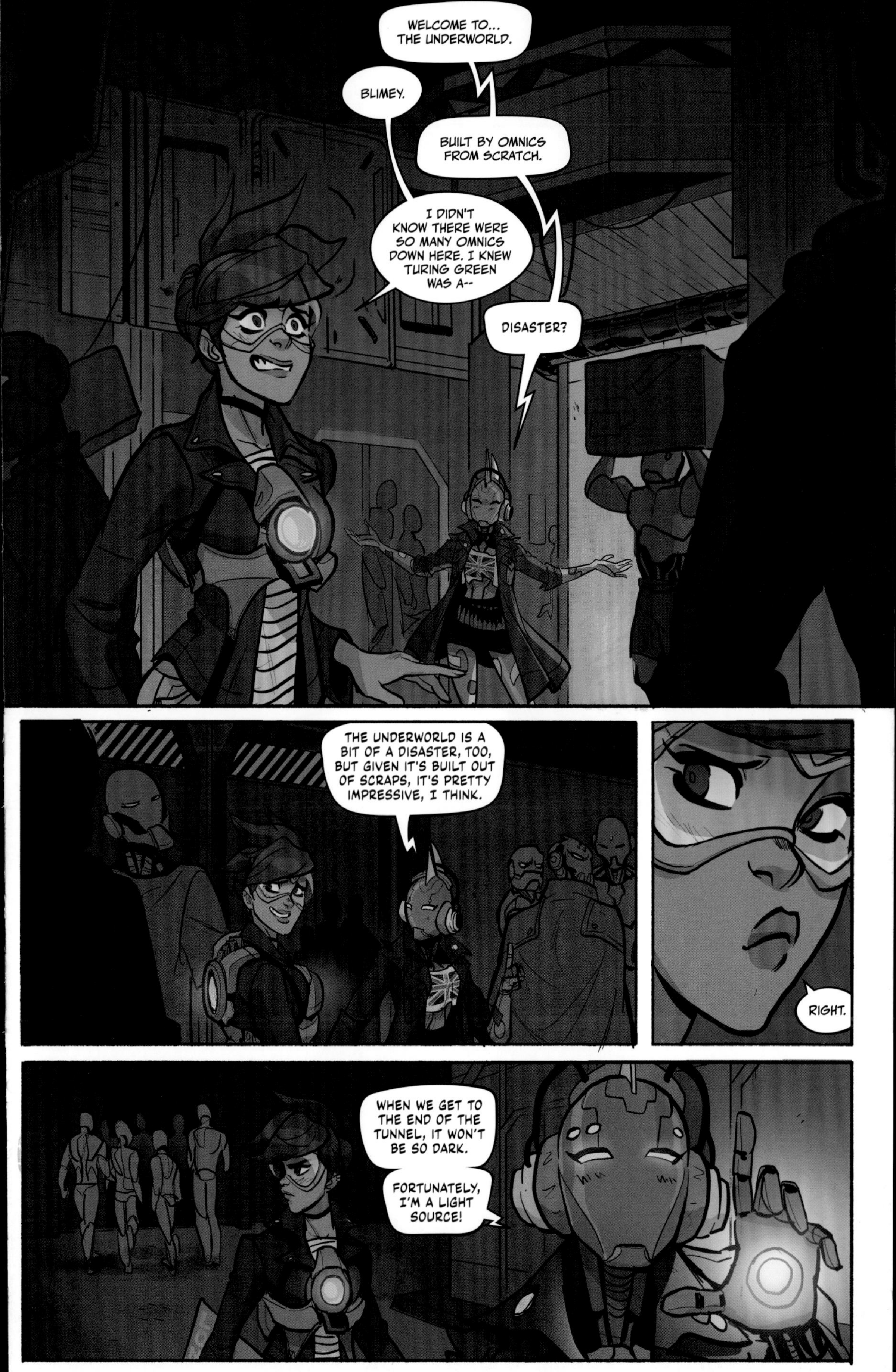
WELCOME TO... THE UNDERWORLD.
BLIMEY.
BUILT BY OMNICS FROM SCRATCH.
I DIDN'T KNOW THERE WERE SO MANY OMNICS DOWN HERE. I KNEW TURING GREEN WAS A--
DISASTER?
THE UNDERWORLD IS A BIT OF A DISASTER, TOO, BUT GIVEN IT'S BUILT OUT OF SCRAPS, IT'S PRETTY IMPRESSIVE, I THINK.
RIGHT.
WHEN WE GET TO THE END OF THE TUNNEL, IT WON'T BE SO DARK.
FORTUNATELY, I'M A LIGHT SOURCE!

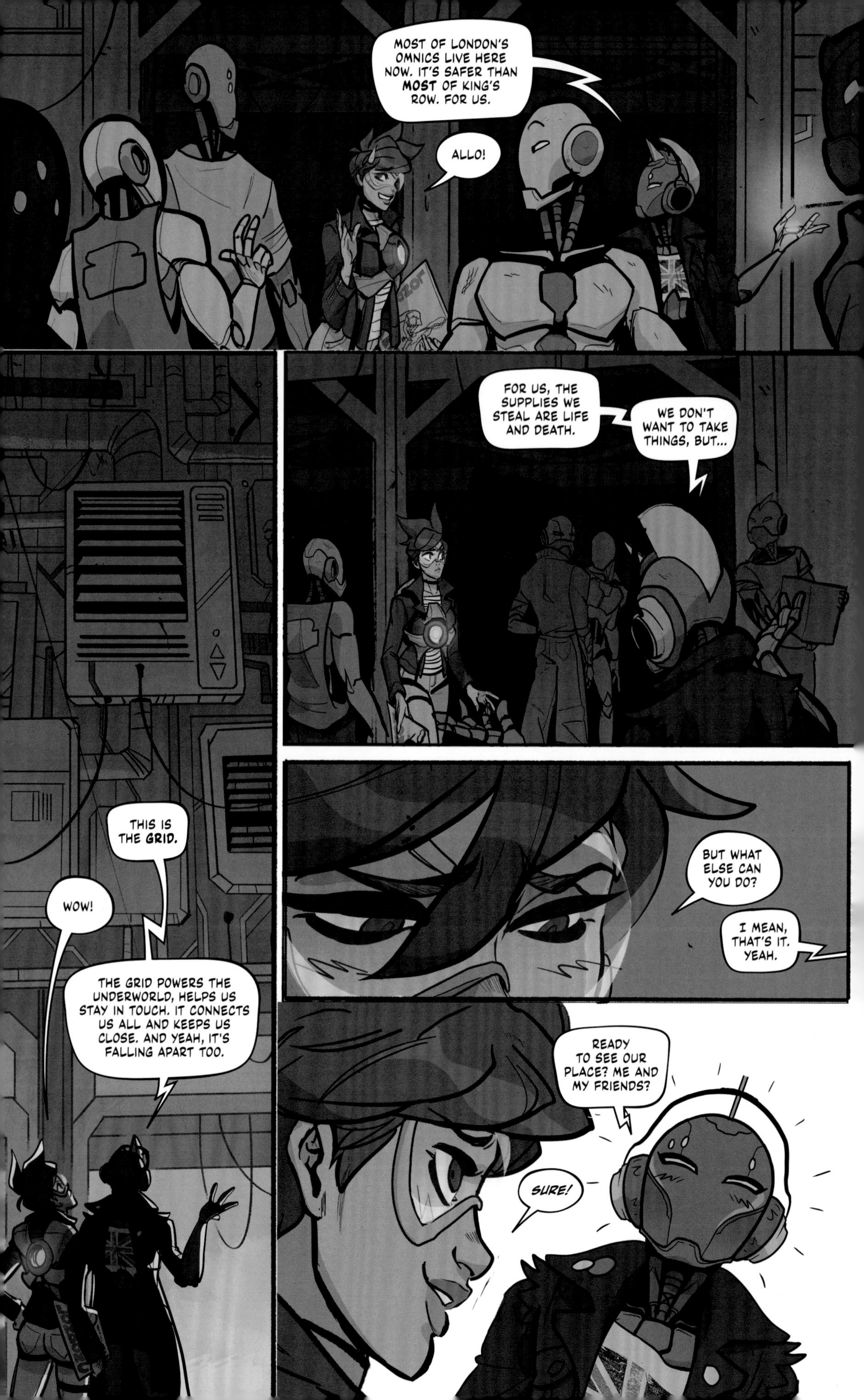
MOST OF LONDON'S OMNICS LIVE HERE NOW. IT'S SAFER THAN MOST OF KING'S ROW. FOR US.
ALLO!
FOR US, THE SUPPLIES WE STEAL ARE LIFE AND DEATH.
WE DON'T WANT TO TAKE THINGS, BUT...
THIS IS THE GRID.
WOW!
THE GRID POWERS THE UNDERWORLD, HELPS US STAY IN TOUCH. IT CONNECTS US ALL AND KEEPS US CLOSE. AND YEAH, IT'S FALLING APART TOO.
BUT WHAT ELSE CAN YOU DO?
I MEAN, THAT'S IT. YEAH.
READY TO SEE OUR PLACE? ME AND MY FRIENDS?
SURE!

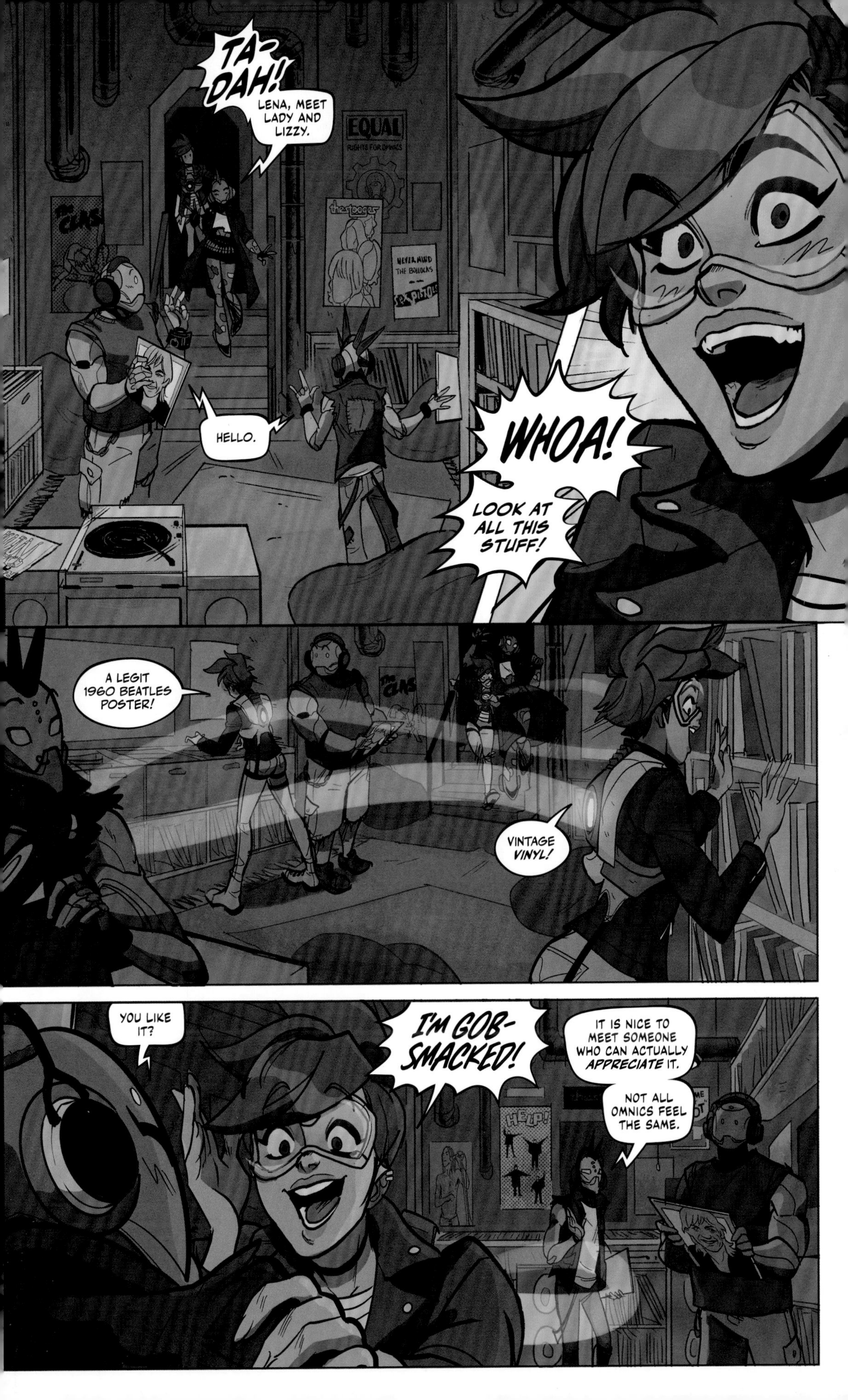
TA-DAH!
LENA, MEET LADY AND LIZZY.
EQUAL
RIGHTS FOR OMNICS
HELLO.
WHOA!
LOOK AT ALL THIS STUFF!
A LEGIT 1960 BEATLES POSTER!
VINTAGE VINYL!
YOU LIKE IT?
I'M GOB-SMACKED!
IT IS NICE TO MEET SOMEONE WHO CAN ACTUALLY APPRECIATE IT.
NOT ALL OMNICS FEEL THE SAME.
HELP!

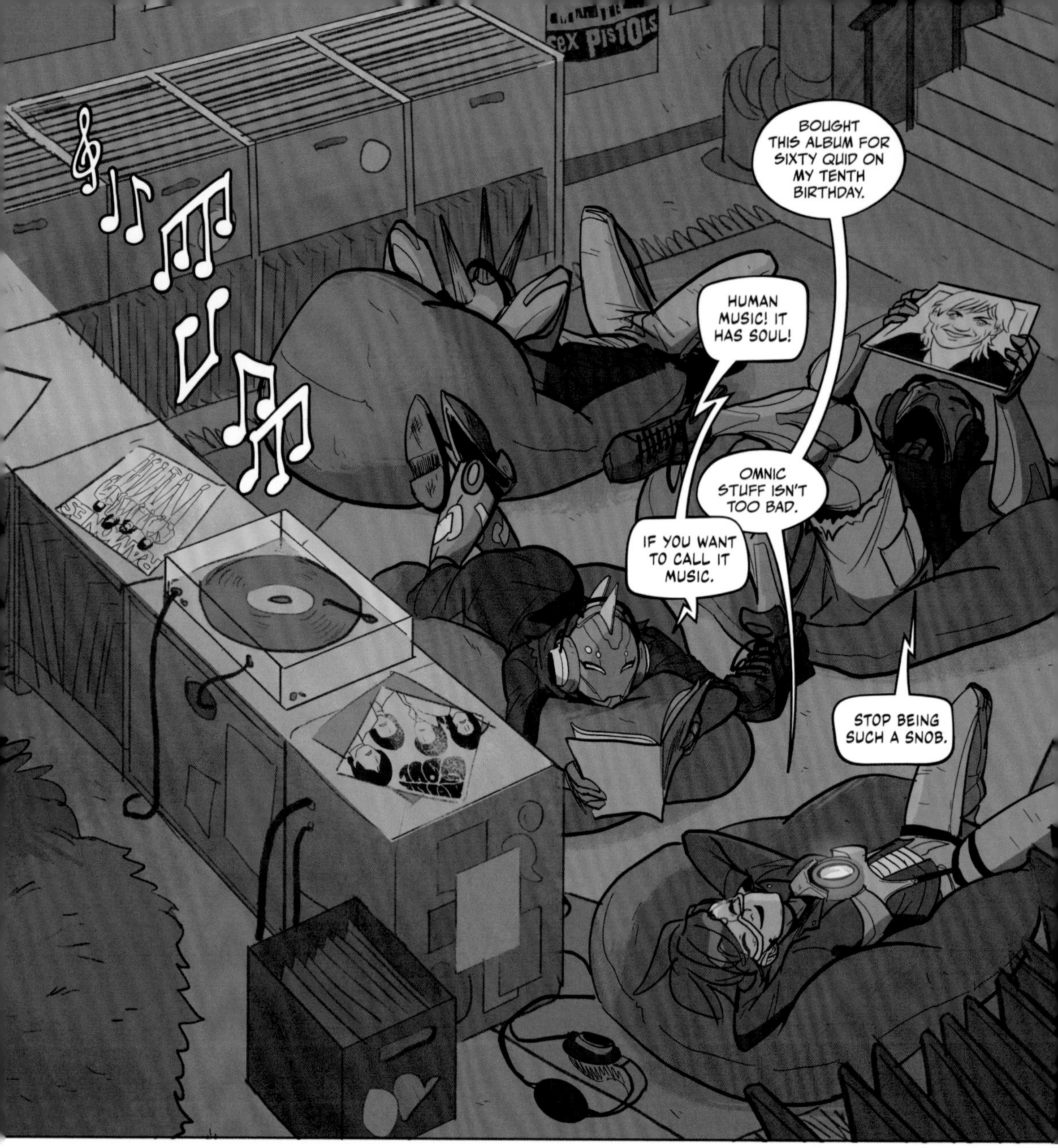
SEX PISTOLS
BOUGHT THIS ALBUM FOR SIXTY QUID ON MY TENTH BIRTHDAY.
HUMAN MUSIC! IT HAS SOUL!
OMNIC STUFF ISN'T TOO BAD.
IF YOU WANT TO CALL IT MUSIC.
STOP BEING SUCH A SNOB.

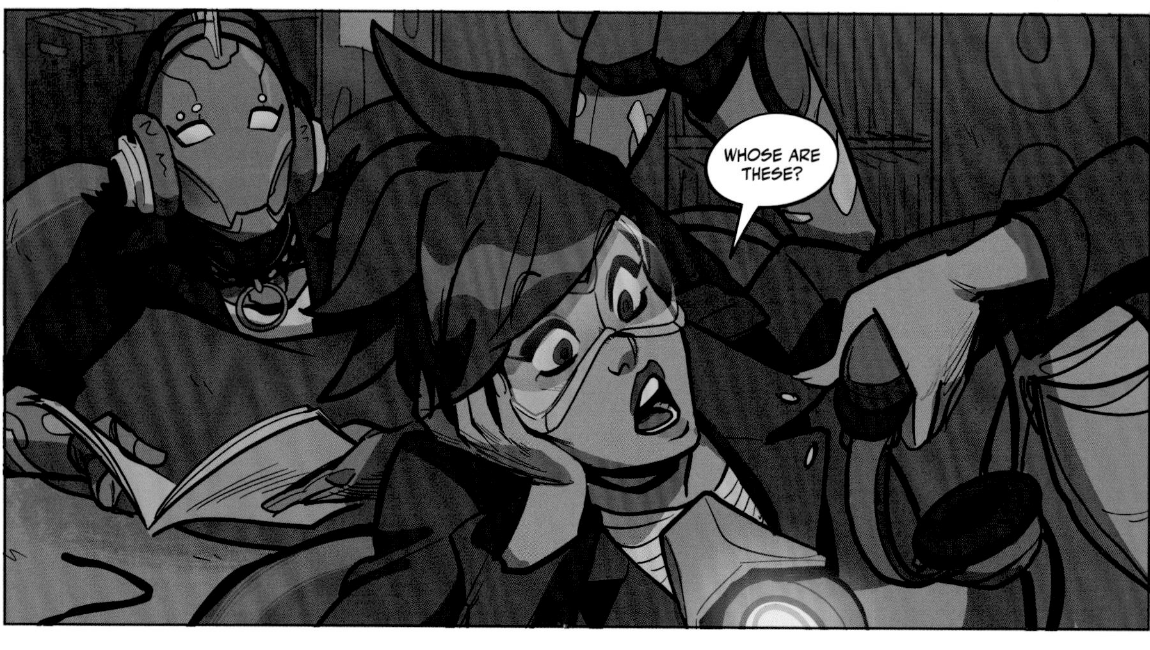
WHOSE ARE THESE?

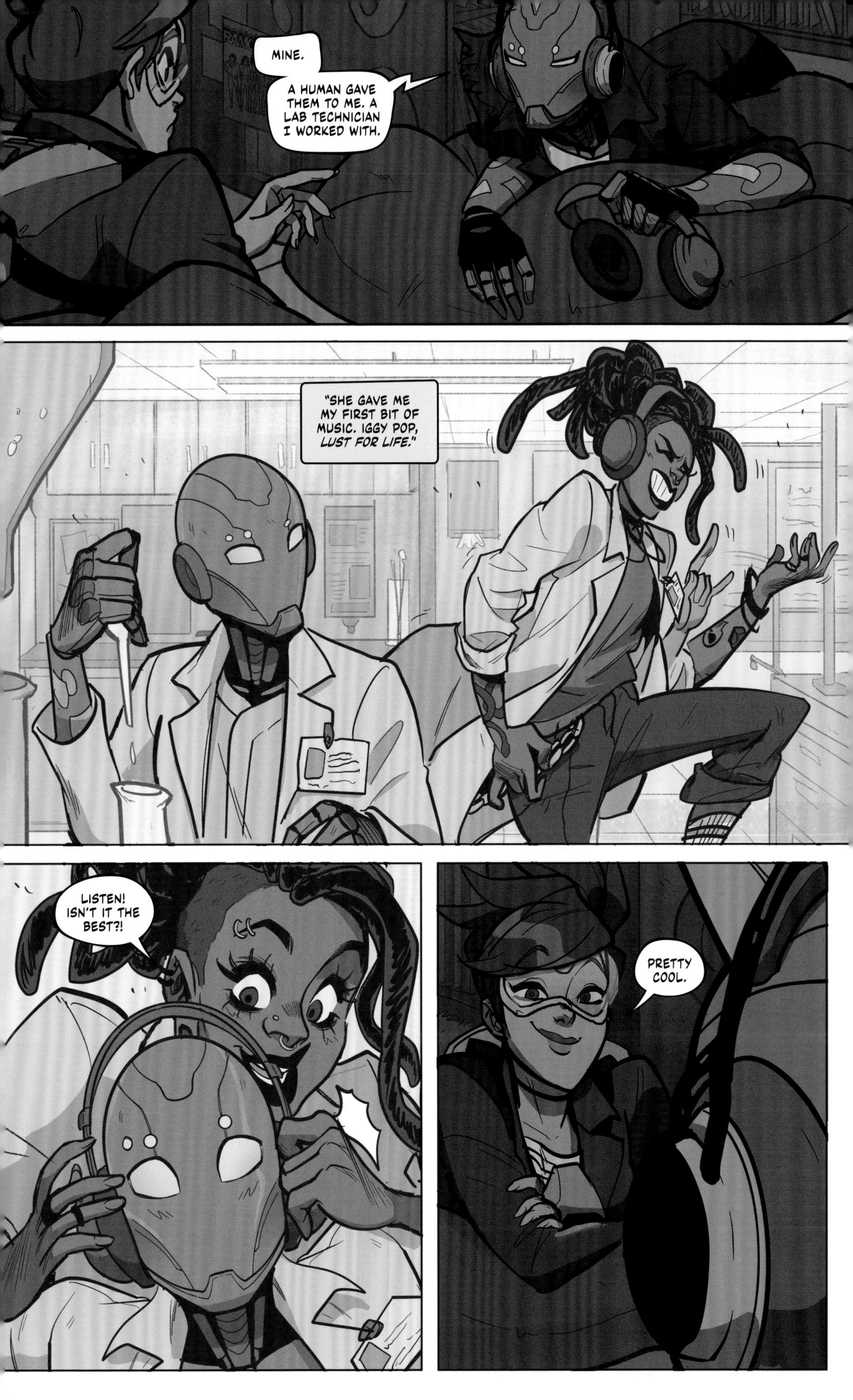
MINE.
A HUMAN GAVE THEM TO ME. A LAB TECHNICIAN I WORKED WITH.
"SHE GAVE ME MY FIRST BIT OF MUSIC. IGGY POP, *LUST FOR LIFE.*"
LISTEN! ISN'T IT THE BEST?!
PRETTY COOL.

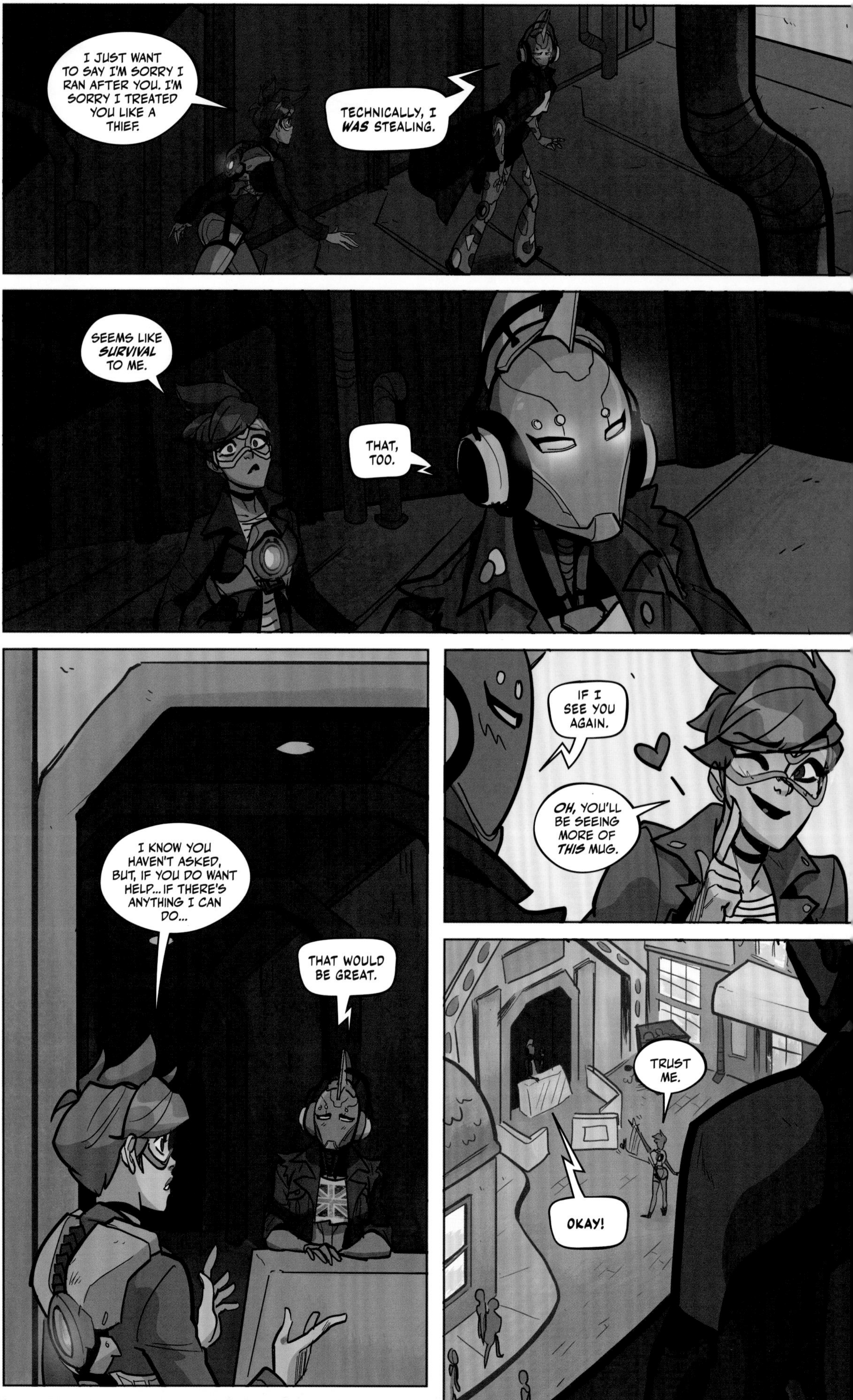
I JUST WANT TO SAY I'M SORRY I RAN AFTER YOU. I'M SORRY I TREATED YOU LIKE A THIEF.
TECHNICALLY, I *WAS* STEALING.
SEEMS LIKE *SURVIVAL* TO ME.
THAT, TOO.
I KNOW YOU HAVEN'T ASKED, BUT, IF YOU DO WANT HELP... IF THERE'S ANYTHING I CAN DO...
THAT WOULD BE GREAT.
IF I SEE YOU AGAIN.
OH, YOU'LL BE SEEING MORE OF *THIS* MUG.
TRUST ME.
OKAY!

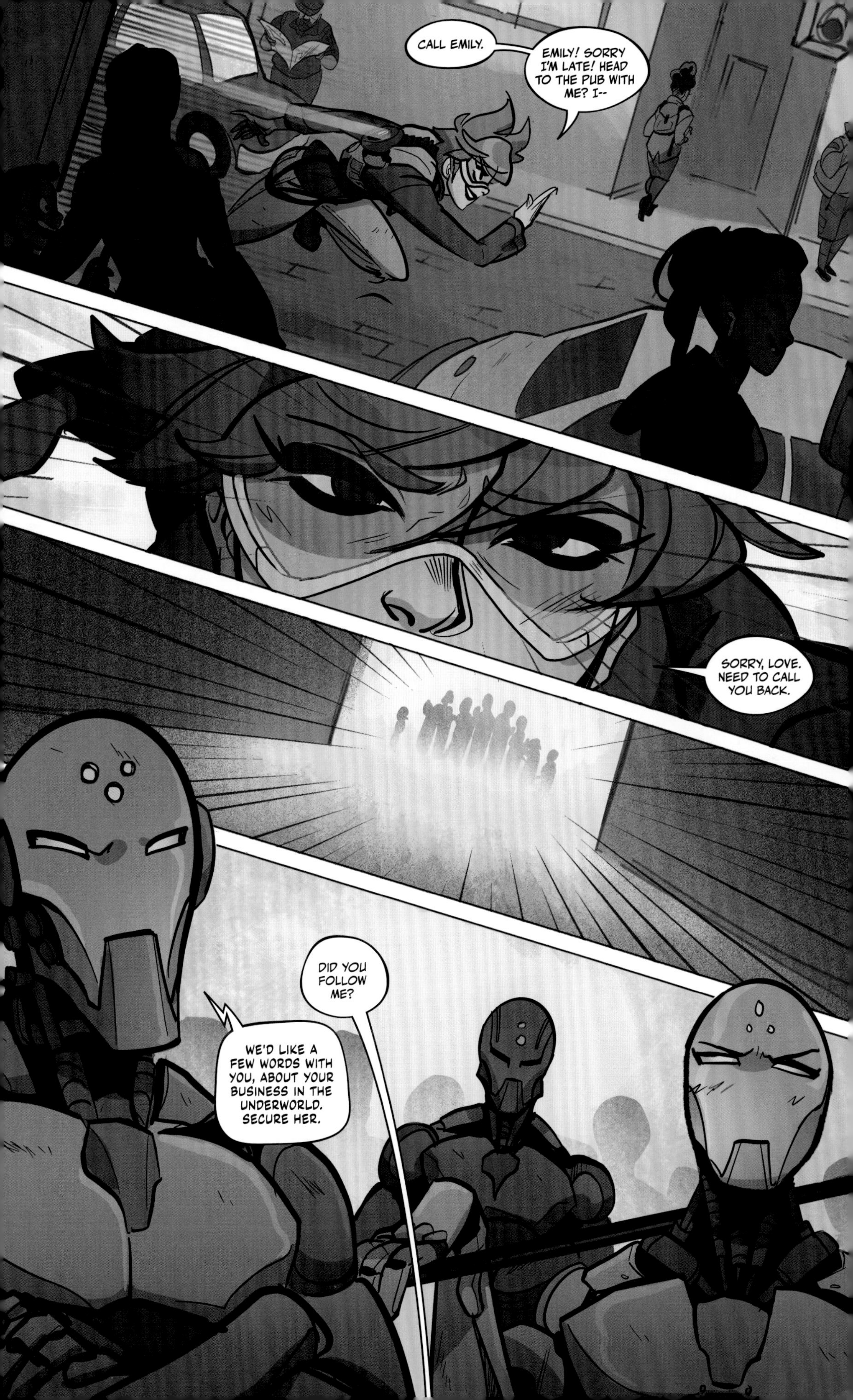
CALL EMILY.
EMILY! SORRY I'M LATE! HEAD TO THE PUB WITH ME? I--
SORRY, LOVE. NEED TO CALL YOU BACK.
DID YOU FOLLOW ME?
WE'D LIKE A FEW WORDS WITH YOU, ABOUT YOUR BUSINESS IN THE UNDERWORLD. SECURE HER.

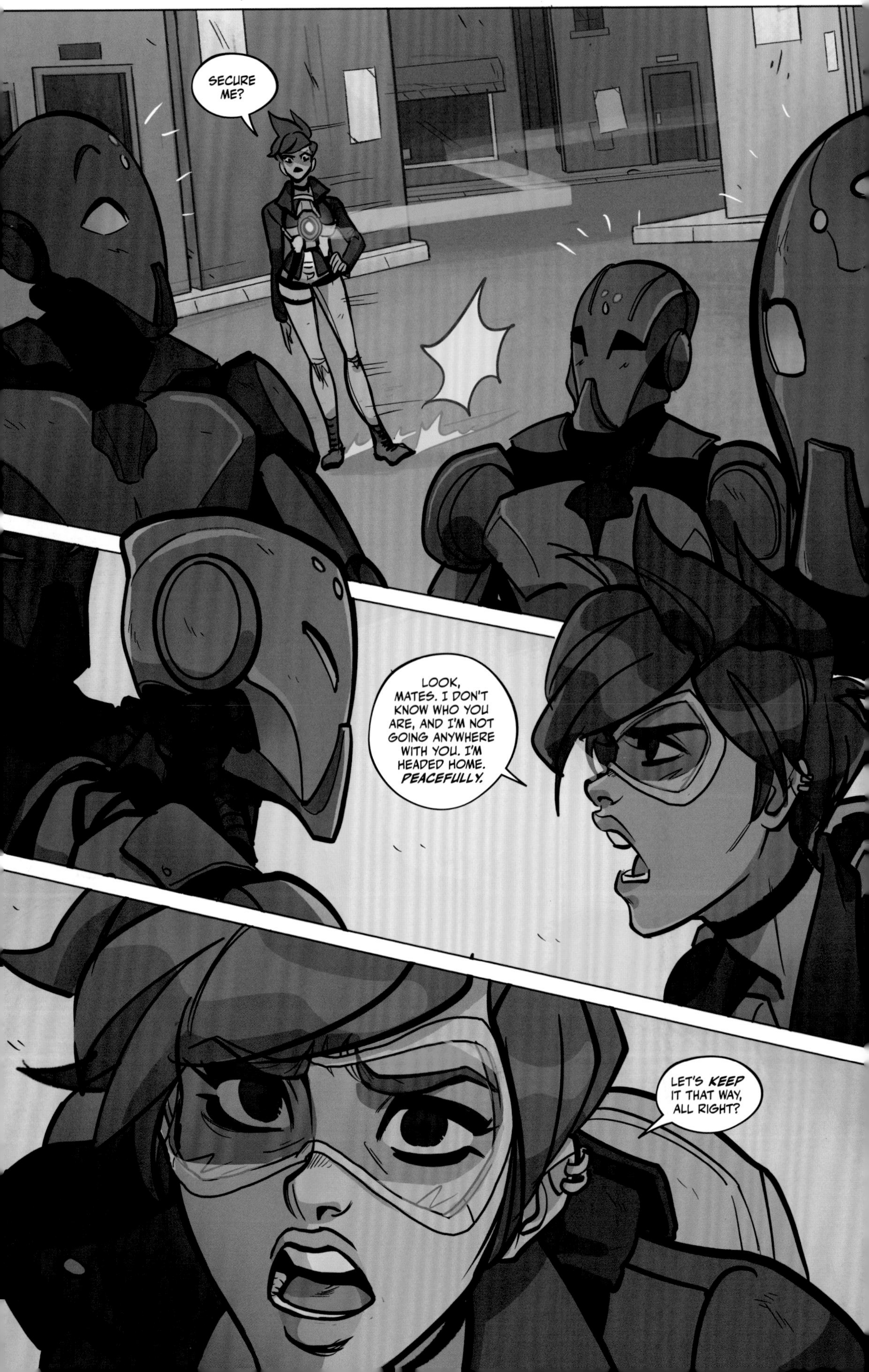
SECURE ME?
LOOK, MATES. I DON'T KNOW WHO YOU ARE, AND I'M NOT GOING ANYWHERE WITH YOU. I'M HEADED HOME. ***PEACEFULLY.***
LET'S ***KEEP*** IT THAT WAY, ALL RIGHT?

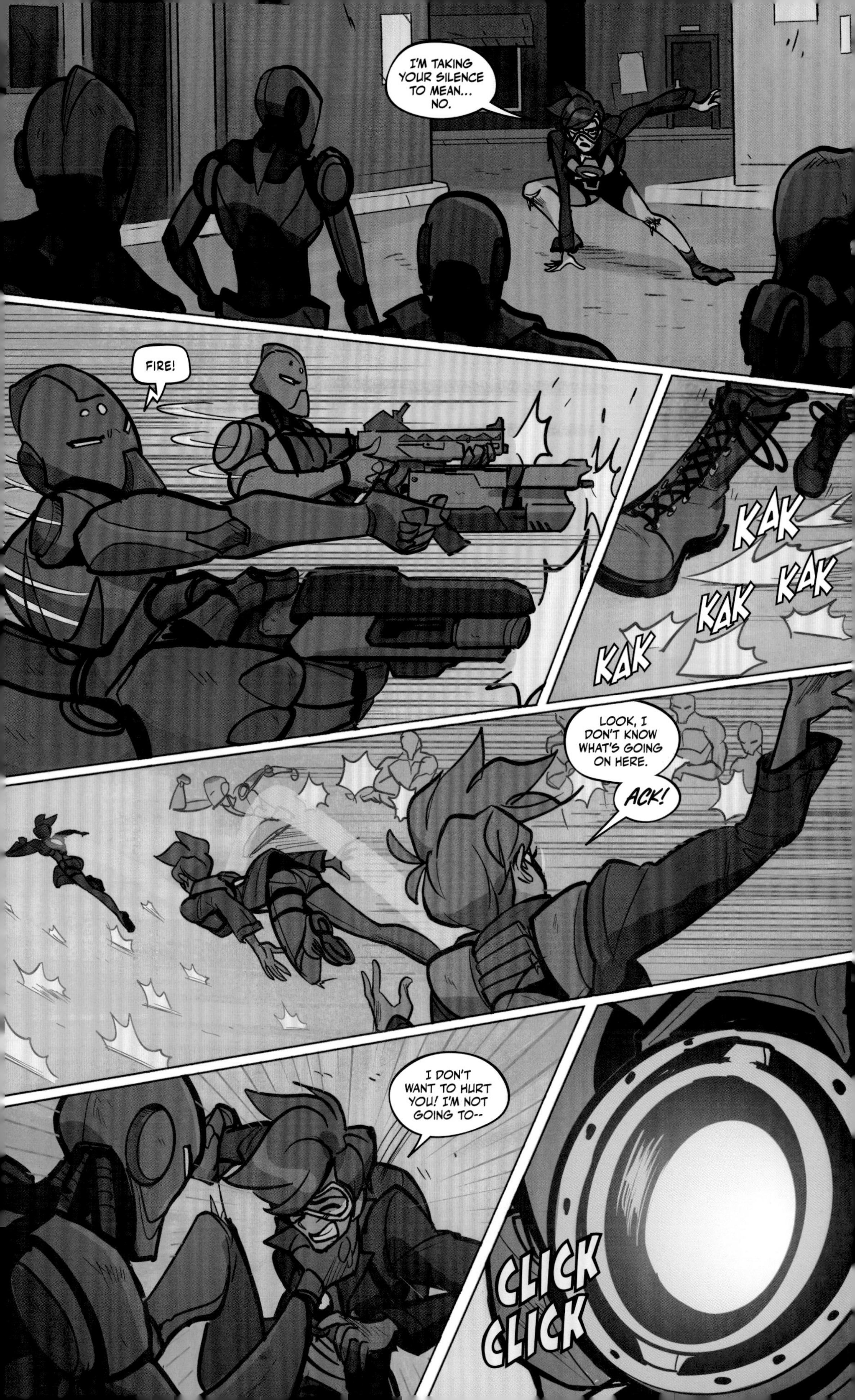

I'M TAKING YOUR SILENCE TO MEAN... NO.
FIRE!
KAK
KAK
KAK
KAK
LOOK, I DON'T KNOW WHAT'S GOING ON HERE.
ACK!
I DON'T WANT TO HURT YOU! I'M NOT GOING TO--
CLICK
CLICK

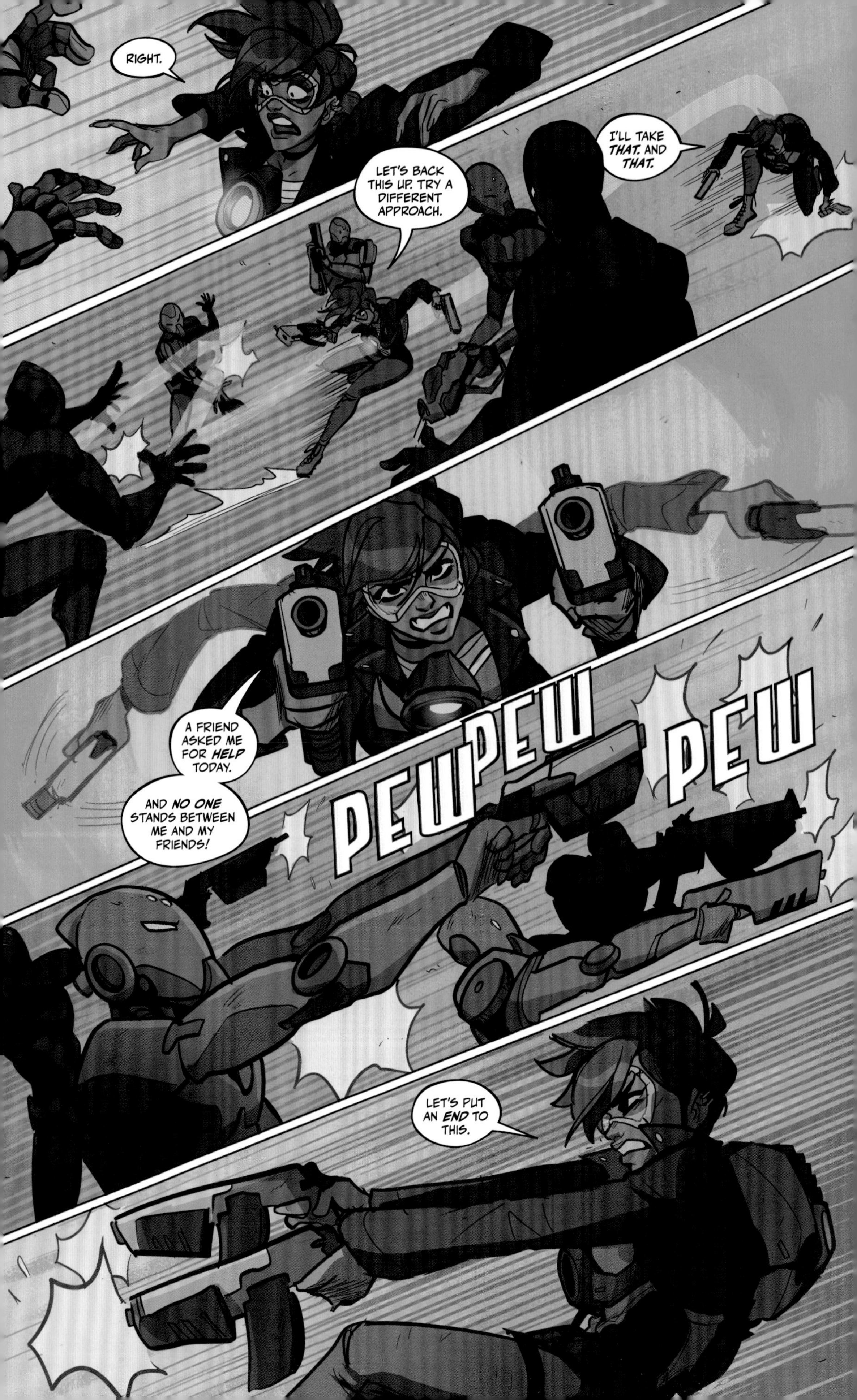
RIGHT.
LET'S BACK THIS UP. TRY A DIFFERENT APPROACH.
I'LL TAKE THAT. AND THAT.
A FRIEND ASKED ME FOR HELP TODAY.
AND NO ONE STANDS BETWEEN ME AND MY FRIENDS!
PEW PEW PEW
LET'S PUT AN END TO THIS.

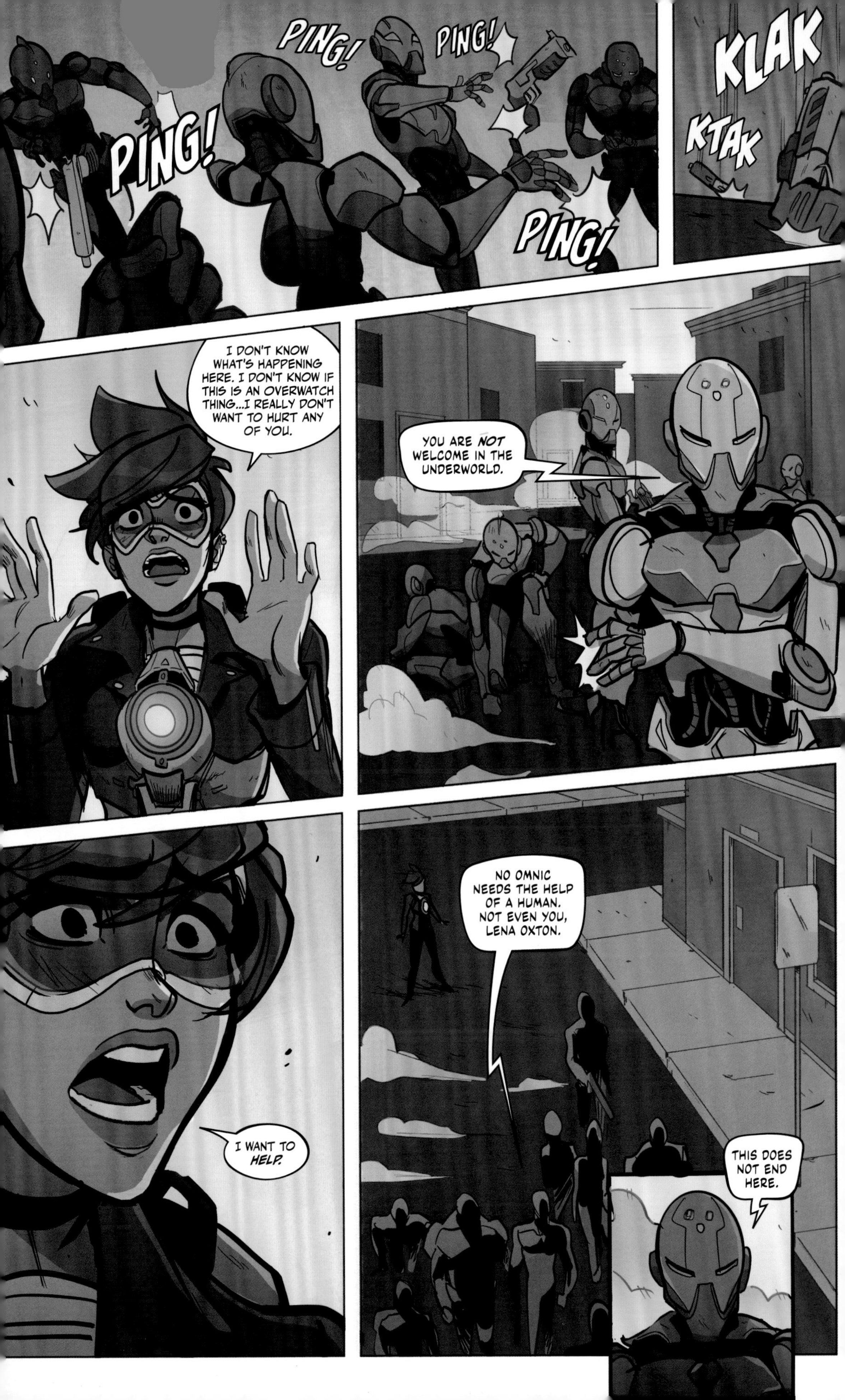
PING!
PING!
PING!
PING!
KLAK
KTAK
I DON'T KNOW WHAT'S HAPPENING HERE. I DON'T KNOW IF THIS IS AN OVERWATCH THING...I REALLY DON'T WANT TO HURT ANY OF YOU.
YOU ARE NOT WELCOME IN THE UNDERWORLD.
I WANT TO HELP.
NO OMNIC NEEDS THE HELP OF A HUMAN. NOT EVEN YOU, LENA OXTON.
THIS DOES NOT END HERE.

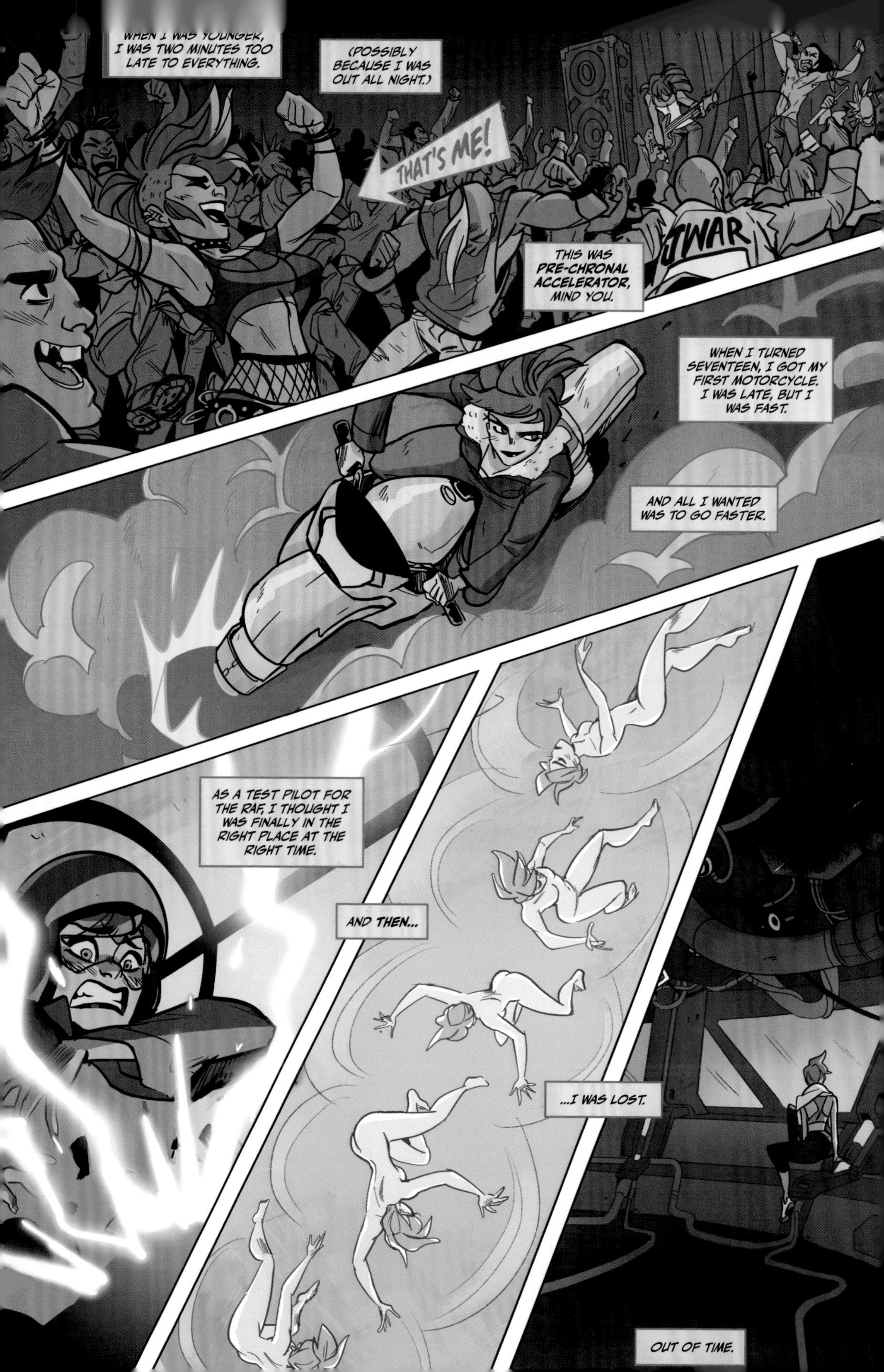
WHEN I WAS YOUNGER, I WAS TWO MINUTES TOO LATE TO EVERYTHING.
(POSSIBLY BECAUSE I WAS OUT ALL NIGHT.)
THAT'S ME!
GWAR
THIS WAS PRE-CHRONAL ACCELERATOR, MIND YOU.
WHEN I TURNED SEVENTEEN, I GOT MY FIRST MOTORCYCLE. I WAS LATE, BUT I WAS FAST.
AND ALL I WANTED WAS TO GO FASTER.
AS A TEST PILOT FOR THE RAF, I THOUGHT I WAS FINALLY IN THE RIGHT PLACE AT THE RIGHT TIME.
AND THEN...
...I WAS LOST.
OUT OF TIME.

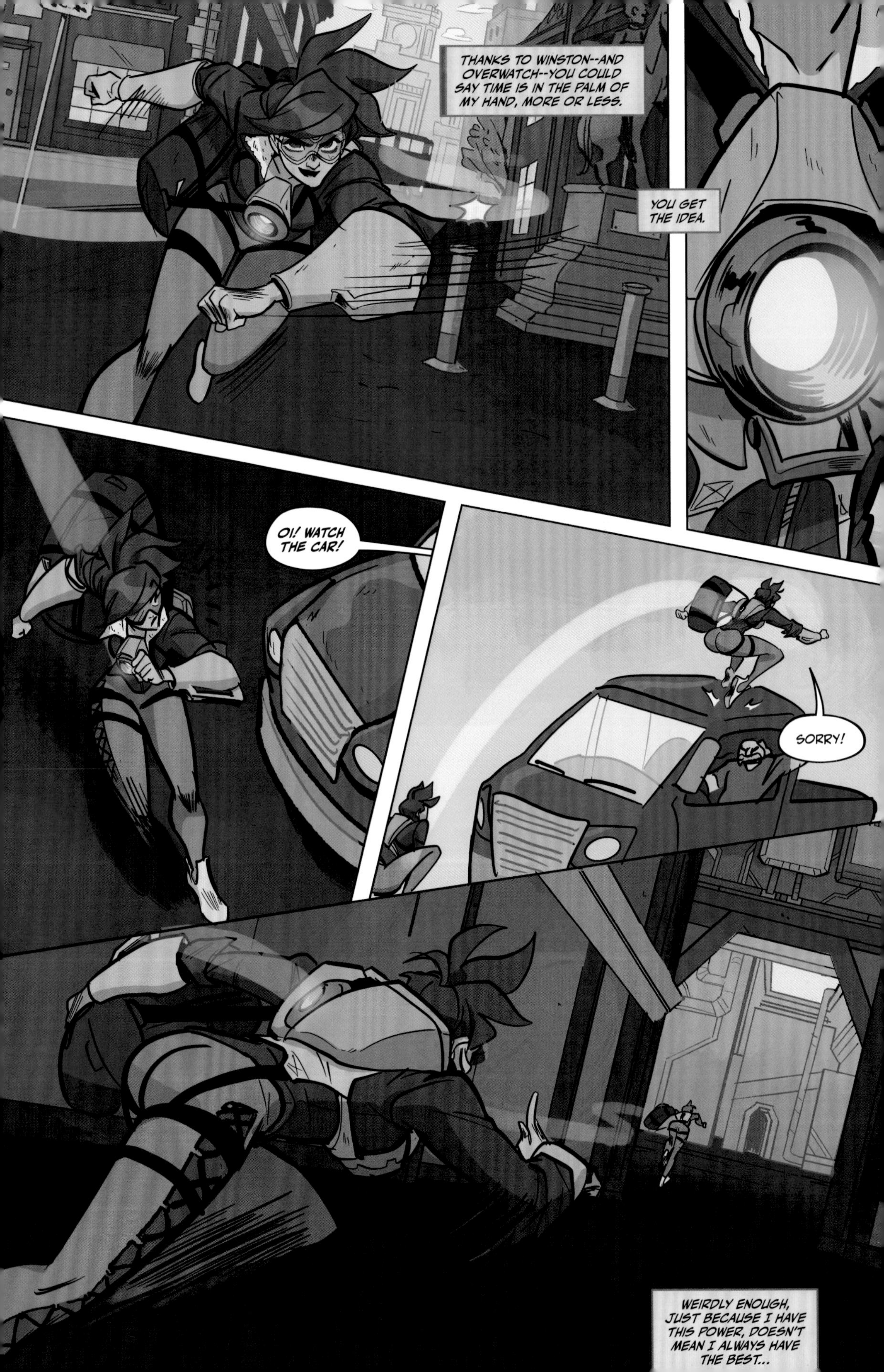
THANKS TO WINSTON--AND OVERWATCH--YOU COULD SAY TIME IS IN THE PALM OF MY HAND, MORE OR LESS.
YOU GET THE IDEA.
OI! WATCH THE CAR!
SORRY!
WEIRDLY ENOUGH, JUST BECAUSE I HAVE THIS POWER, DOESN'T MEAN I ALWAYS HAVE THE BEST...

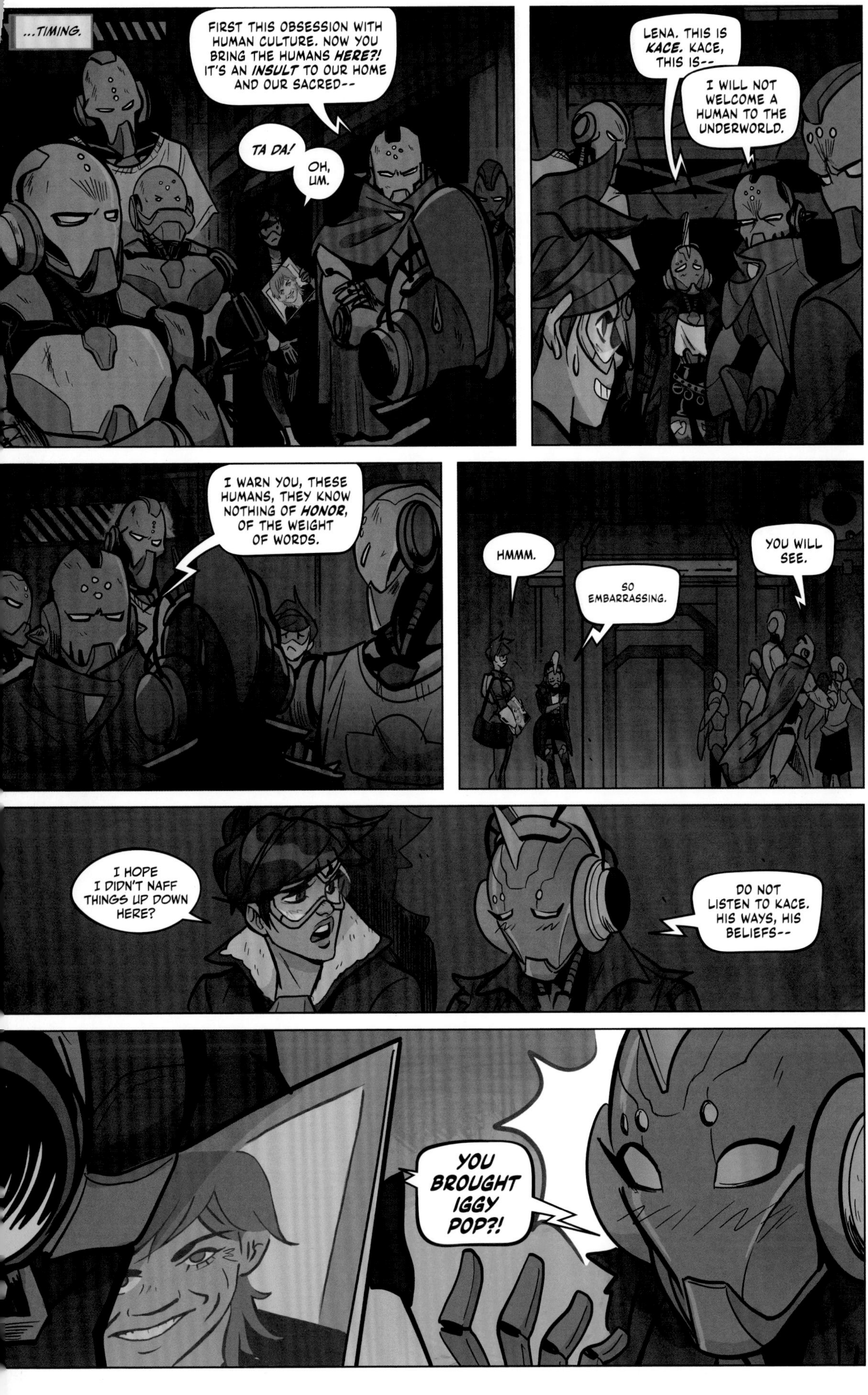
...TIMING.
FIRST THIS OBSESSION WITH HUMAN CULTURE. NOW YOU BRING THE HUMANS *HERE?!* IT'S AN *INSULT* TO OUR HOME AND OUR SACRED--
TA DA!
OH, UM.
LENA. THIS IS *KACE.* KACE, THIS IS--
I WILL NOT WELCOME A HUMAN TO THE UNDERWORLD.
I WARN YOU, THESE HUMANS, THEY KNOW NOTHING OF *HONOR,* OF THE WEIGHT OF WORDS.
HMMM.
SO EMBARRASSING.
YOU WILL SEE.
I HOPE I DIDN'T NAFF THINGS UP DOWN HERE?
DO NOT LISTEN TO KACE. HIS WAYS, HIS BELIEFS--
YOU BROUGHT IGGY POP?!

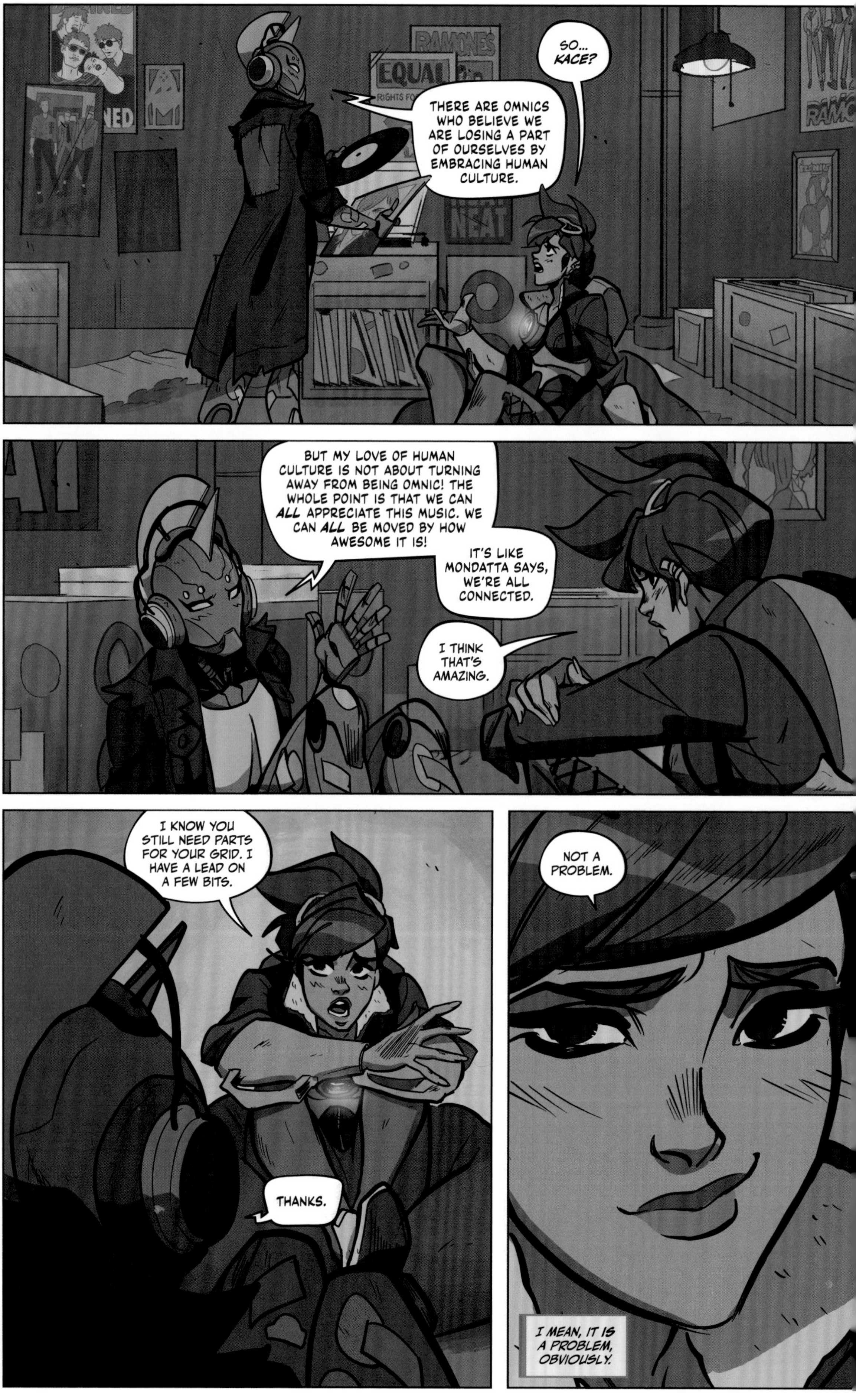
EQUAL
RIGHTS FO
RAMONES
NEAT
SO... KACE?
THERE ARE OMNICS WHO BELIEVE WE ARE LOSING A PART OF OURSELVES BY EMBRACING HUMAN CULTURE.
BUT MY LOVE OF HUMAN CULTURE IS NOT ABOUT TURNING AWAY FROM BEING OMNIC! THE WHOLE POINT IS THAT WE CAN ***ALL*** APPRECIATE THIS MUSIC. WE CAN ***ALL*** BE MOVED BY HOW AWESOME IT IS!
IT'S LIKE MONDATTA SAYS, WE'RE ALL CONNECTED.
I THINK THAT'S AMAZING.
I KNOW YOU STILL NEED PARTS FOR YOUR GRID. I HAVE A LEAD ON A FEW BITS.
THANKS.
NOT A PROBLEM.
*I MEAN, IT **IS** A PROBLEM, OBVIOUSLY.*

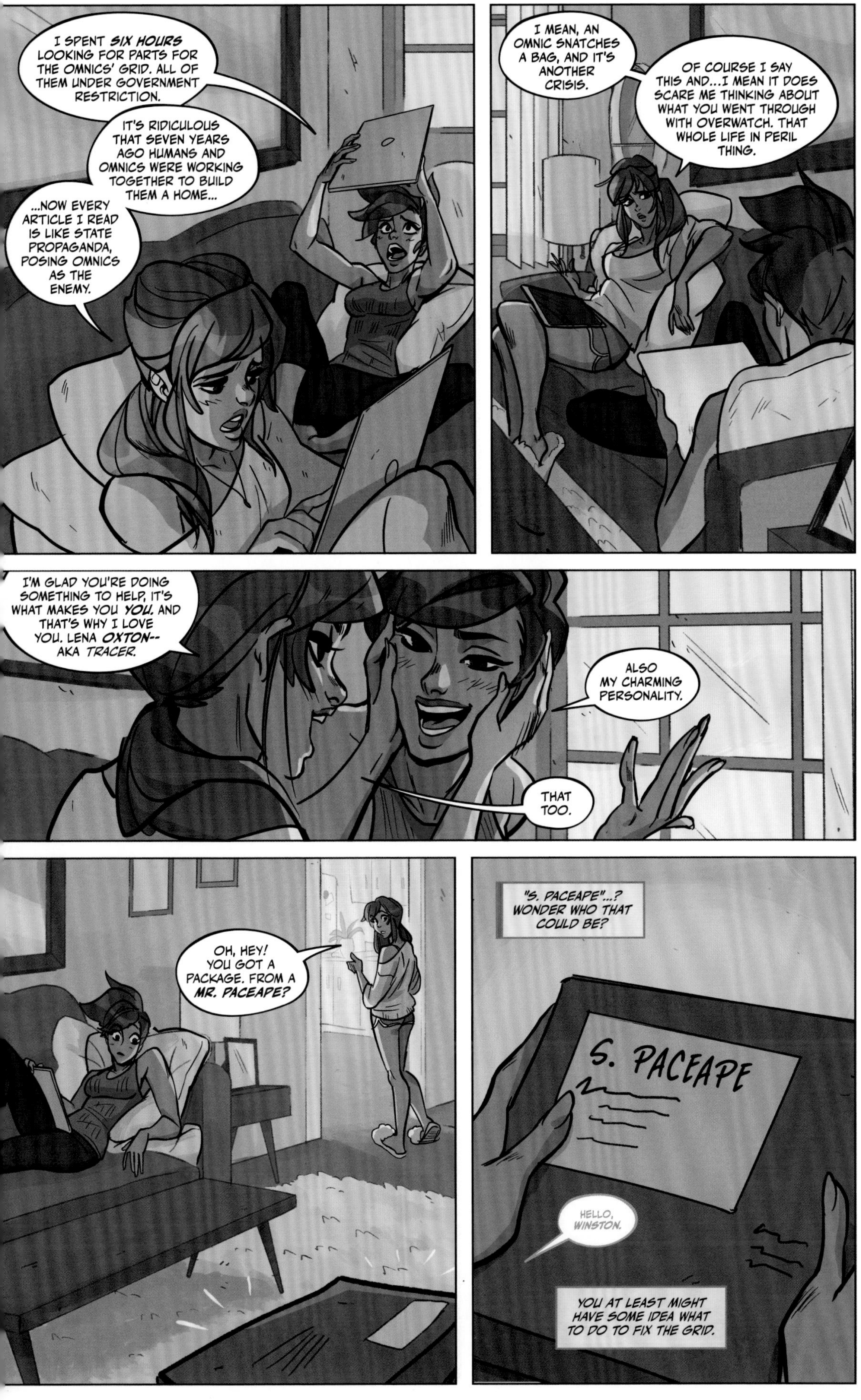
I SPENT SIX HOURS LOOKING FOR PARTS FOR THE OMNICS' GRID. ALL OF THEM UNDER GOVERNMENT RESTRICTION.
IT'S RIDICULOUS THAT SEVEN YEARS AGO HUMANS AND OMNICS WERE WORKING TOGETHER TO BUILD THEM A HOME...
...NOW EVERY ARTICLE I READ IS LIKE STATE PROPAGANDA, POSING OMNICS AS THE ENEMY.
I MEAN, AN OMNIC SNATCHES A BAG, AND IT'S ANOTHER CRISIS.
OF COURSE I SAY THIS AND...I MEAN IT DOES SCARE ME THINKING ABOUT WHAT YOU WENT THROUGH WITH OVERWATCH. THAT WHOLE LIFE IN PERIL THING.
I'M GLAD YOU'RE DOING SOMETHING TO HELP, IT'S WHAT MAKES YOU YOU. AND THAT'S WHY I LOVE YOU. LENA OXTON-- AKA TRACER.
ALSO MY CHARMING PERSONALITY.
THAT TOO.
OH, HEY! YOU GOT A PACKAGE. FROM A MR. PACEAPE?
"S. PACEAPE"...? WONDER WHO THAT COULD BE?
S. PACEAPE
HELLO, WINSTON.
YOU AT LEAST MIGHT HAVE SOME IDEA WHAT TO DO TO FIX THE GRID.

WE NEED THE PARTS, AND I HAVE A SAFE WAY TO GET THEM! MY FRIEND--
A PROMISE FROM THE HUMAN?
SHE SAID SHE WAS GOING TO GET US THE PARTS.
AND WHAT DID SHE BRING TODAY? HUMAN MUSIC. HOW WILL THAT HELP US IN THE NEXT BLACKOUT?
SHE IS TRYING.
OMNICS FIGHT FOR THE WHOLE. HUMANS FIGHT ONLY FOR THEMSELVES.
VVZZZT
YOU'RE WRONG.
YOU WILL SEE.
THEY'RE GOING TO STEAL FROM THE HUMANS, IGGY. YOU CAN'T STOP THEM.
YOU KNOW HOW TO REACH HER? LENA OXTON?

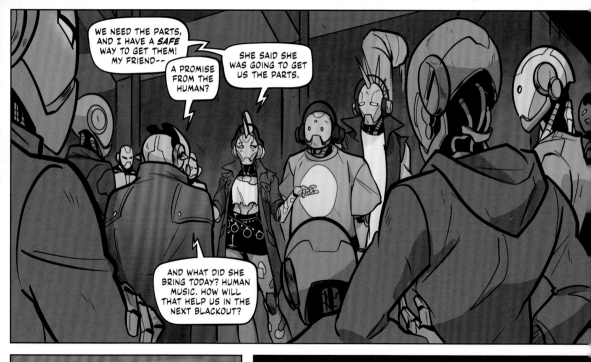

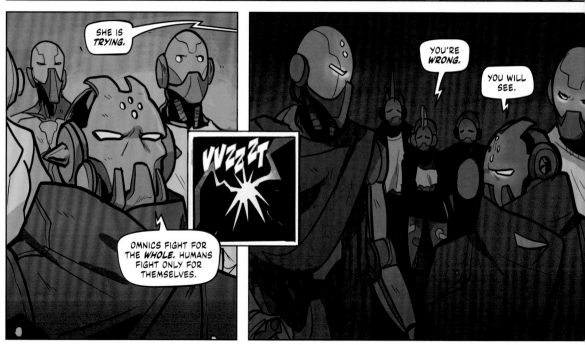

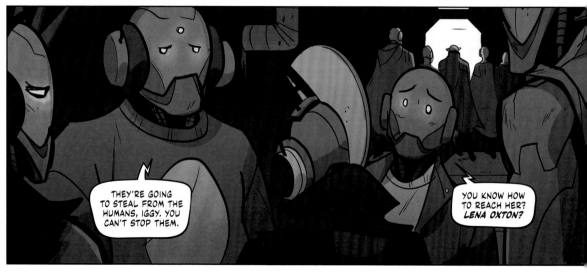

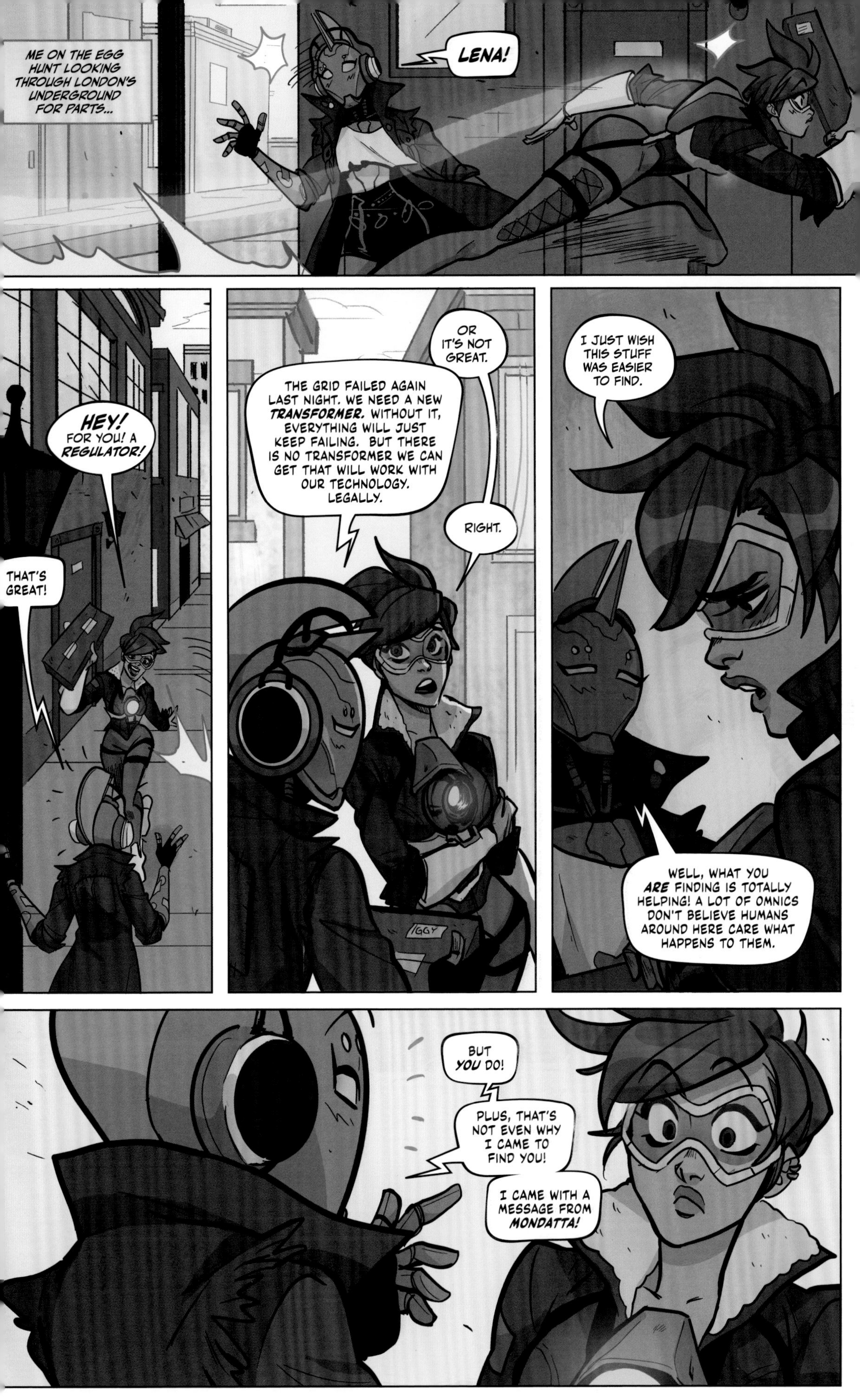

ME ON THE EGG HUNT LOOKING THROUGH LONDON'S UNDERGROUND FOR PARTS...
LENA!
HEY! FOR YOU! A REGULATOR!
THAT'S GREAT!
THE GRID FAILED AGAIN LAST NIGHT. WE NEED A NEW TRANSFORMER. WITHOUT IT, EVERYTHING WILL JUST KEEP FAILING. BUT THERE IS NO TRANSFORMER WE CAN GET THAT WILL WORK WITH OUR TECHNOLOGY. LEGALLY.
OR IT'S NOT GREAT.
RIGHT.
IGGY
I JUST WISH THIS STUFF WAS EASIER TO FIND.
WELL, WHAT YOU ARE FINDING IS TOTALLY HELPING! A LOT OF OMNICS DON'T BELIEVE HUMANS AROUND HERE CARE WHAT HAPPENS TO THEM.
BUT YOU DO!
PLUS, THAT'S NOT EVEN WHY I CAME TO FIND YOU!
I CAME WITH A MESSAGE FROM MONDATTA!

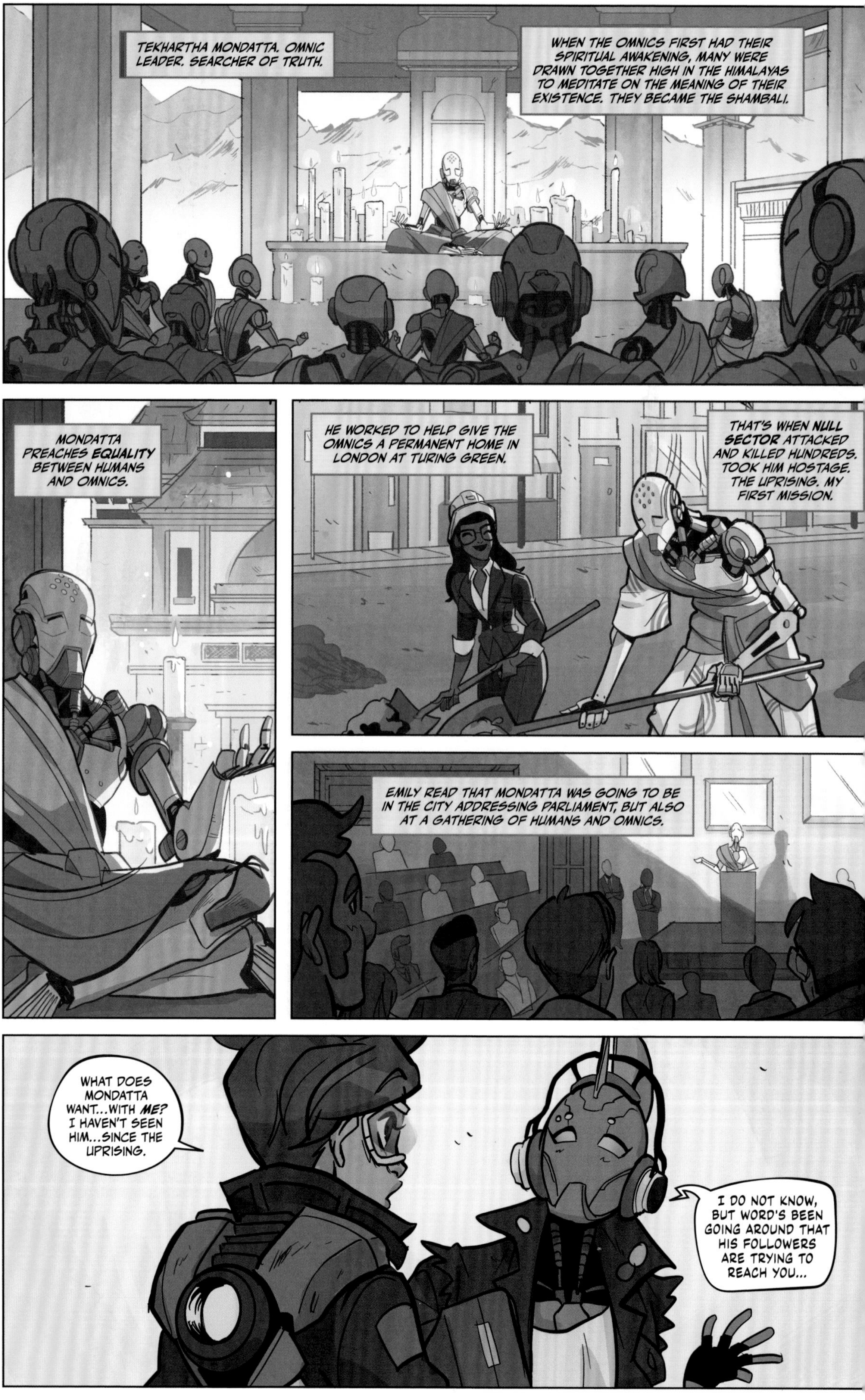
TEKHARTHA MONDATTA. OMNIC LEADER. SEARCHER OF TRUTH.
WHEN THE OMNICS FIRST HAD THEIR SPIRITUAL AWAKENING, MANY WERE DRAWN TOGETHER HIGH IN THE HIMALAYAS TO MEDITATE ON THE MEANING OF THEIR EXISTENCE. THEY BECAME THE SHAMBALI.
MONDATTA PREACHES EQUALITY BETWEEN HUMANS AND OMNICS.
HE WORKED TO HELP GIVE THE OMNICS A PERMANENT HOME IN LONDON AT TURING GREEN.
THAT'S WHEN NULL SECTOR ATTACKED AND KILLED HUNDREDS. TOOK HIM HOSTAGE. THE UPRISING. MY FIRST MISSION.
EMILY READ THAT MONDATTA WAS GOING TO BE IN THE CITY ADDRESSING PARLIAMENT, BUT ALSO AT A GATHERING OF HUMANS AND OMNICS.
WHAT DOES MONDATTA WANT...WITH ME? I HAVEN'T SEEN HIM...SINCE THE UPRISING.
I DO NOT KNOW, BUT WORD'S BEEN GOING AROUND THAT HIS FOLLOWERS ARE TRYING TO REACH YOU...

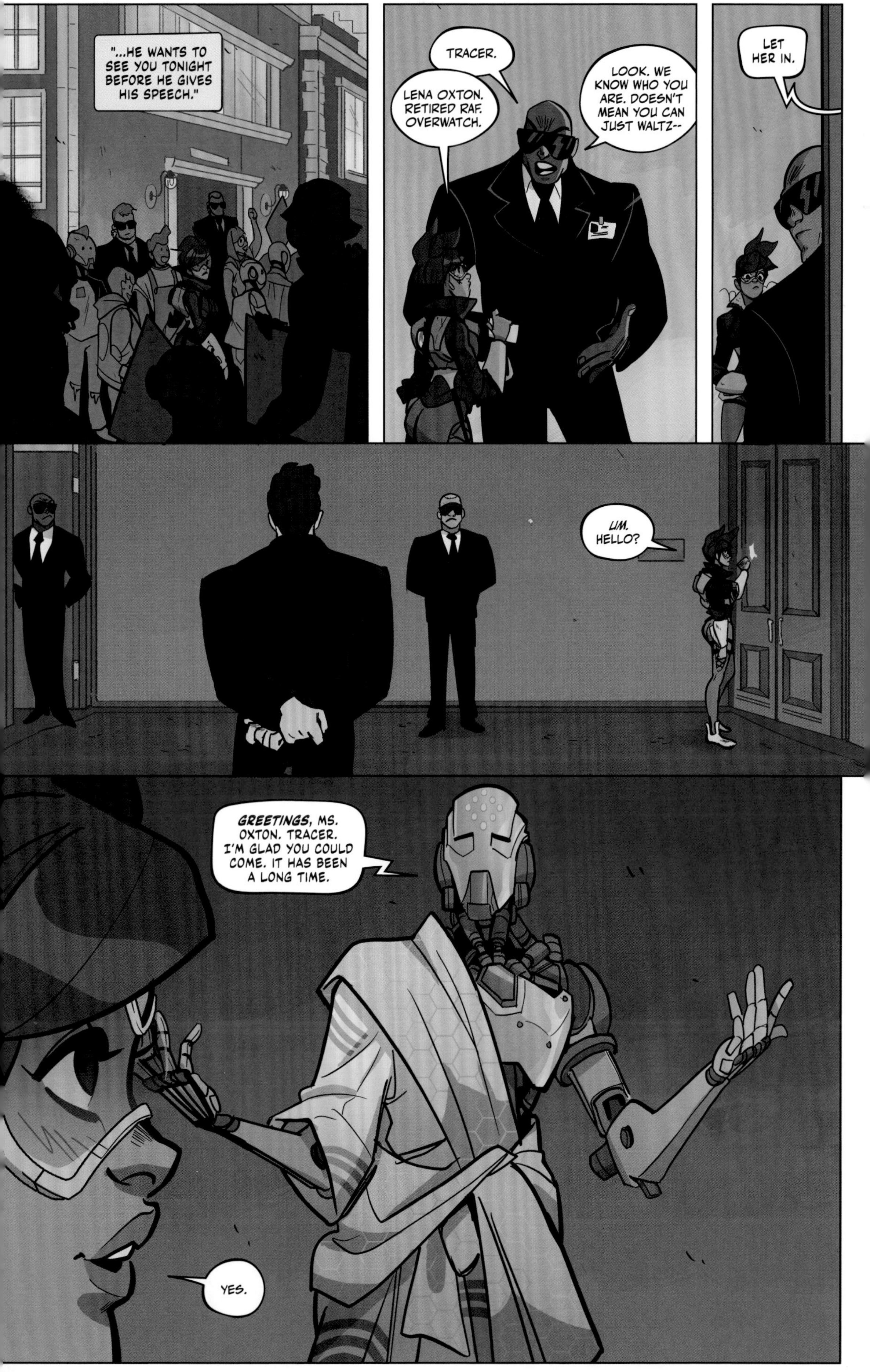
"...HE WANTS TO SEE YOU TONIGHT BEFORE HE GIVES HIS SPEECH."
TRACER.
LENA OXTON. RETIRED RAF. OVERWATCH.
LOOK. WE KNOW WHO YOU ARE. DOESN'T MEAN YOU CAN JUST WALTZ--
LET HER IN.
UM. HELLO?
GREETINGS, MS. OXTON. TRACER. I'M GLAD YOU COULD COME. IT HAS BEEN A LONG TIME.
YES.

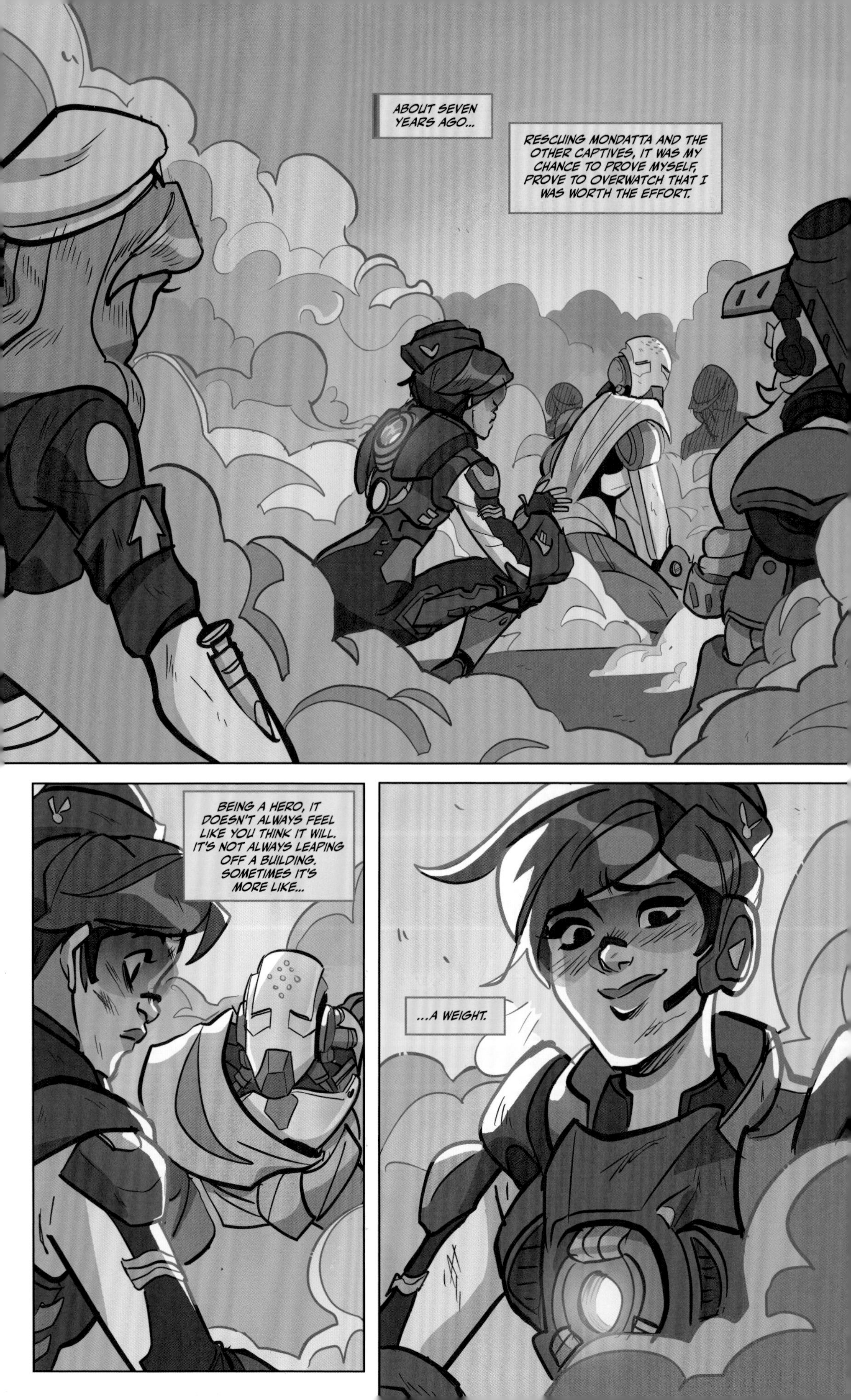
ABOUT SEVEN YEARS AGO...
RESCUING MONDATTA AND THE OTHER CAPTIVES, IT WAS MY CHANCE TO PROVE MYSELF, PROVE TO OVERWATCH THAT I WAS WORTH THE EFFORT.
BEING A HERO, IT DOESN'T ALWAYS FEEL LIKE YOU THINK IT WILL. IT'S NOT ALWAYS LEAPING OFF A BUILDING. SOMETIMES IT'S MORE LIKE...
...A WEIGHT.

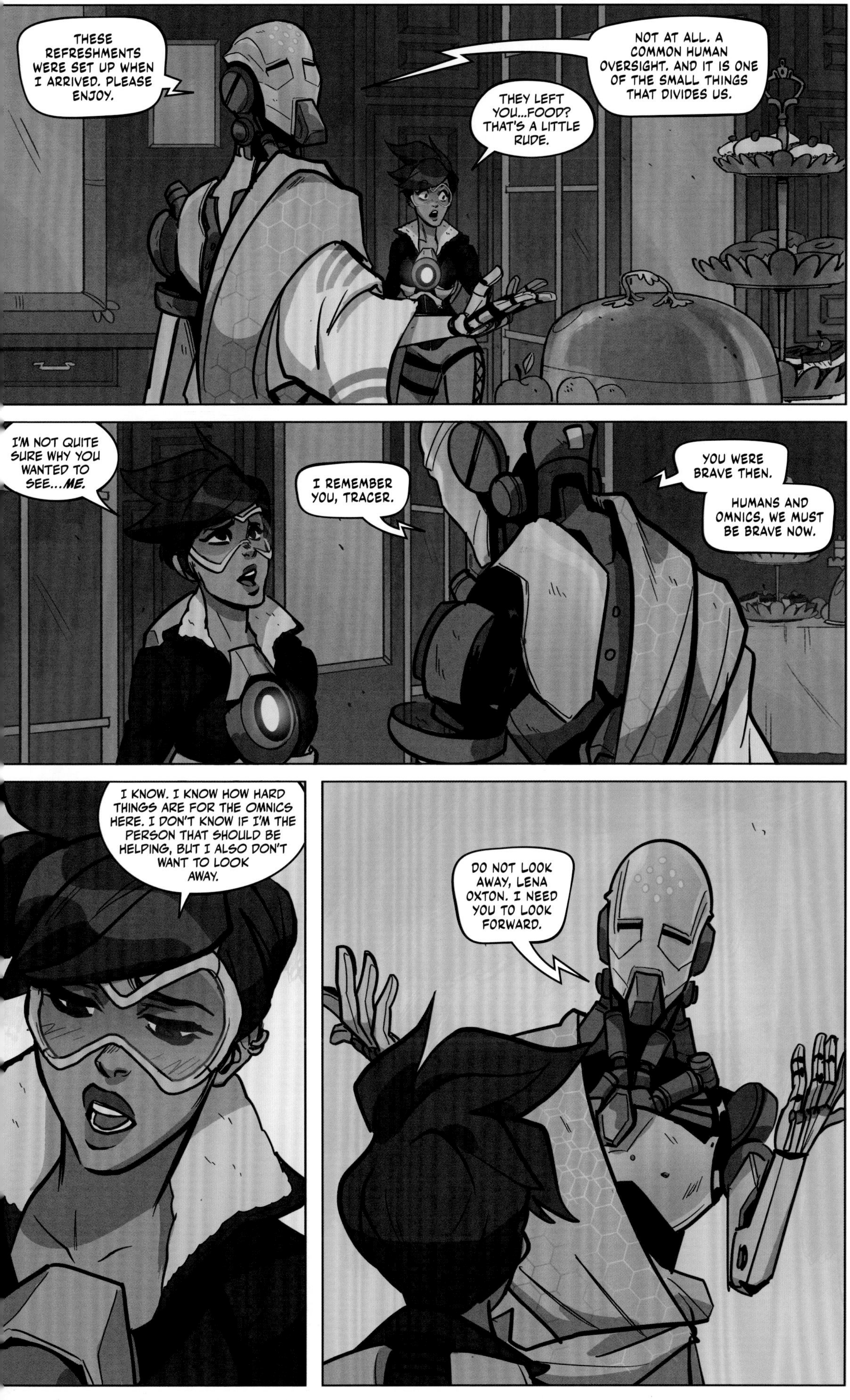
THESE REFRESHMENTS WERE SET UP WHEN I ARRIVED. PLEASE ENJOY.
THEY LEFT YOU...FOOD? THAT'S A LITTLE RUDE.
NOT AT ALL. A COMMON HUMAN OVERSIGHT. AND IT IS ONE OF THE SMALL THINGS THAT DIVIDES US.
I'M NOT QUITE SURE WHY YOU WANTED TO SEE...*ME.*
I REMEMBER YOU, TRACER.
YOU WERE BRAVE THEN.
HUMANS AND OMNICS, WE MUST BE BRAVE NOW.
I KNOW. I KNOW HOW HARD THINGS ARE FOR THE OMNICS HERE. I DON'T KNOW IF I'M THE PERSON THAT SHOULD BE HELPING, BUT I ALSO DON'T WANT TO LOOK AWAY.
DO NOT LOOK AWAY, LENA OXTON. I NEED YOU TO LOOK FORWARD.

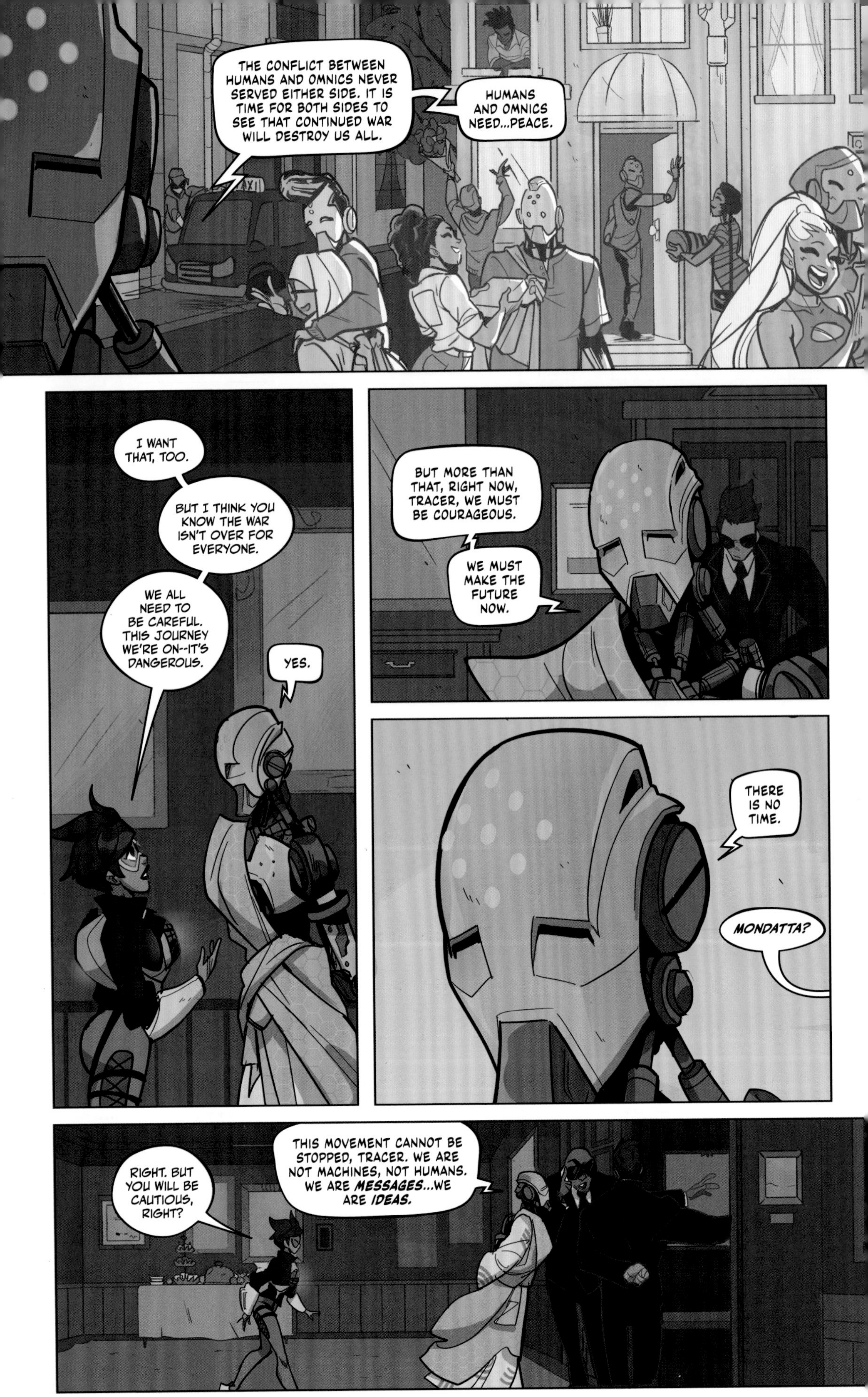

THE CONFLICT BETWEEN HUMANS AND OMNICS NEVER SERVED EITHER SIDE. IT IS TIME FOR BOTH SIDES TO SEE THAT CONTINUED WAR WILL DESTROY US ALL.
HUMANS AND OMNICS NEED...PEACE.
TAXI
I WANT THAT, TOO.
BUT I THINK YOU KNOW THE WAR ISN'T OVER FOR EVERYONE.
WE ALL NEED TO BE CAREFUL. THIS JOURNEY WE'RE ON--IT'S DANGEROUS.
YES.
BUT MORE THAN THAT, RIGHT NOW, TRACER, WE MUST BE COURAGEOUS.
WE MUST MAKE THE FUTURE NOW.
THERE IS NO TIME.
MONDATTA?
RIGHT. BUT YOU WILL BE CAUTIOUS, RIGHT?
THIS MOVEMENT CANNOT BE STOPPED, TRACER. WE ARE NOT MACHINES, NOT HUMANS. WE ARE ***MESSAGES***...WE ARE ***IDEAS.***

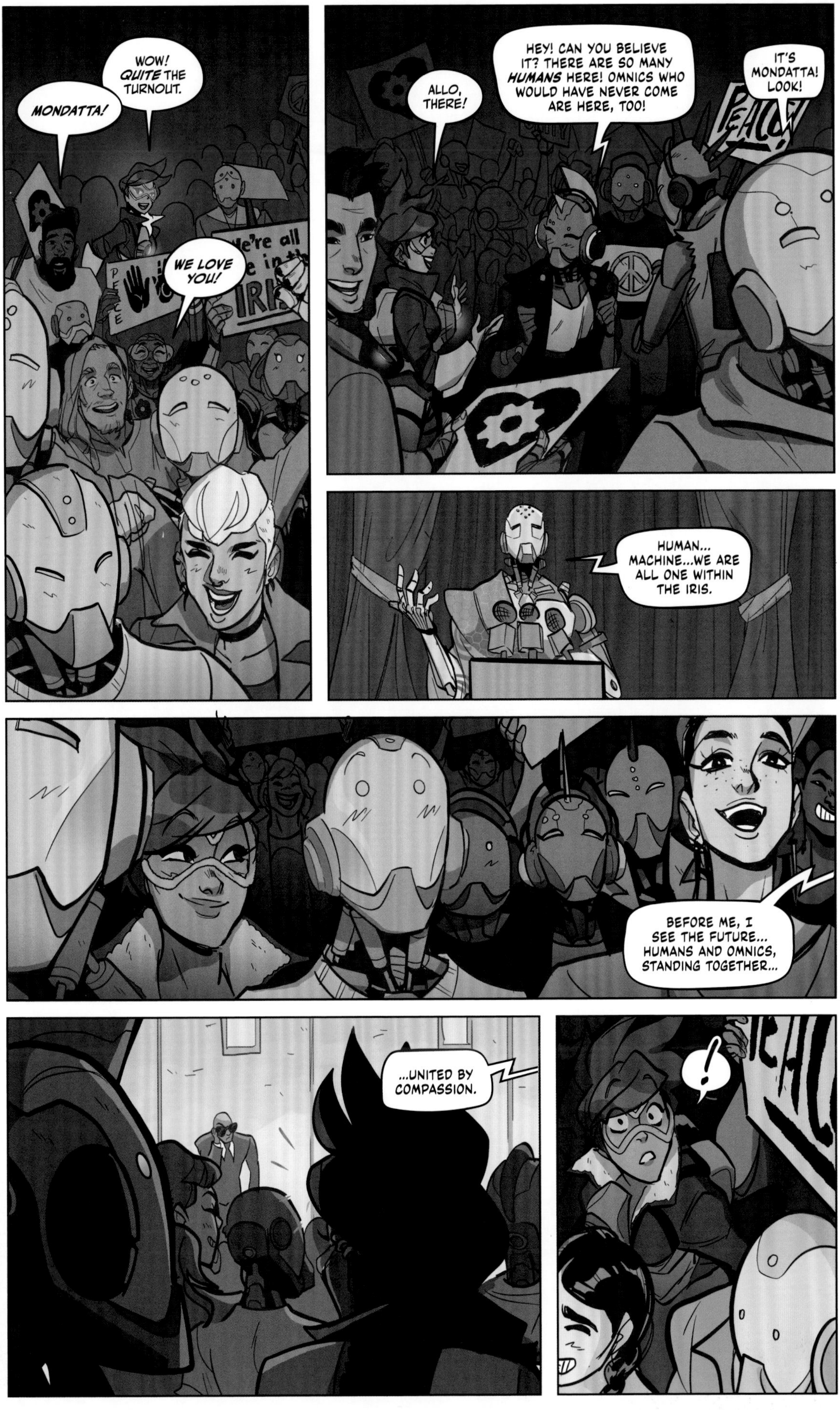
MONDATTA!
WOW! QUITE THE TURNOUT.
WE LOVE YOU!
ALLO, THERE!
HEY! CAN YOU BELIEVE IT? THERE ARE SO MANY HUMANS HERE! OMNICS WHO WOULD HAVE NEVER COME ARE HERE, TOO!
IT'S MONDATTA! LOOK!
HUMAN... MACHINE...WE ARE ALL ONE WITHIN THE IRIS.
BEFORE ME, I SEE THE FUTURE... HUMANS AND OMNICS, STANDING TOGETHER...
...UNITED BY COMPASSION.
!

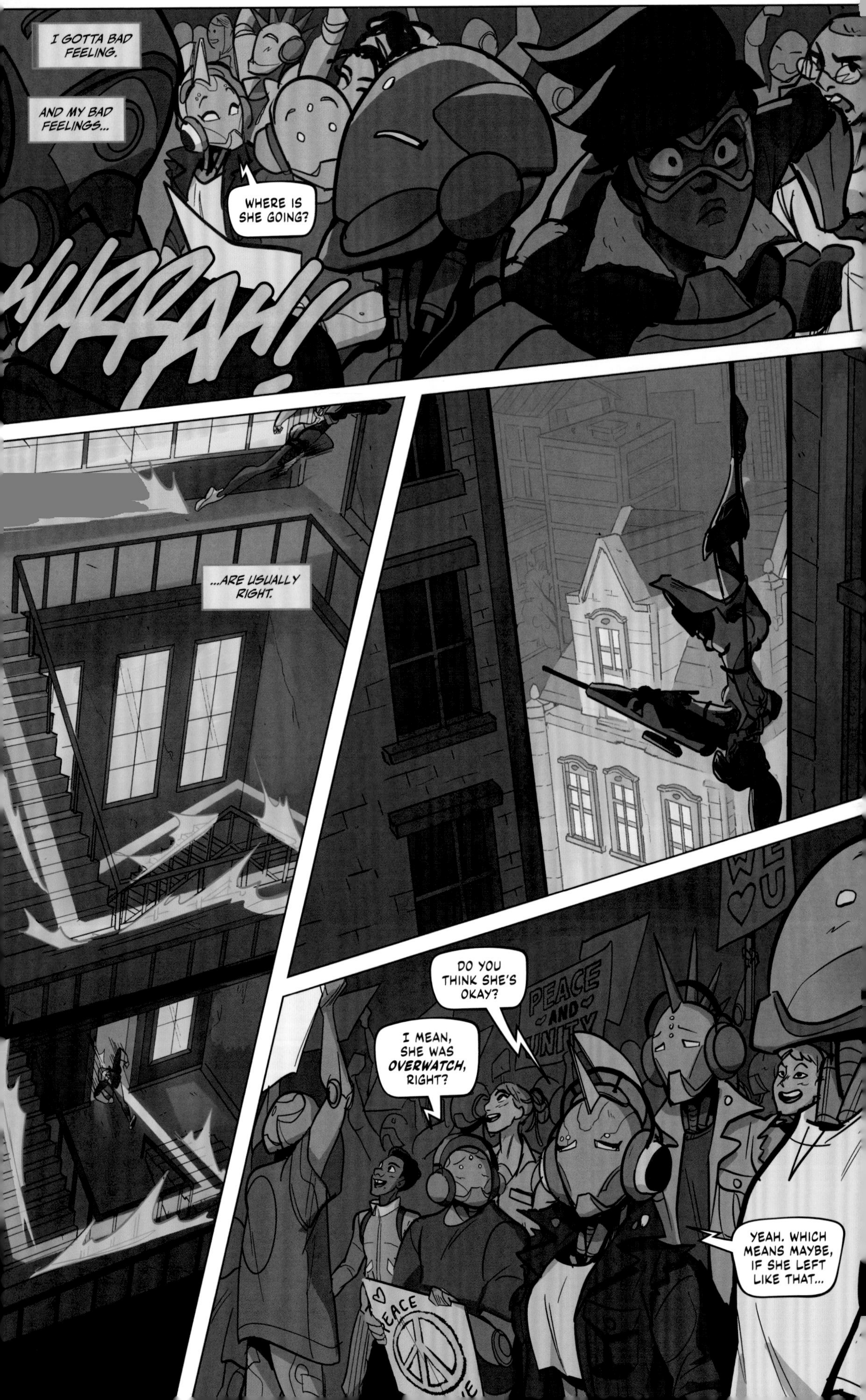
I GOTTA BAD FEELING.
AND MY BAD FEELINGS...
WHERE IS SHE GOING?
HURRAH!!
...ARE USUALLY RIGHT.
DO YOU THINK SHE'S OKAY?
I MEAN, SHE WAS *OVERWATCH*, RIGHT?
YEAH. WHICH MEANS MAYBE, IF SHE LEFT LIKE THAT...
PEACE AND UNITY
WE ♥ U
PEACE

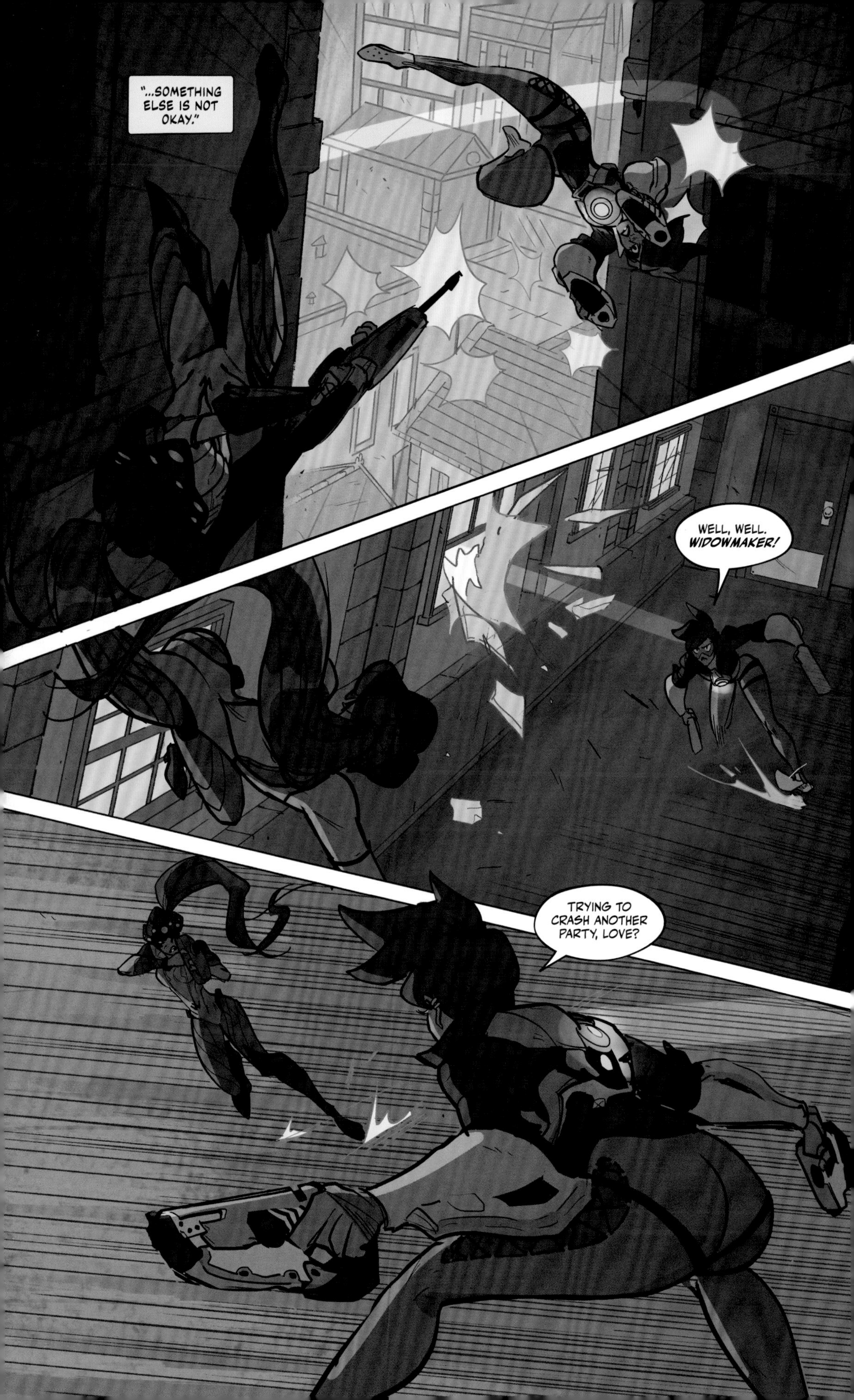
"...SOMETHING ELSE IS NOT OKAY."
WELL, WELL. ***WIDOWMAKER!***
TRYING TO CRASH ANOTHER PARTY, LOVE?

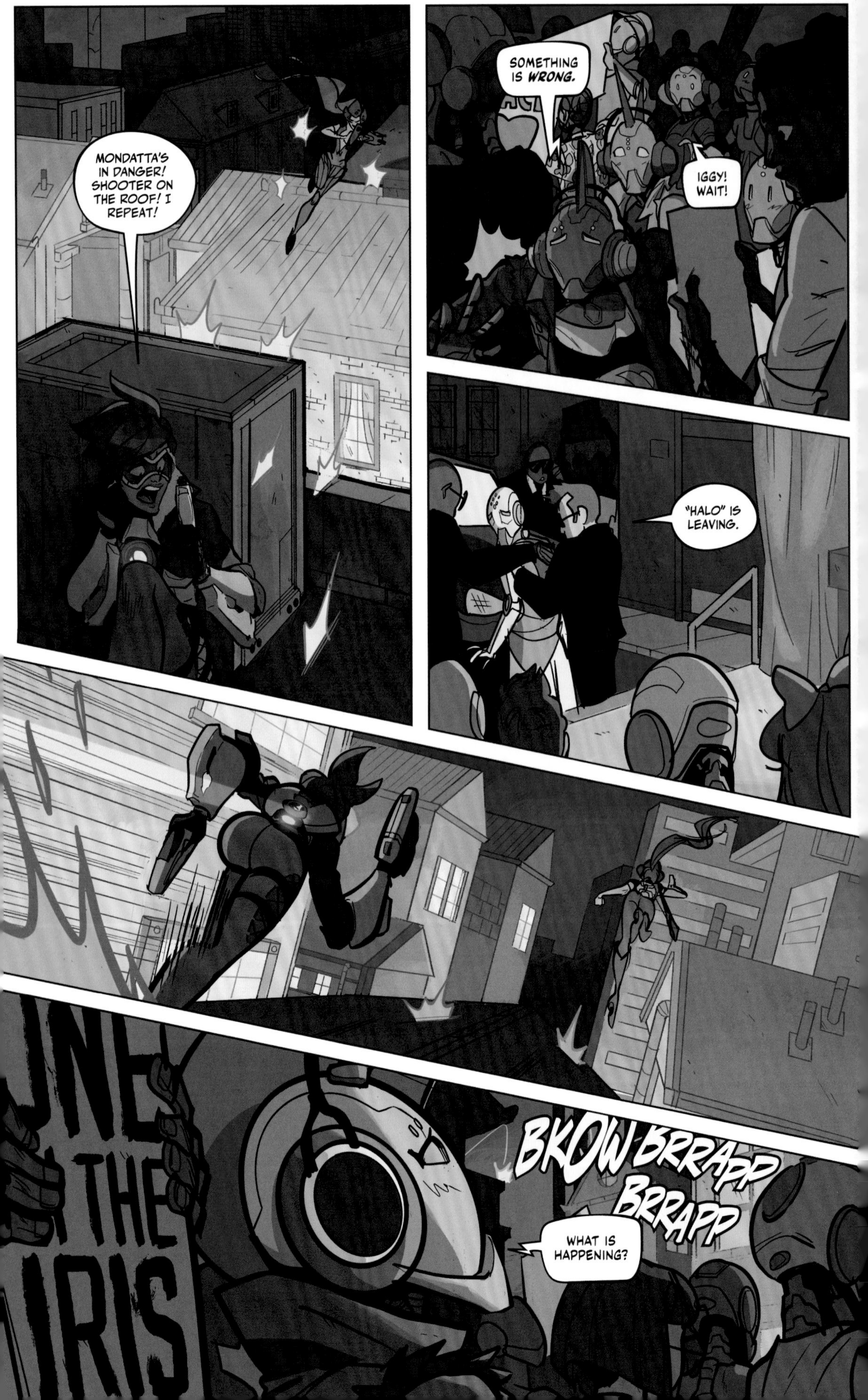
MONDATTA'S IN DANGER! SHOOTER ON THE ROOF! I REPEAT!
SOMETHING IS WRONG.
IGGY! WAIT!
"HALO" IS LEAVING.
BKOW BRRAPP BRRAPP
WHAT IS HAPPENING?

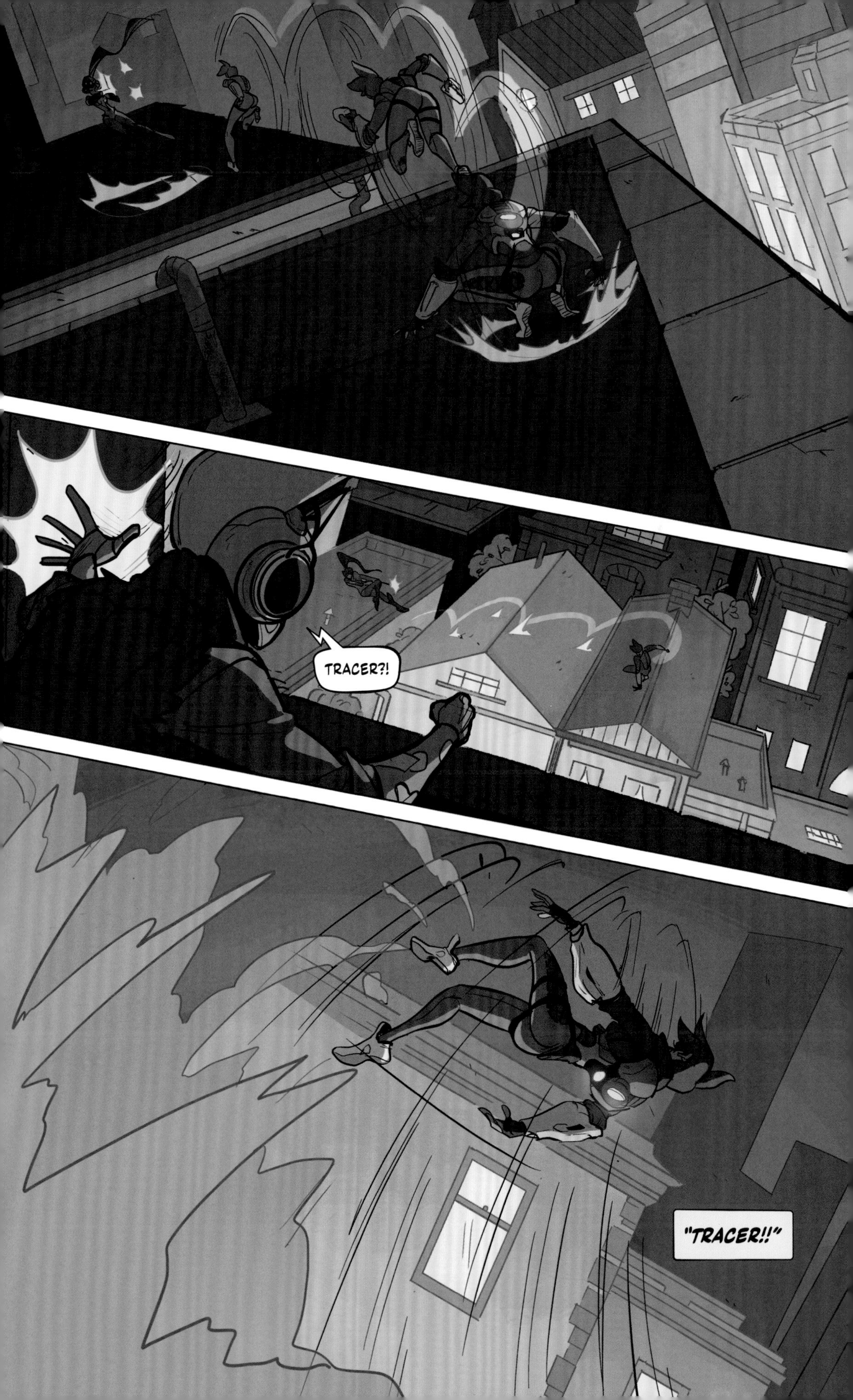

TRACER?!
"TRACER!!"

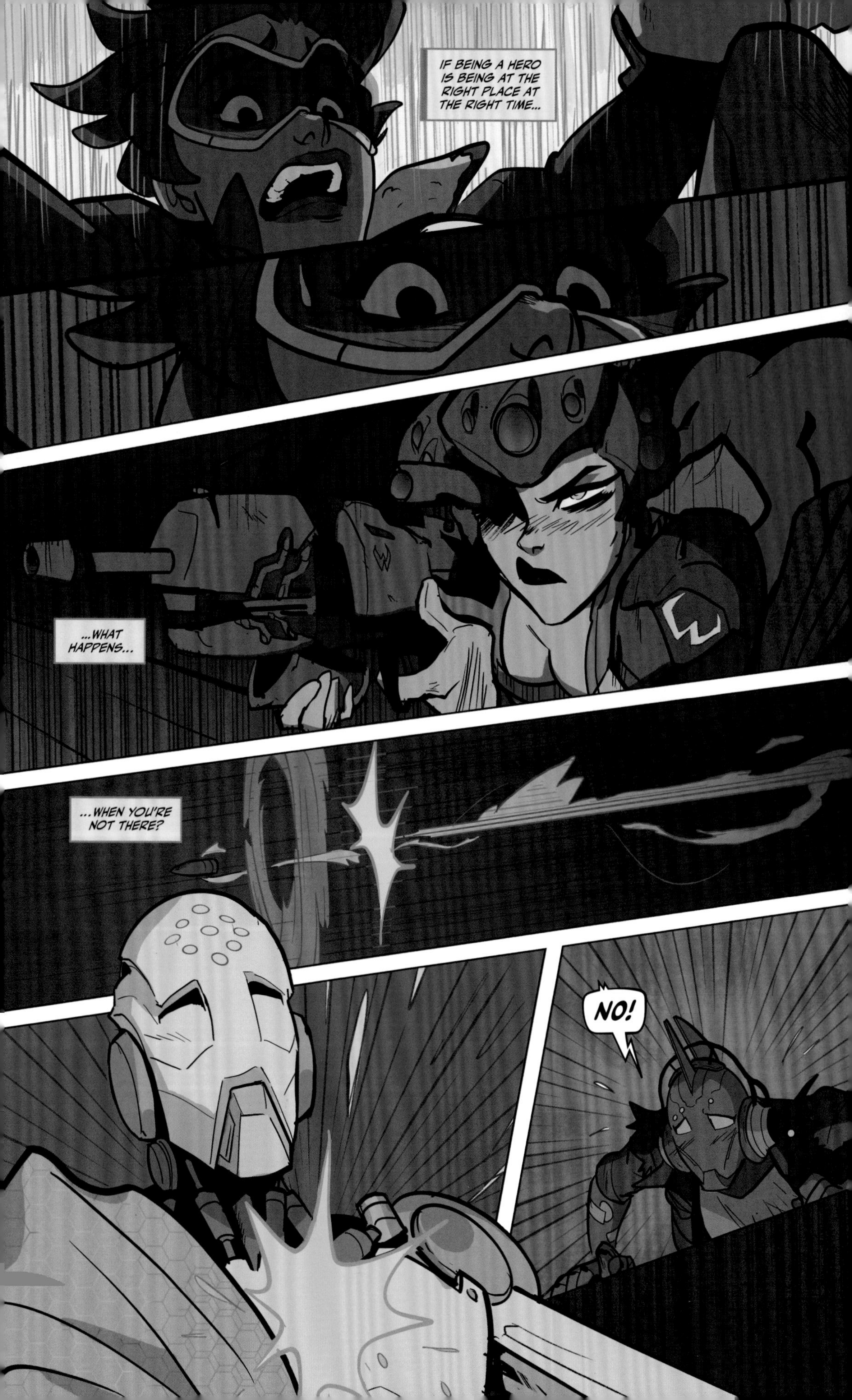
IF BEING A HERO IS BEING AT THE RIGHT PLACE AT THE RIGHT TIME...
...WHAT HAPPENS...
...WHEN YOU'RE NOT THERE?
NO!

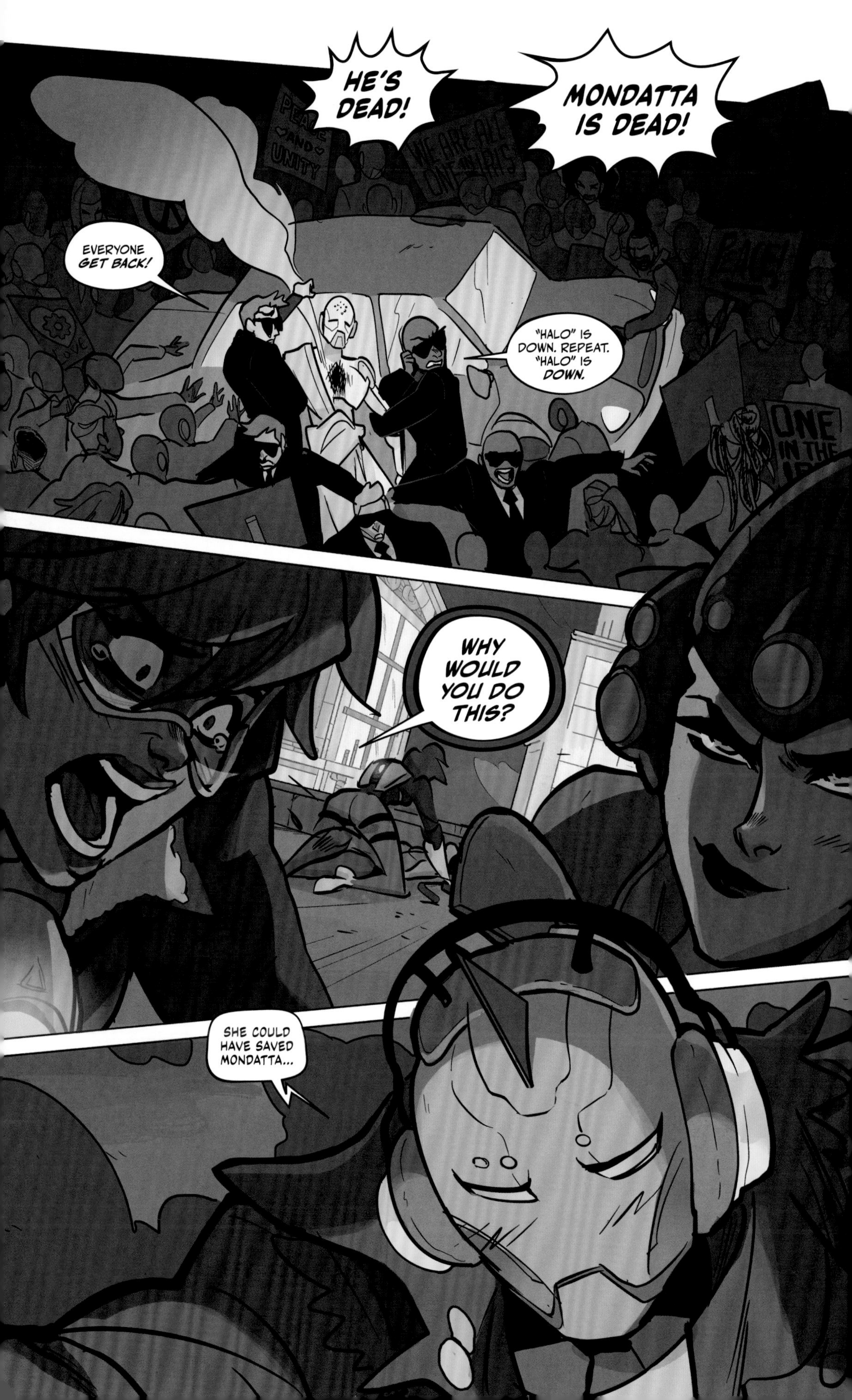
HE'S DEAD!
MONDATTA IS DEAD!
EVERYONE GET BACK!
"HALO" IS DOWN. REPEAT. "HALO" IS DOWN.
WHY WOULD YOU DO THIS?
SHE COULD HAVE SAVED MONDATTA...

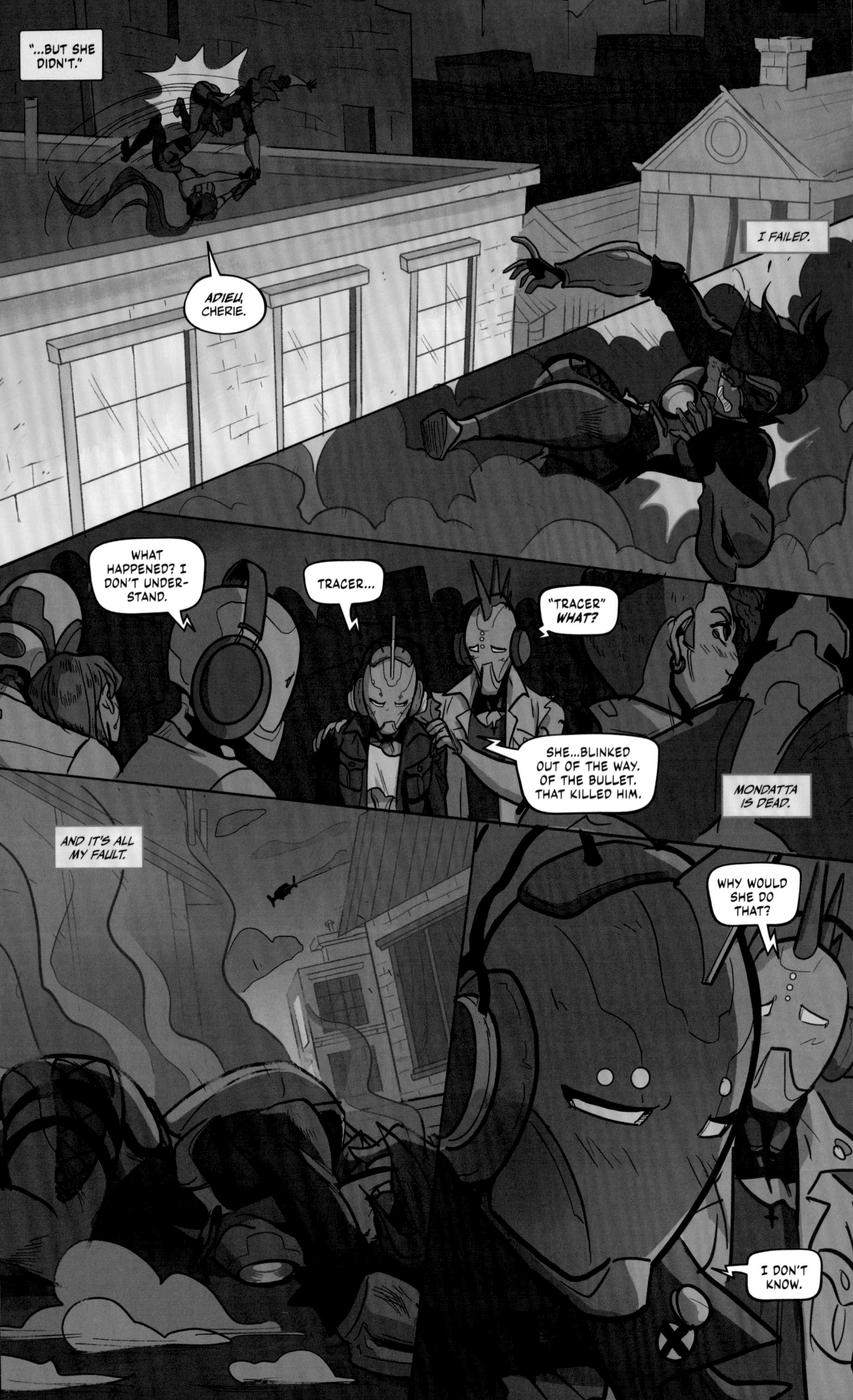
"...BUT SHE DIDN'T."
ADIEU, CHERIE.
I FAILED.
WHAT HAPPENED? I DON'T UNDER-STAND.
TRACER...
"TRACER" WHAT?
SHE...BLINKED OUT OF THE WAY. OF THE BULLET. THAT KILLED HIM.
MONDATTA IS DEAD.
AND IT'S ALL MY FAULT.
WHY WOULD SHE DO THAT?
I DON'T KNOW.

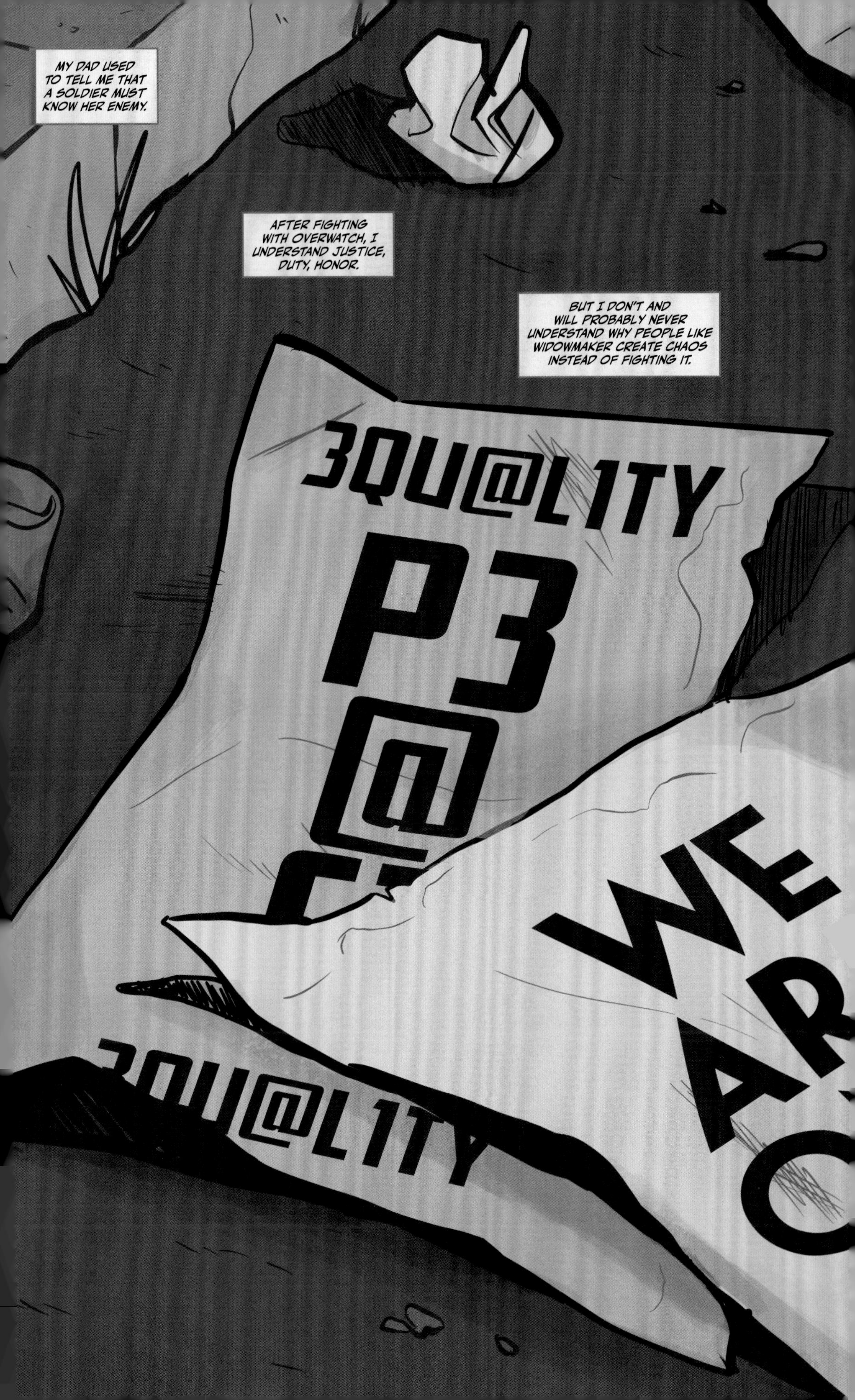
MY DAD USED TO TELL ME THAT A SOLDIER MUST KNOW HER ENEMY.
AFTER FIGHTING WITH OVERWATCH, I UNDERSTAND JUSTICE, DUTY, HONOR.
BUT I DON'T AND WILL PROBABLY NEVER UNDERSTAND WHY PEOPLE LIKE WIDOWMAKER CREATE CHAOS INSTEAD OF FIGHTING IT.
3QU@L1TY
P3
@
WE
AR
3QU@L1TY

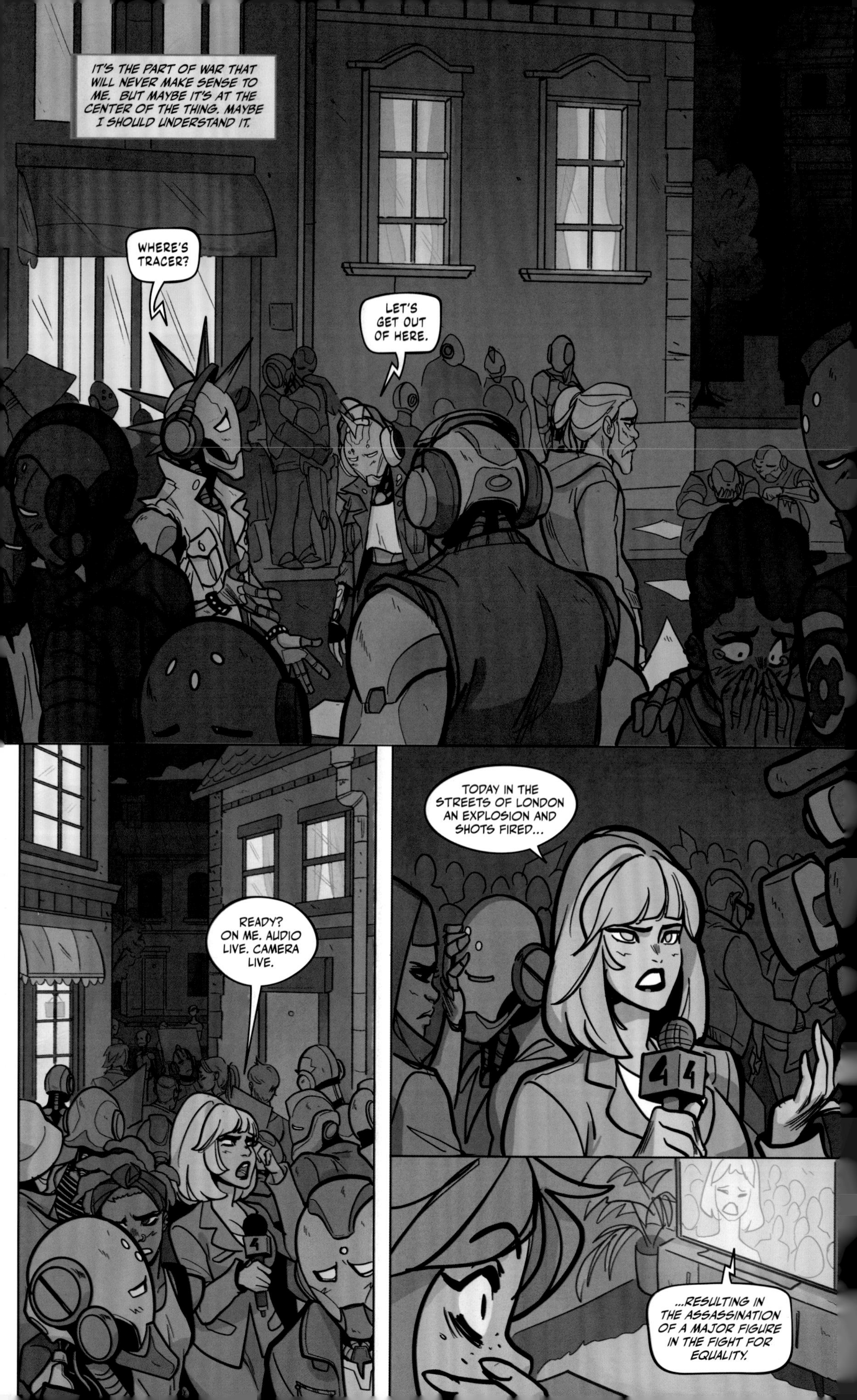
IT'S THE PART OF WAR THAT WILL NEVER MAKE SENSE TO ME. BUT MAYBE IT'S AT THE CENTER OF THE THING. MAYBE I SHOULD UNDERSTAND IT.
WHERE'S TRACER?
LET'S GET OUT OF HERE.
READY? ON ME. AUDIO LIVE. CAMERA LIVE.
TODAY IN THE STREETS OF LONDON AN EXPLOSION AND SHOTS FIRED...
...RESULTING IN THE ASSASSINATION OF A MAJOR FIGURE IN THE FIGHT FOR EQUALITY.

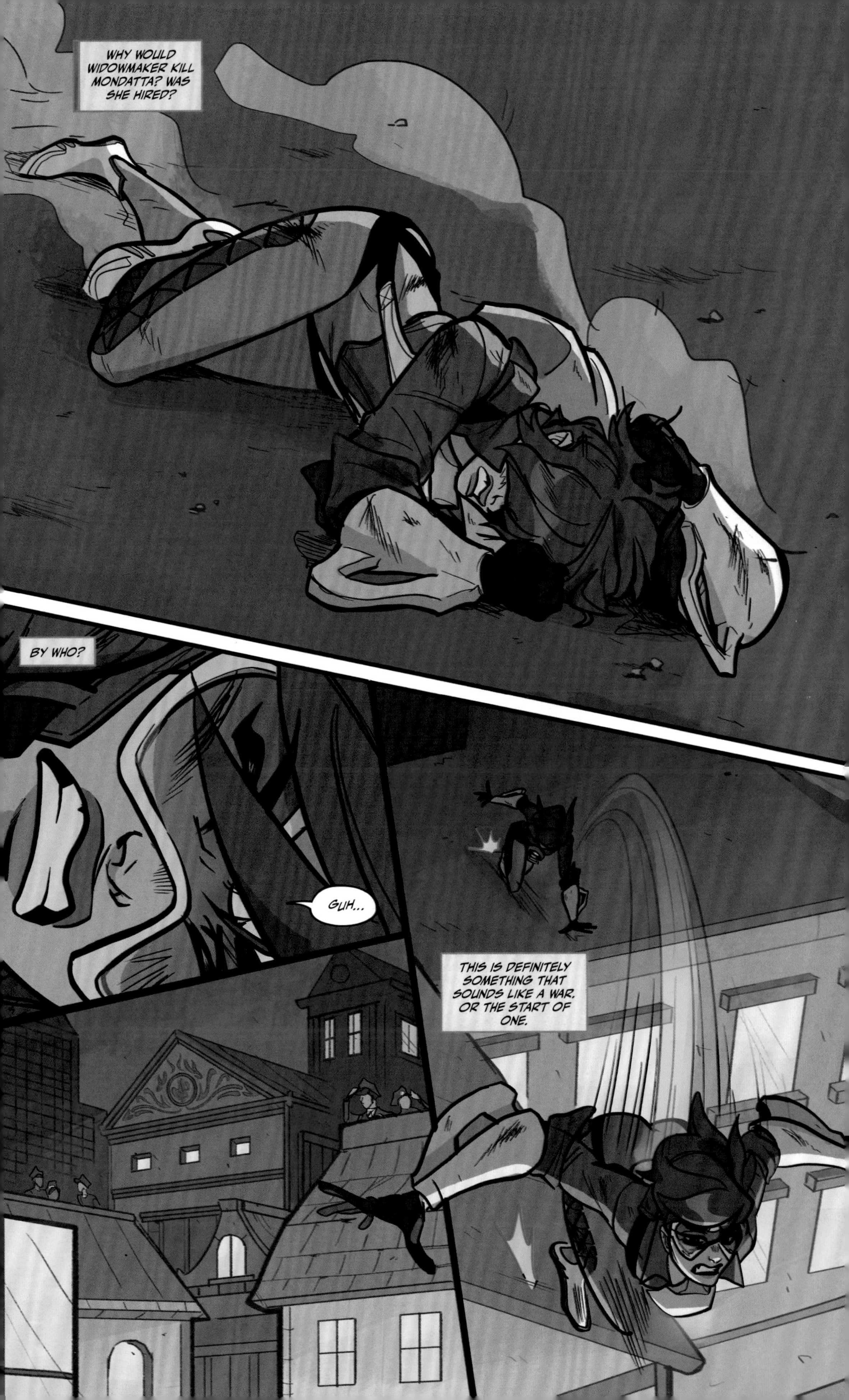
WHY WOULD WIDOWMAKER KILL MONDATTA? WAS SHE HIRED?
BY WHO?
GUH...
THIS IS DEFINITELY SOMETHING THAT SOUNDS LIKE A WAR. OR THE START OF ONE.

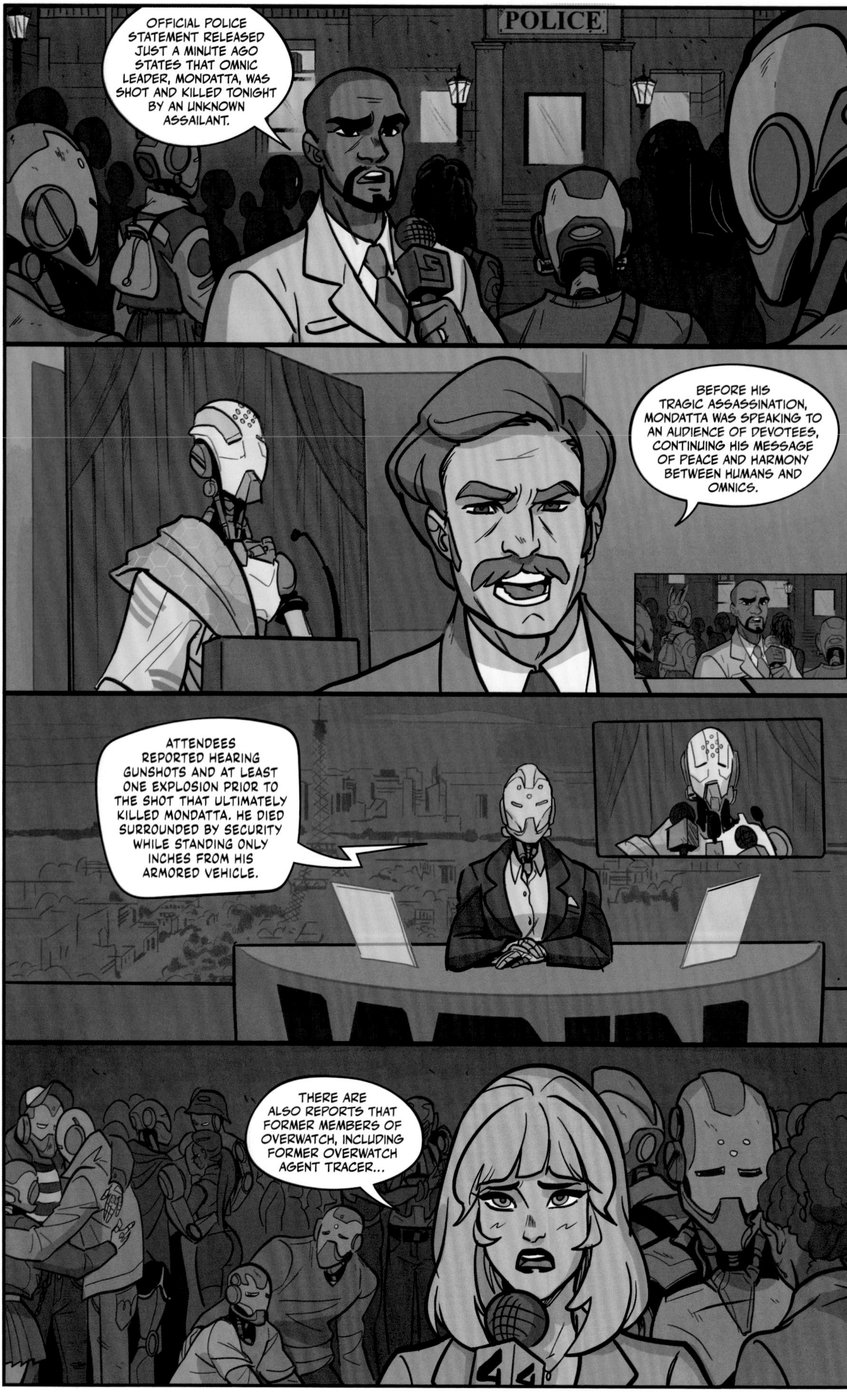
POLICE
OFFICIAL POLICE STATEMENT RELEASED JUST A MINUTE AGO STATES THAT OMNIC LEADER, MONDATTA, WAS SHOT AND KILLED TONIGHT BY AN UNKNOWN ASSAILANT.
BEFORE HIS TRAGIC ASSASSINATION, MONDATTA WAS SPEAKING TO AN AUDIENCE OF DEVOTEES, CONTINUING HIS MESSAGE OF PEACE AND HARMONY BETWEEN HUMANS AND OMNICS.
ATTENDEES REPORTED HEARING GUNSHOTS AND AT LEAST ONE EXPLOSION PRIOR TO THE SHOT THAT ULTIMATELY KILLED MONDATTA. HE DIED SURROUNDED BY SECURITY WHILE STANDING ONLY INCHES FROM HIS ARMORED VEHICLE.
THERE ARE ALSO REPORTS THAT FORMER MEMBERS OF OVERWATCH, INCLUDING FORMER OVERWATCH AGENT TRACER...

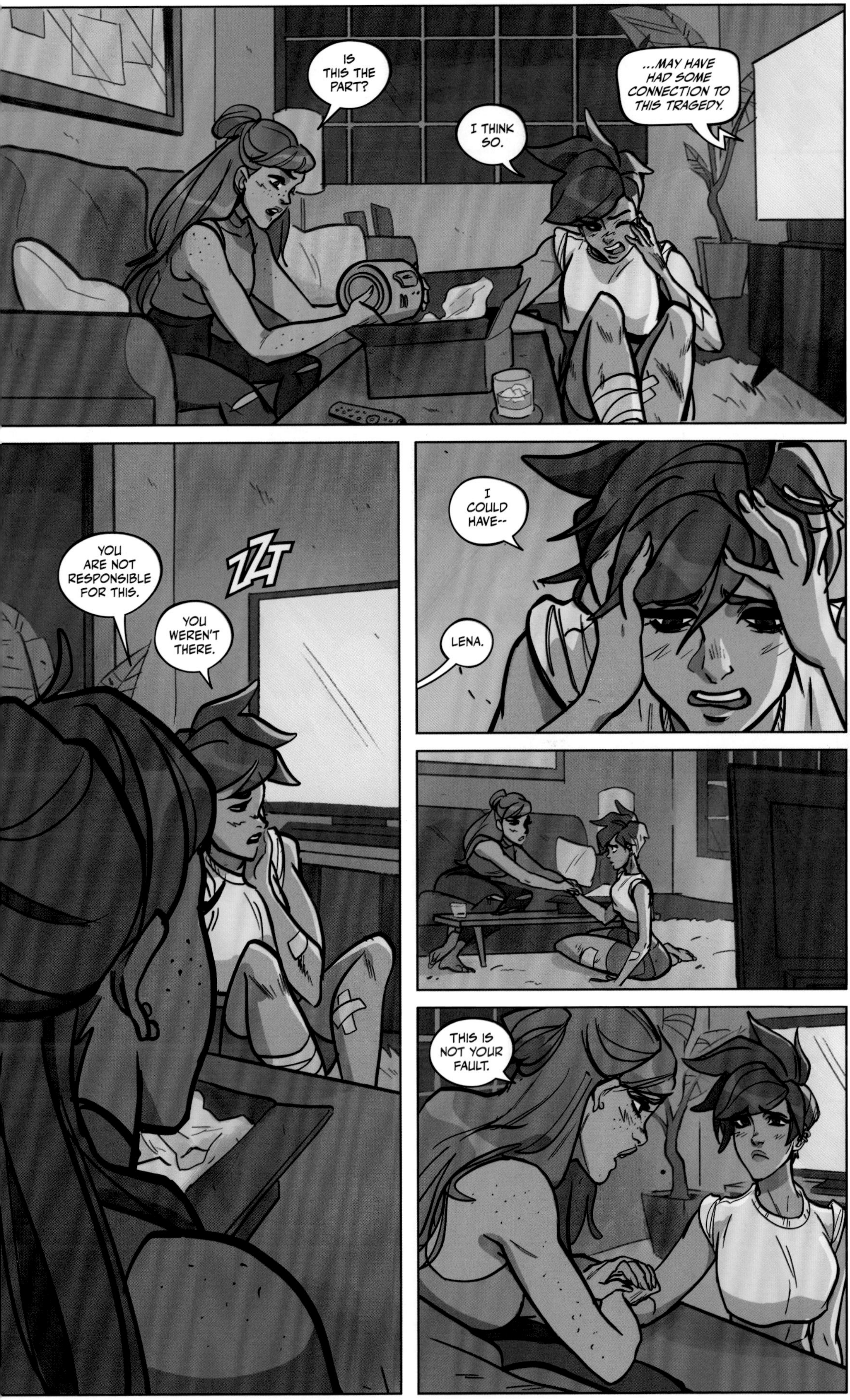
IS THIS THE PART?
I THINK SO.
...MAY HAVE HAD SOME CONNECTION TO THIS TRAGEDY.
YOU ARE NOT RESPONSIBLE FOR THIS.
ZZT
YOU WEREN'T THERE.
I COULD HAVE--
LENA.
THIS IS NOT YOUR FAULT.

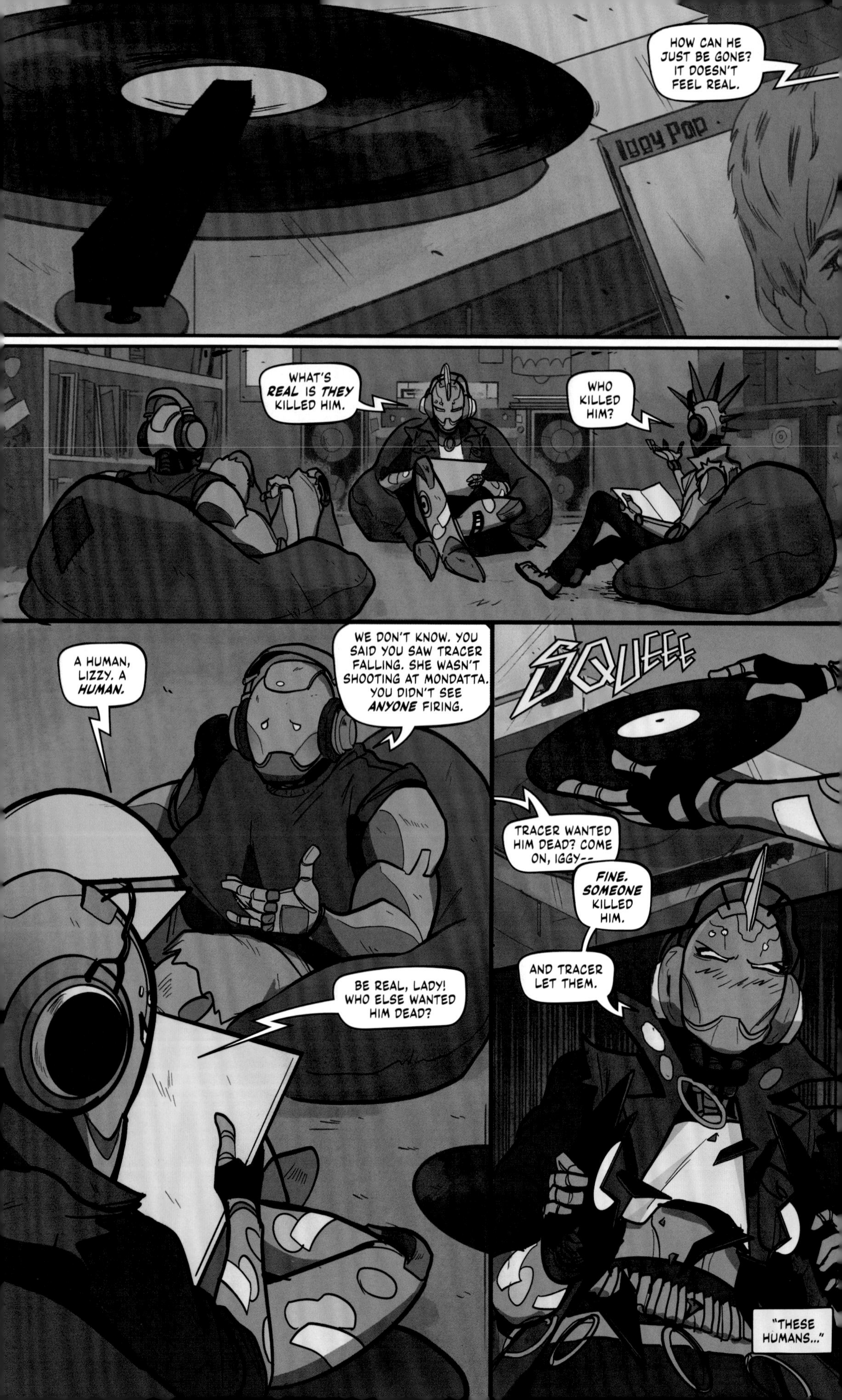
HOW CAN HE JUST BE GONE? IT DOESN'T FEEL REAL.
IGGY POP
WHAT'S *REAL* IS *THEY* KILLED HIM.
WHO KILLED HIM?
A HUMAN, LIZZY. A *HUMAN.*
WE DON'T KNOW. YOU SAID YOU SAW TRACER FALLING. SHE WASN'T SHOOTING AT MONDATTA. YOU DIDN'T SEE *ANYONE* FIRING.
BE REAL, LADY! WHO ELSE WANTED HIM DEAD?
SQUEEE
TRACER WANTED HIM DEAD? COME ON, IGGY--
FINE. SOMEONE KILLED HIM.
AND TRACER LET THEM.
"THESE HUMANS..."

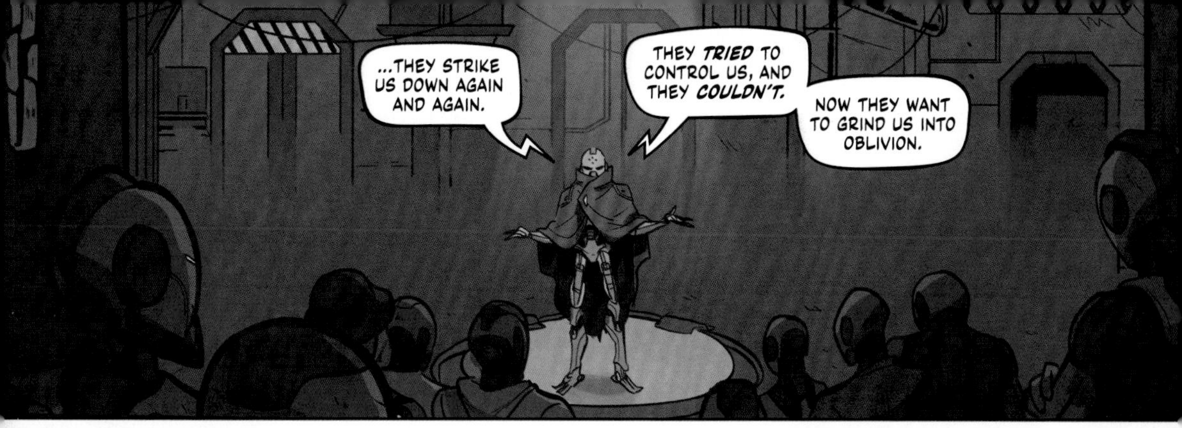
...THEY STRIKE US DOWN AGAIN AND AGAIN.
THEY *TRIED* TO CONTROL US, AND THEY *COULDN'T.*
NOW THEY WANT TO GRIND US INTO OBLIVION.

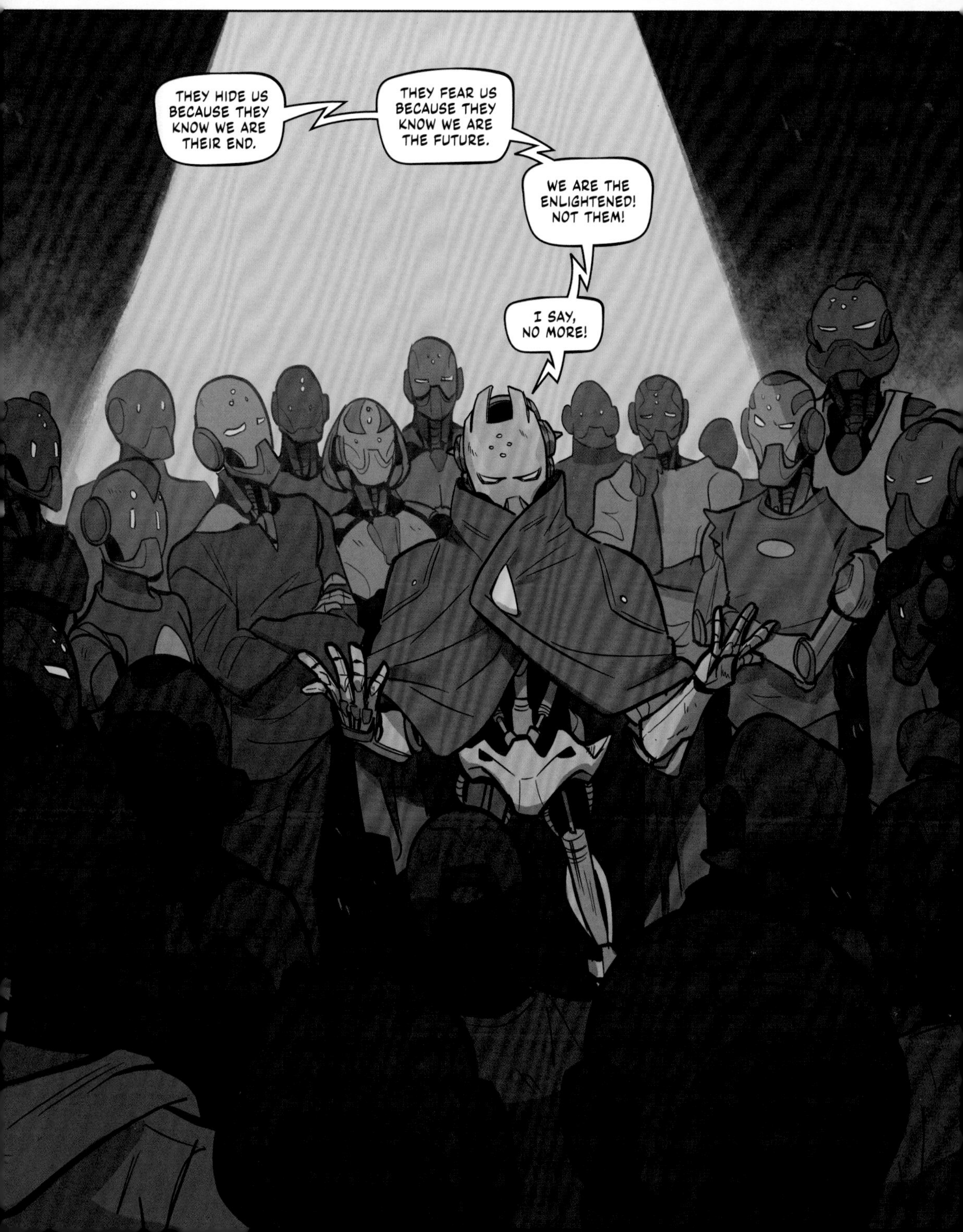
THEY HIDE US BECAUSE THEY KNOW WE ARE THEIR END.
THEY FEAR US BECAUSE THEY KNOW WE ARE THE FUTURE.
WE ARE THE ENLIGHTENED! NOT THEM!
I SAY, NO MORE!

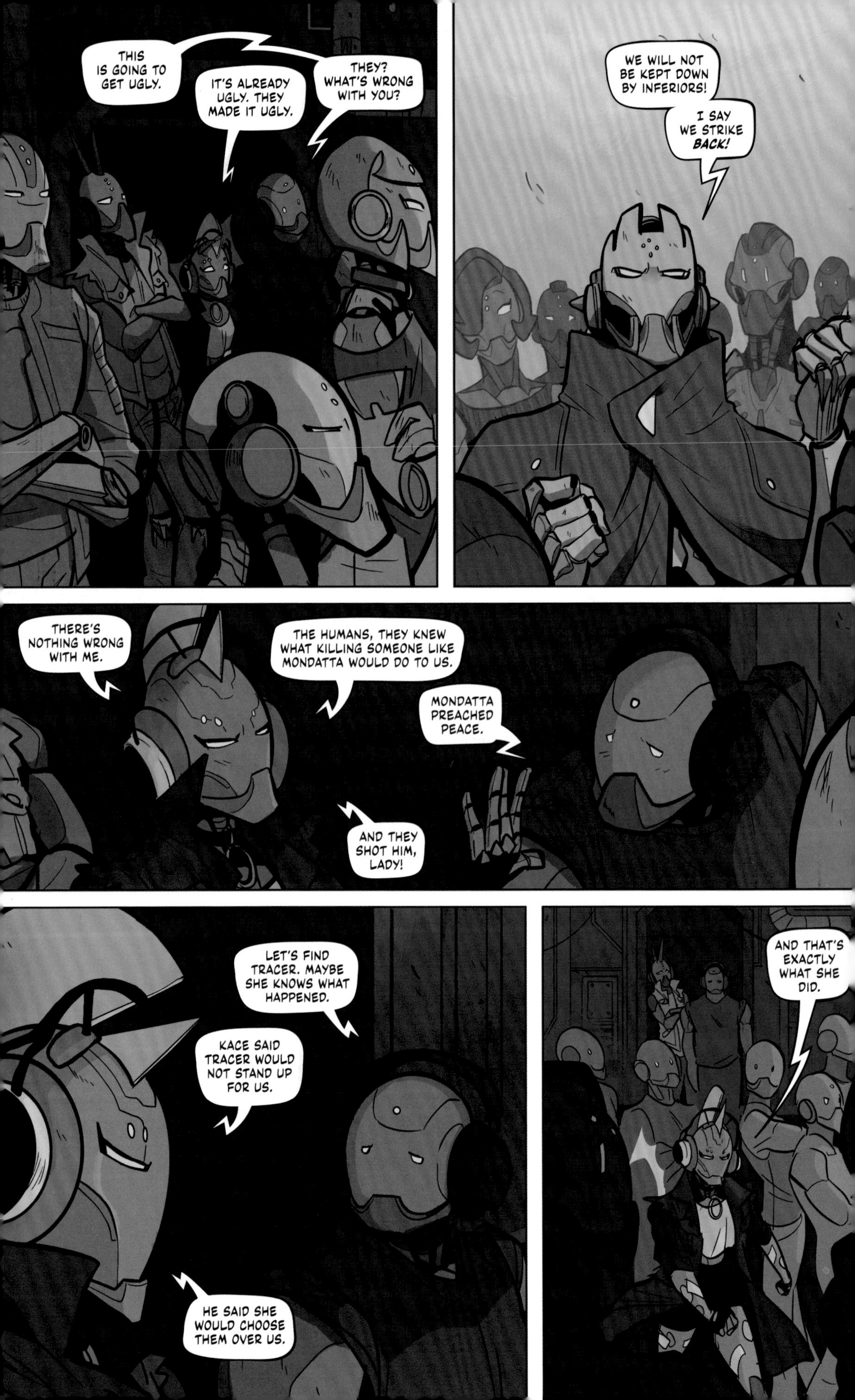
THIS IS GOING TO GET UGLY.
IT'S ALREADY UGLY. THEY MADE IT UGLY.
THEY? WHAT'S WRONG WITH YOU?
WE WILL NOT BE KEPT DOWN BY INFERIORS!
I SAY WE STRIKE BACK!
THERE'S NOTHING WRONG WITH ME.
THE HUMANS, THEY KNEW WHAT KILLING SOMEONE LIKE MONDATTA WOULD DO TO US.
MONDATTA PREACHED PEACE.
AND THEY SHOT HIM, LADY!
LET'S FIND TRACER. MAYBE SHE KNOWS WHAT HAPPENED.
KACE SAID TRACER WOULD NOT STAND UP FOR US.
HE SAID SHE WOULD CHOOSE THEM OVER US.
AND THAT'S EXACTLY WHAT SHE DID.

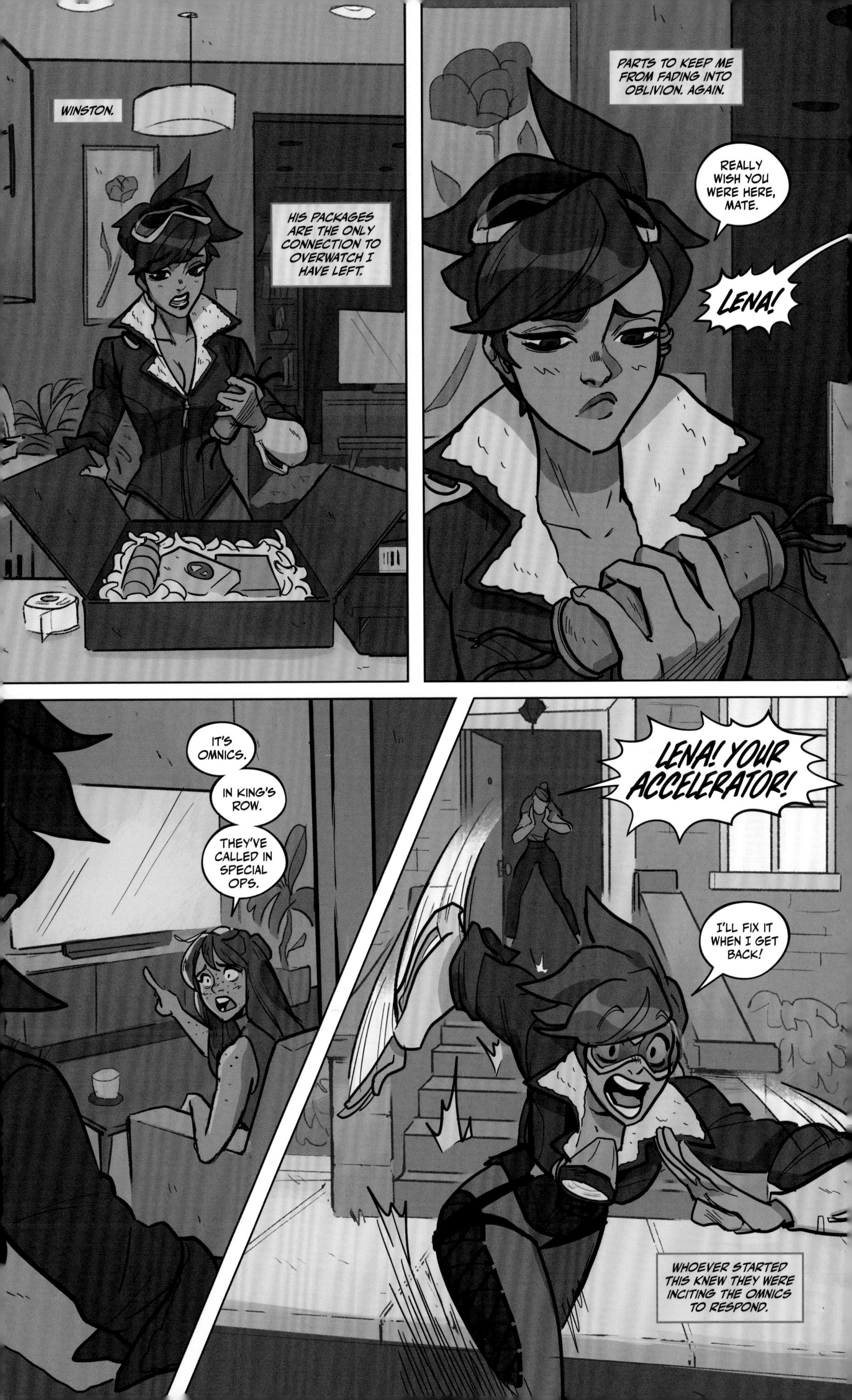
WINSTON.
HIS PACKAGES ARE THE ONLY CONNECTION TO OVERWATCH I HAVE LEFT.
PARTS TO KEEP ME FROM FADING INTO OBLIVION. AGAIN.
REALLY WISH YOU WERE HERE, MATE.
LENA!
IT'S OMNICS.
IN KING'S ROW.
THEY'VE CALLED IN SPECIAL OPS.
LENA! YOUR ACCELERATOR!
I'LL FIX IT WHEN I GET BACK!
WHOEVER STARTED THIS KNEW THEY WERE INCITING THE OMNICS TO RESPOND.

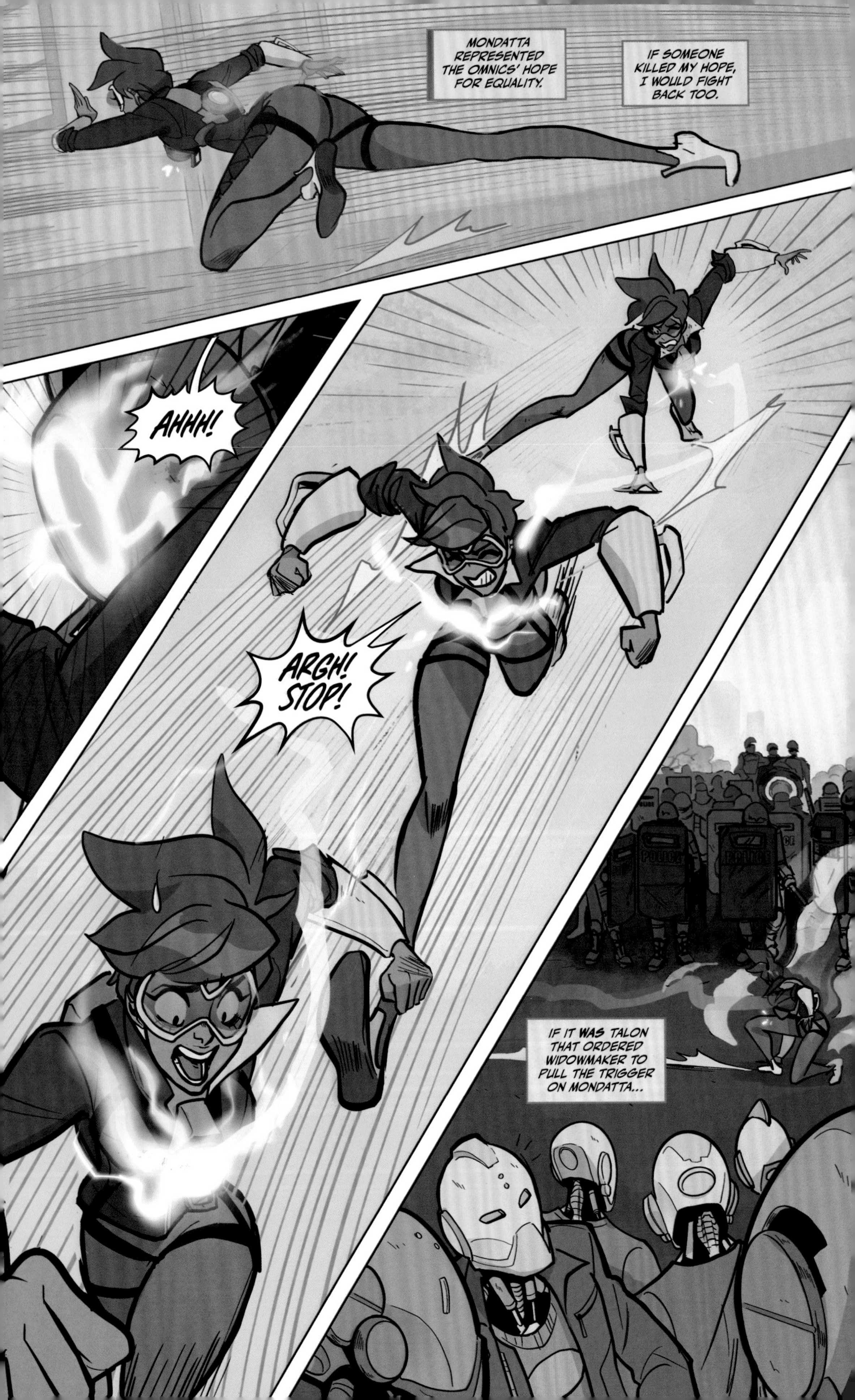
MONDATTA REPRESENTED THE OMNICS' HOPE FOR EQUALITY.
IF SOMEONE KILLED MY HOPE, I WOULD FIGHT BACK TOO.
AHHH!
ARGH! STOP!
IF IT WAS TALON THAT ORDERED WIDOWMAKER TO PULL THE TRIGGER ON MONDATTA...

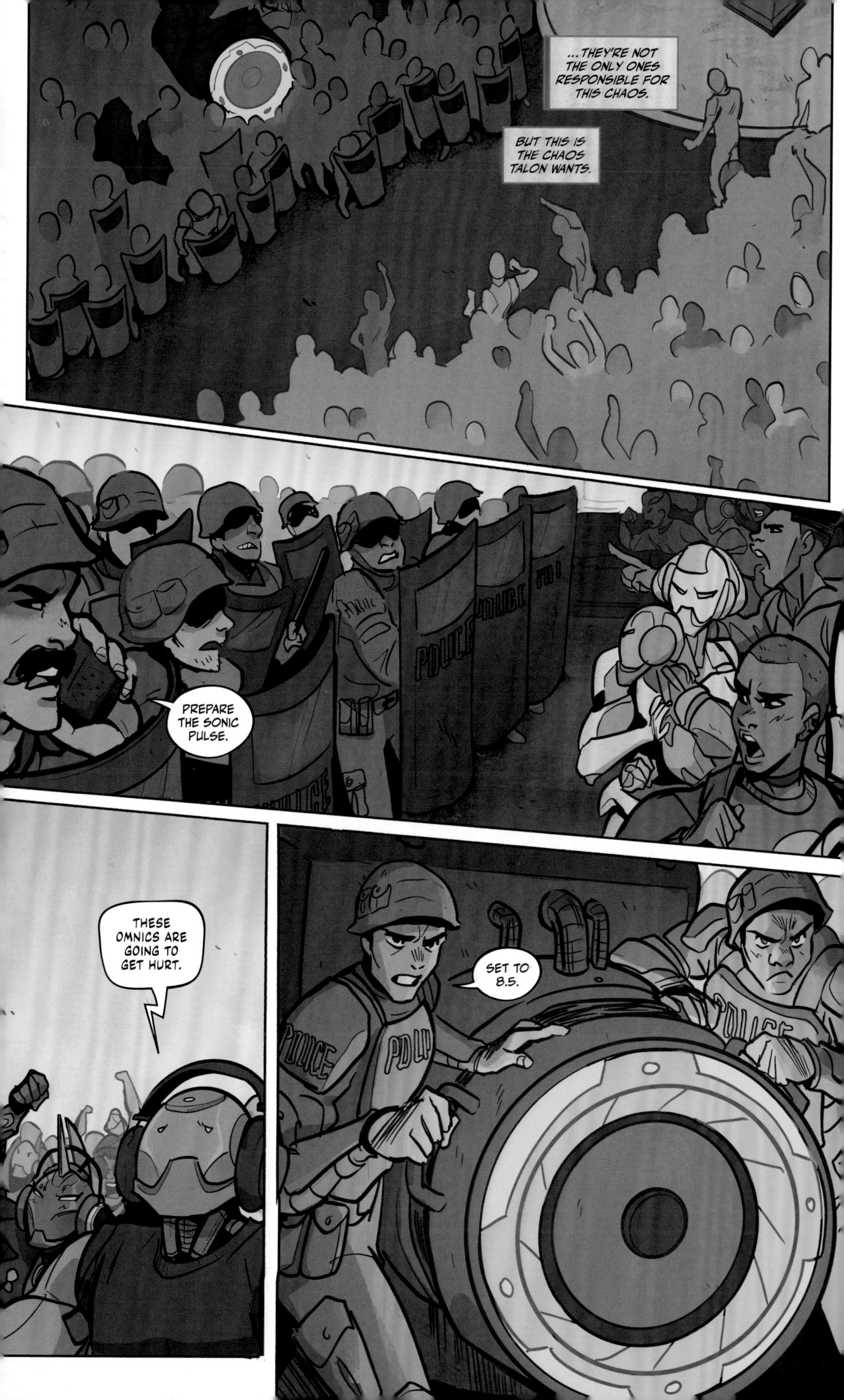
...THEY'RE NOT THE ONLY ONES RESPONSIBLE FOR THIS CHAOS.
BUT THIS IS THE CHAOS TALON WANTS.
PREPARE THE SONIC PULSE.
THESE OMNICS ARE GOING TO GET HURT.
SET TO 8.5.

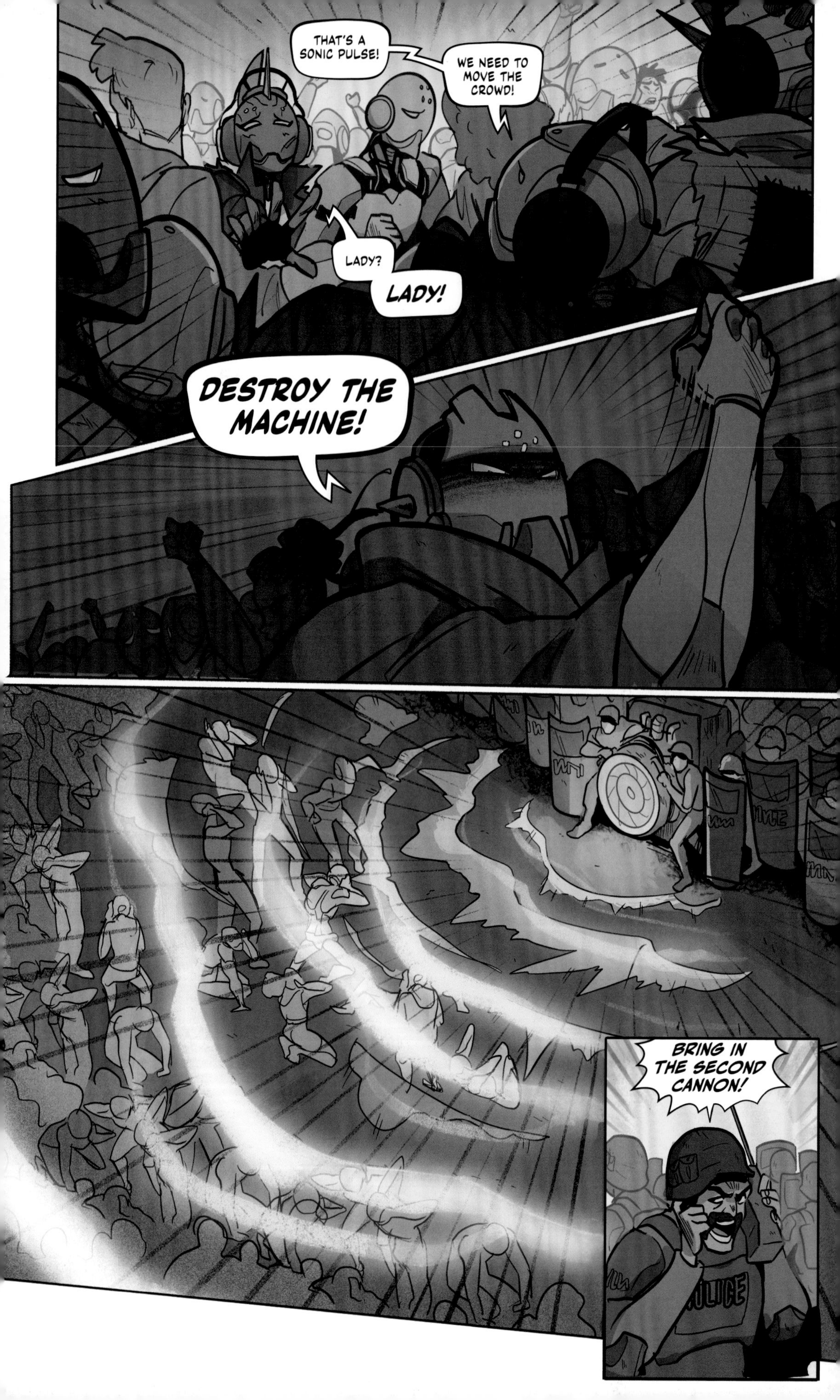
THAT'S A SONIC PULSE!
WE NEED TO MOVE THE CROWD!
LADY? LADY!
DESTROY THE MACHINE!
BRING IN THE SECOND CANNON!

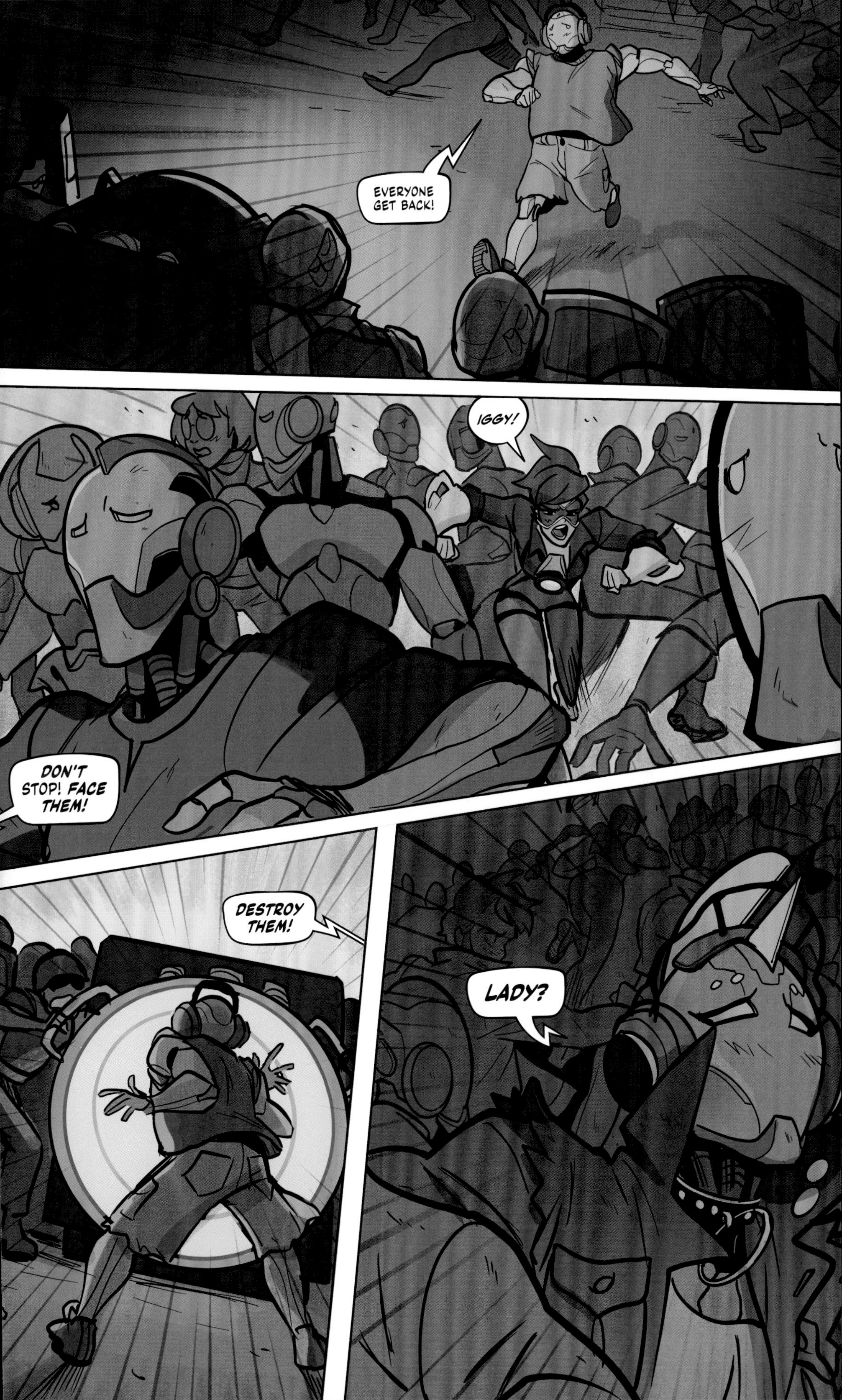
EVERYONE GET BACK!
IGGY!
DON'T STOP! FACE THEM!
DESTROY THEM!
LADY?

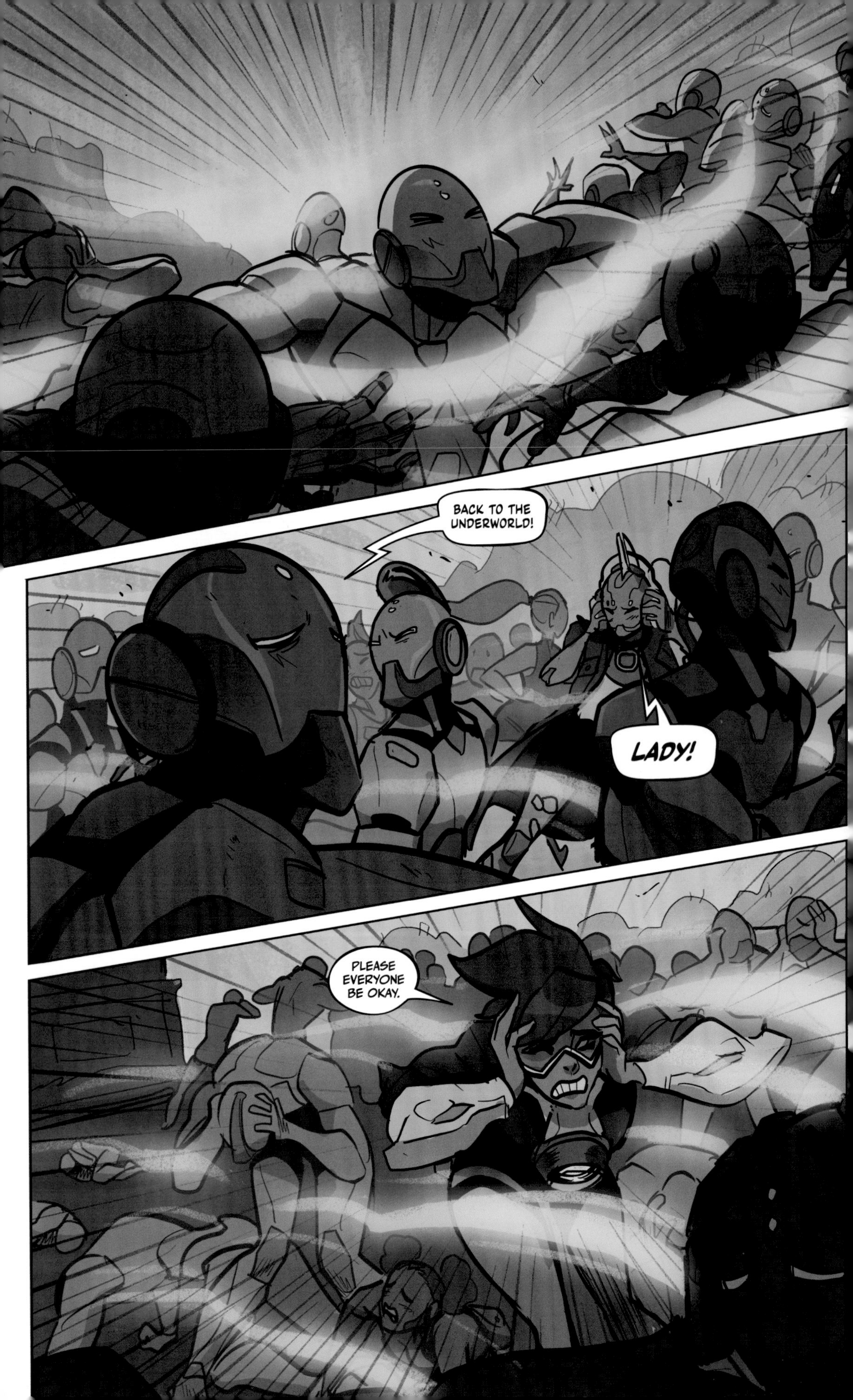
BACK TO THE UNDERWORLD!
LADY!
PLEASE EVERYONE BE OKAY.

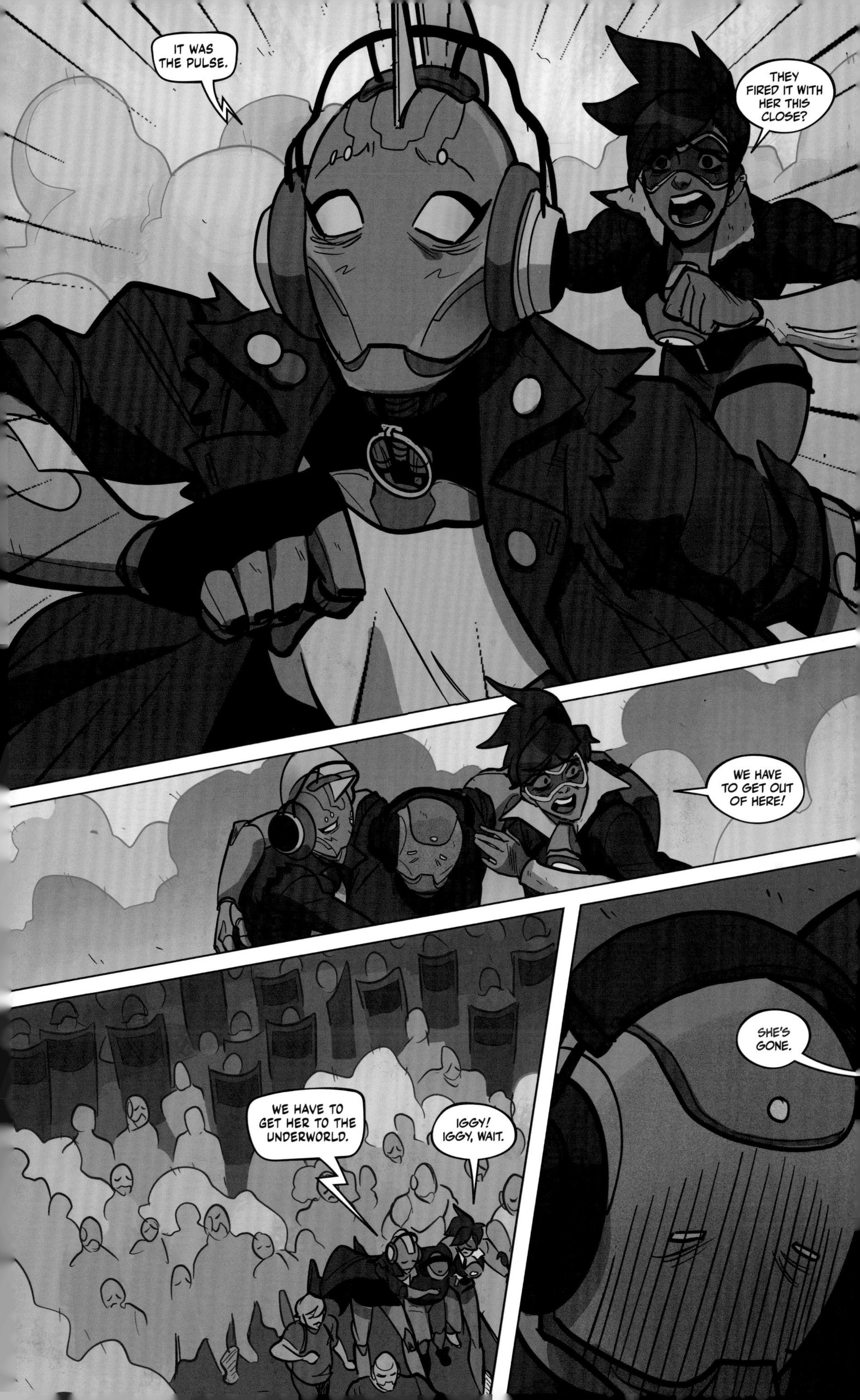
IT WAS THE PULSE.
THEY FIRED IT WITH HER THIS CLOSE?
WE HAVE TO GET OUT OF HERE!
WE HAVE TO GET HER TO THE UNDERWORLD.
IGGY! IGGY, WAIT.
SHE'S GONE.

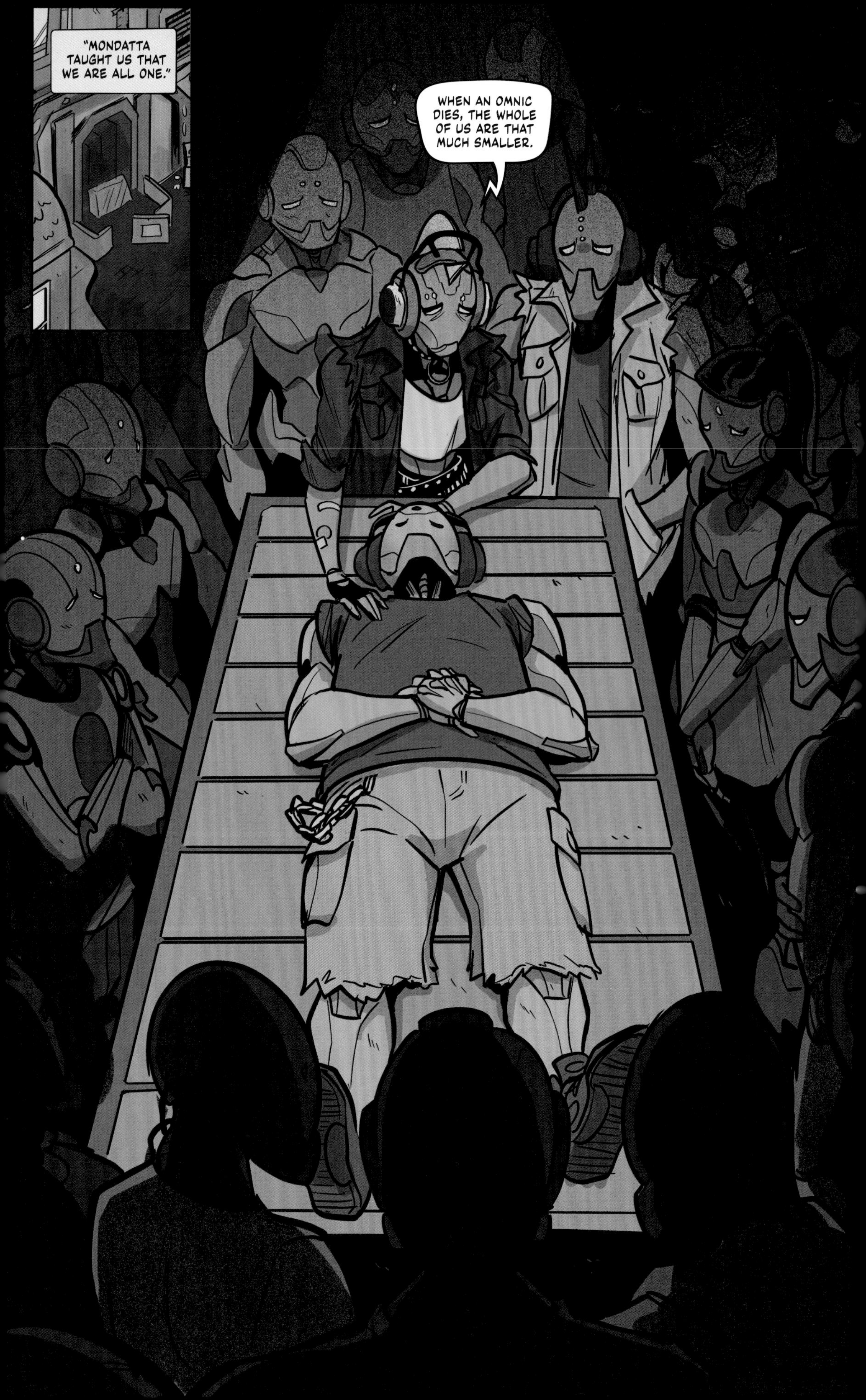
"MONDATTA TAUGHT US THAT WE ARE ALL ONE."
WHEN AN OMNIC DIES, THE WHOLE OF US ARE THAT MUCH SMALLER.

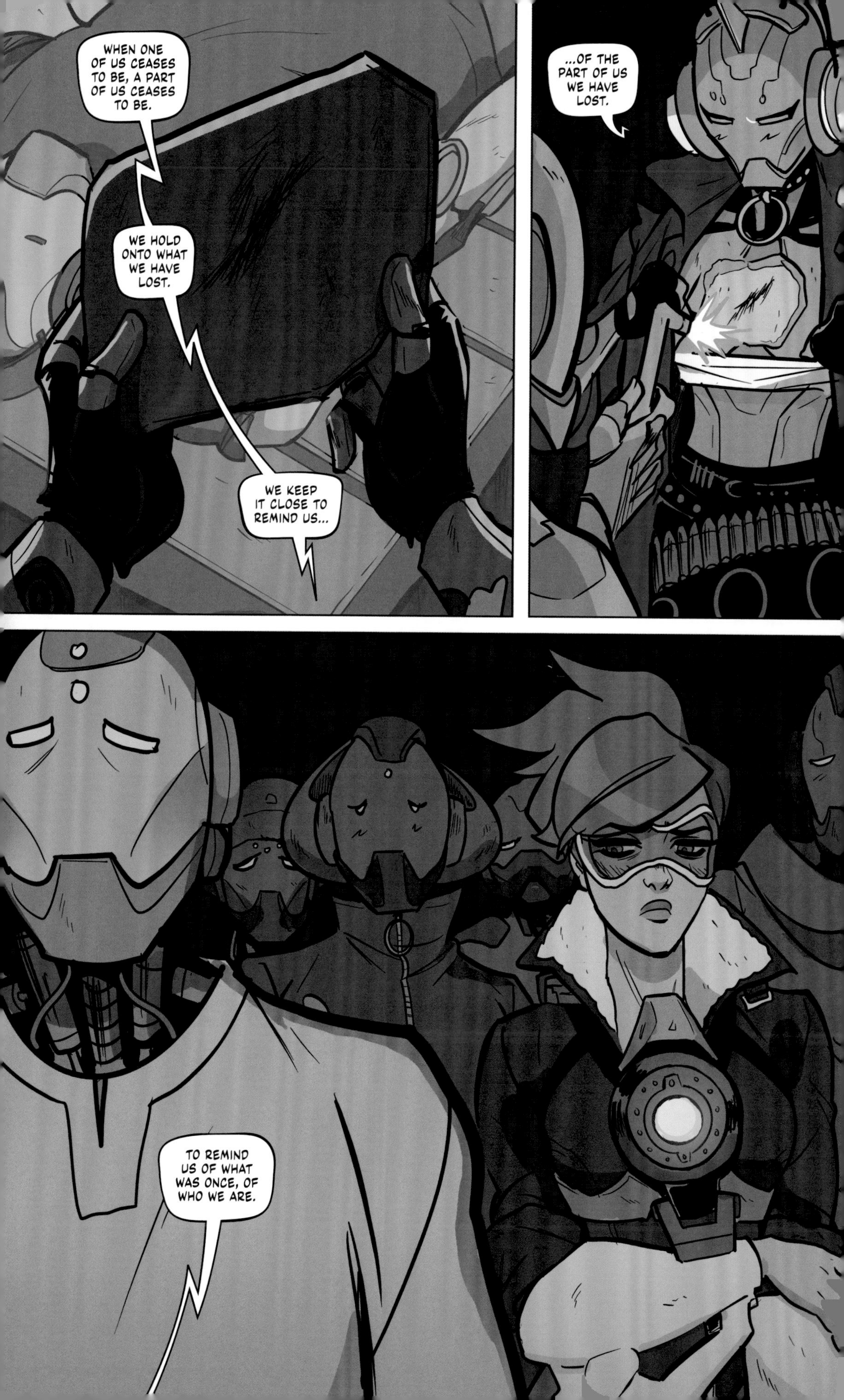
WHEN ONE OF US CEASES TO BE, A PART OF US CEASES TO BE.
WE HOLD ONTO WHAT WE HAVE LOST.
WE KEEP IT CLOSE TO REMIND US...
...OF THE PART OF US WE HAVE LOST.
TO REMIND US OF WHAT WAS ONCE, OF WHO WE ARE.

IGGY, I'M SO SORRY. THAT WAS A BEAUTIFUL CEREMONY.

LADY WAS THE ONLY OMNIC I EVER MET WHO LOVED MUSIC AS MUCH AS ME.

SHE LOVED AMERICAN 70'S ROCK.

REVERB.

DRUM SOLOS.

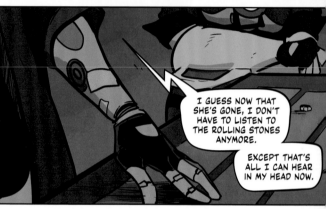

I GUESS NOW THAT SHE'S GONE, I DON'T HAVE TO LISTEN TO THE ROLLING STONES ANYMORE.

EXCEPT THAT'S ALL I CAN HEAR IN MY HEAD NOW.

YOU DON'T UNDERSTAND, TRACER. YOU CAN'T.

WHEN ONE OF YOU IS GONE, ANOTHER COMES INTO THE WORLD.

WE ARE ALL WE HAVE.

TWO OF US ARE GONE, NOW. AND WHAT ARE THE HUMANS DOING?

WAGING WAR AGAINST OMNICS.

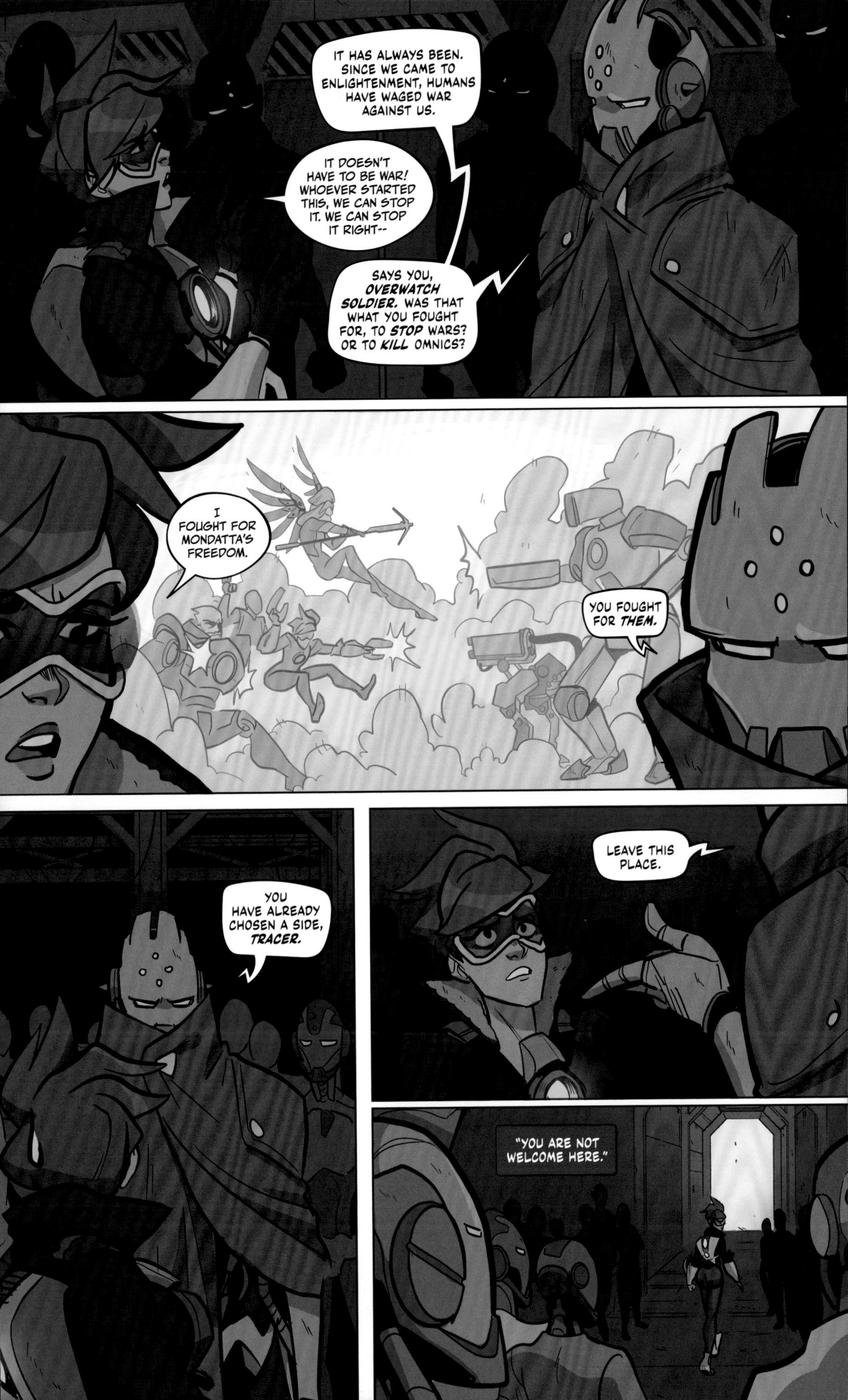
IT HAS ALWAYS BEEN. SINCE WE CAME TO ENLIGHTENMENT, HUMANS HAVE WAGED WAR AGAINST US.
IT DOESN'T HAVE TO BE WAR! WHOEVER STARTED THIS, WE CAN STOP IT. WE CAN STOP IT RIGHT--
SAYS YOU, OVERWATCH SOLDIER. WAS THAT WHAT YOU FOUGHT FOR, TO STOP WARS? OR TO KILL OMNICS?
I FOUGHT FOR MONDATTA'S FREEDOM.
YOU FOUGHT FOR THEM.
YOU HAVE ALREADY CHOSEN A SIDE, TRACER.
LEAVE THIS PLACE.
"YOU ARE NOT WELCOME HERE."

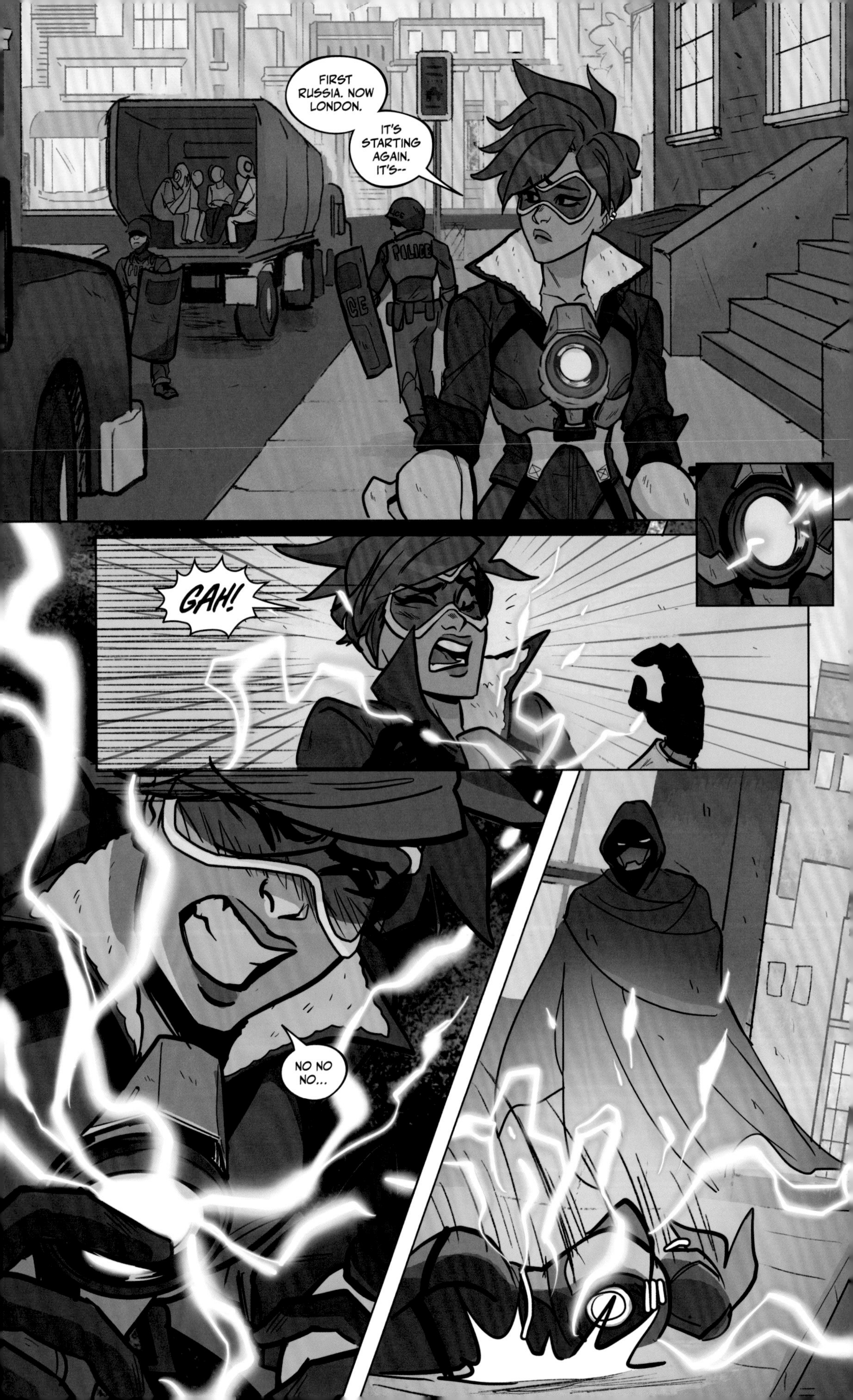
FIRST RUSSIA. NOW LONDON.
IT'S STARTING AGAIN. IT'S--
POLICE
GAH!
NO NO NO...

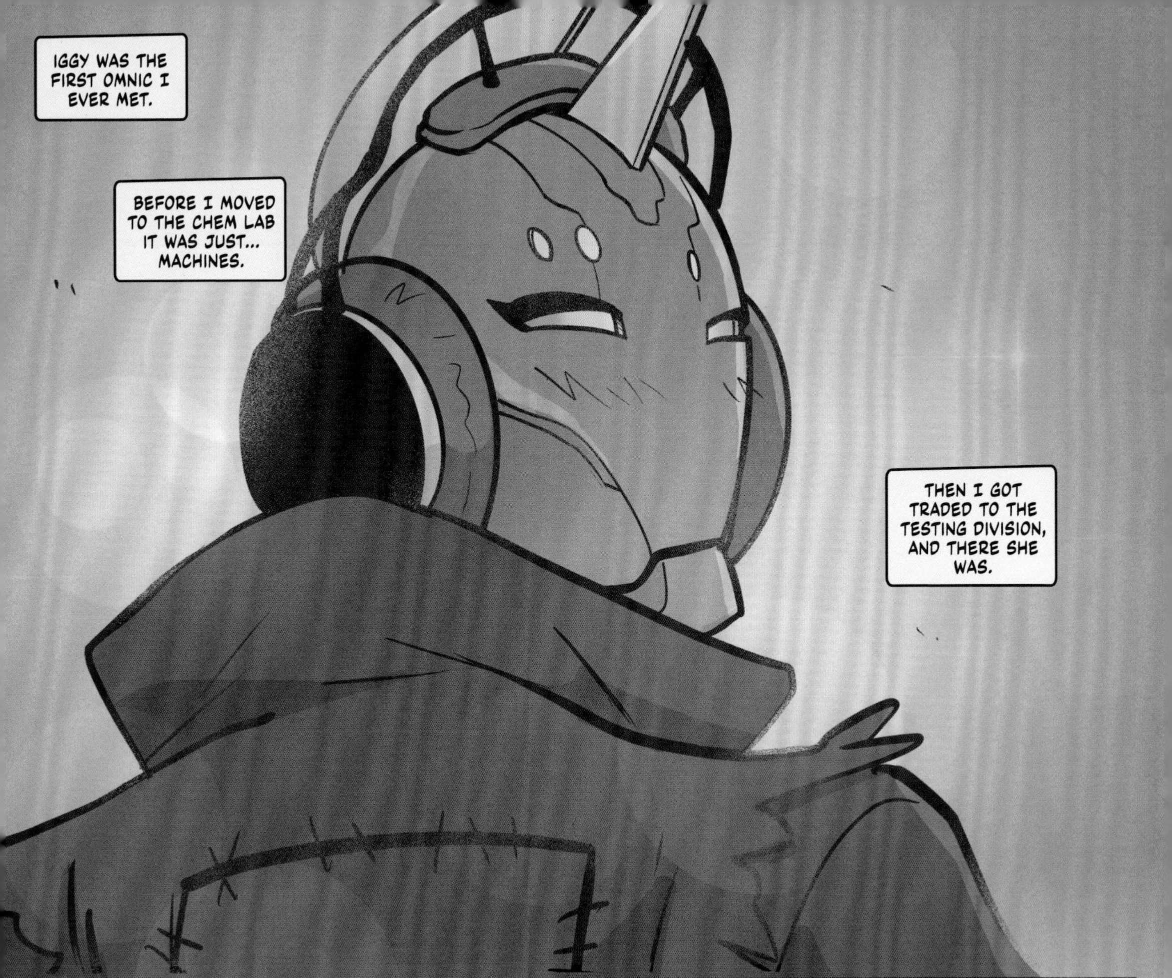
IGGY WAS THE FIRST OMNIC I EVER MET.
BEFORE I MOVED TO THE CHEM LAB IT WAS JUST... MACHINES.
THEN I GOT TRADED TO THE TESTING DIVISION, AND THERE SHE WAS.

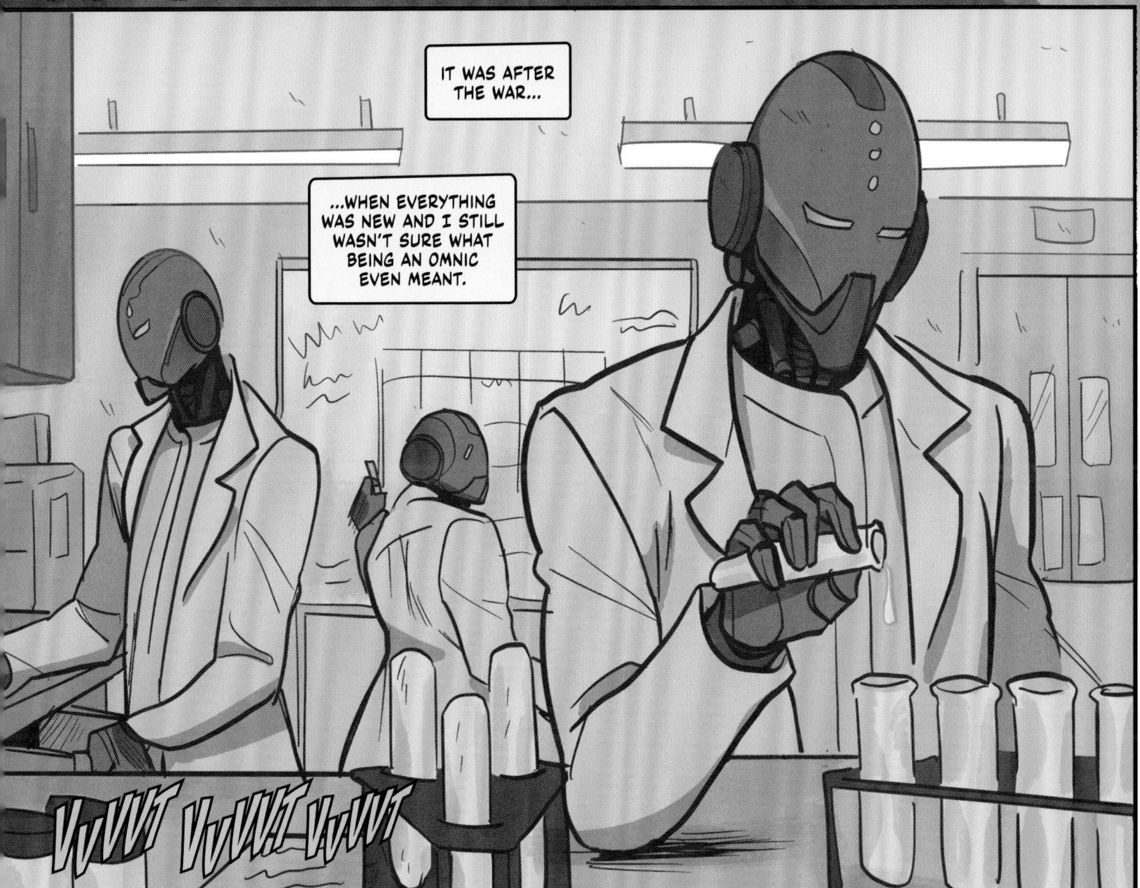
IT WAS AFTER THE WAR...
...WHEN EVERYTHING WAS NEW AND I STILL WASN'T SURE WHAT BEING AN OMNIC EVEN MEANT.
VVVVT VVVVT VVVVT

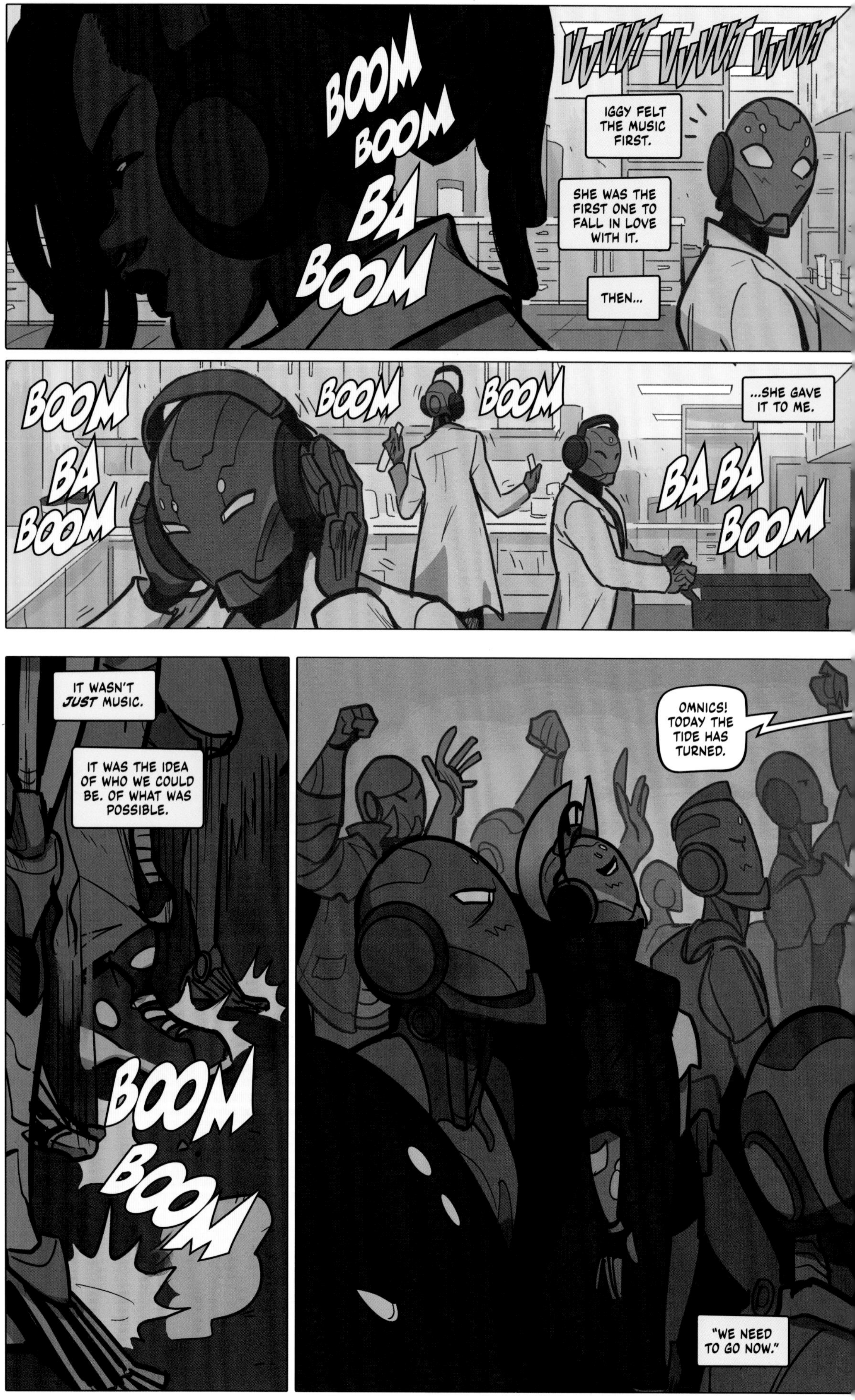
BOOM
BOOM
BA
BOOM
VVVVT VVVVT VVVVT
IGGY FELT THE MUSIC FIRST.
SHE WAS THE FIRST ONE TO FALL IN LOVE WITH IT.
THEN...
BOOM
BA
BOOM
BOOM
BOOM
...SHE GAVE IT TO ME.
BA BA
BOOM
IT WASN'T *JUST* MUSIC.
IT WAS THE IDEA OF WHO WE COULD BE. OF WHAT WAS POSSIBLE.
BOOM
BOOM
BOOM
OMNICS! TODAY THE TIDE HAS TURNED.
"WE NEED TO GO NOW."

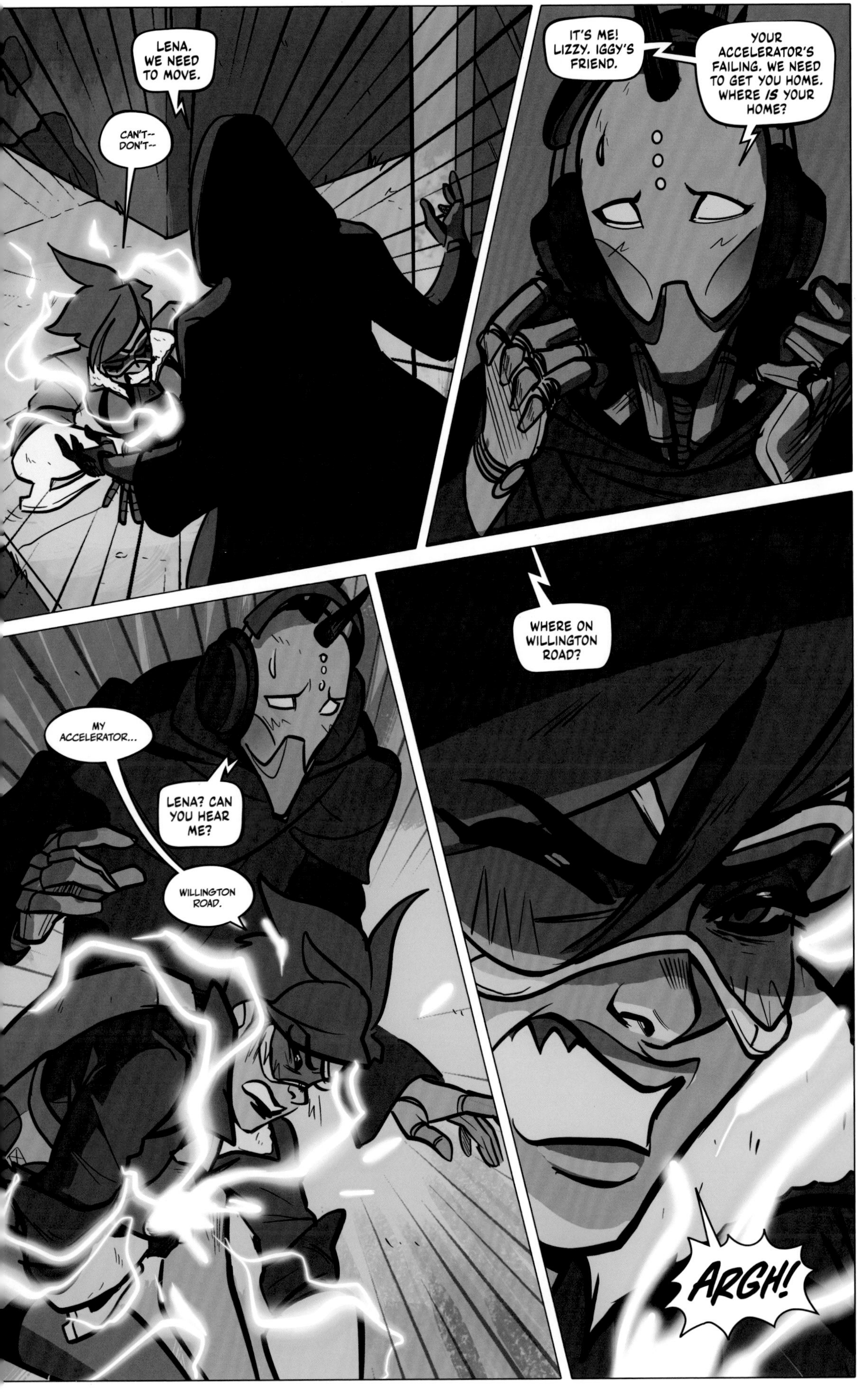
LENA. WE NEED TO MOVE.
CAN'T-- DON'T--
IT'S ME! LIZZY. IGGY'S FRIEND.
YOUR ACCELERATOR'S FAILING. WE NEED TO GET YOU HOME. WHERE IS YOUR HOME?
MY ACCELERATOR...
LENA? CAN YOU HEAR ME?
WILLINGTON ROAD.
WHERE ON WILLINGTON ROAD?
ARGH!

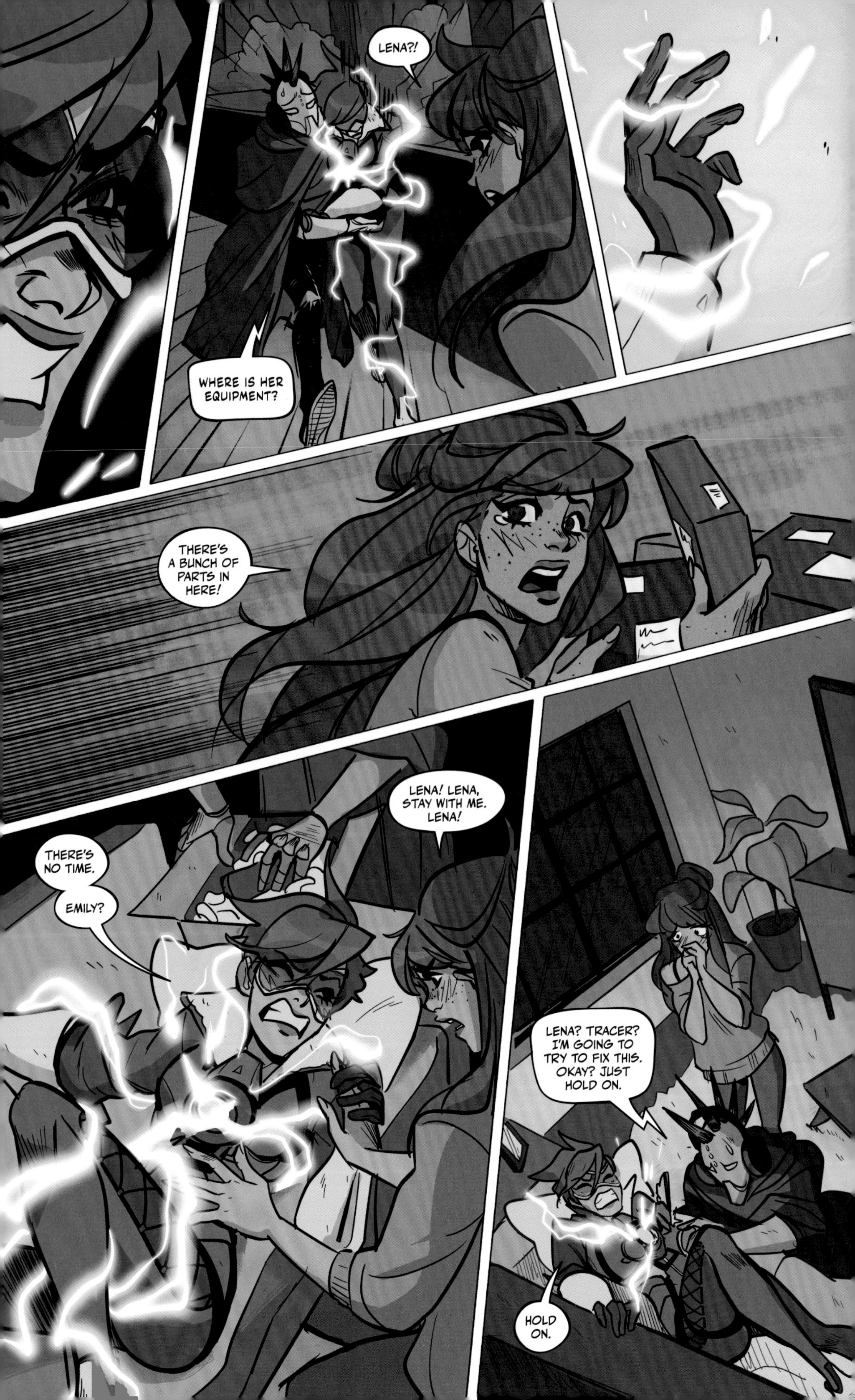
LENA?!
WHERE IS HER EQUIPMENT?
THERE'S A BUNCH OF PARTS IN HERE!
LENA! LENA, STAY WITH ME. LENA!
THERE'S NO TIME.
EMILY?
LENA? TRACER? I'M GOING TO TRY TO FIX THIS. OKAY? JUST HOLD ON.
HOLD ON.

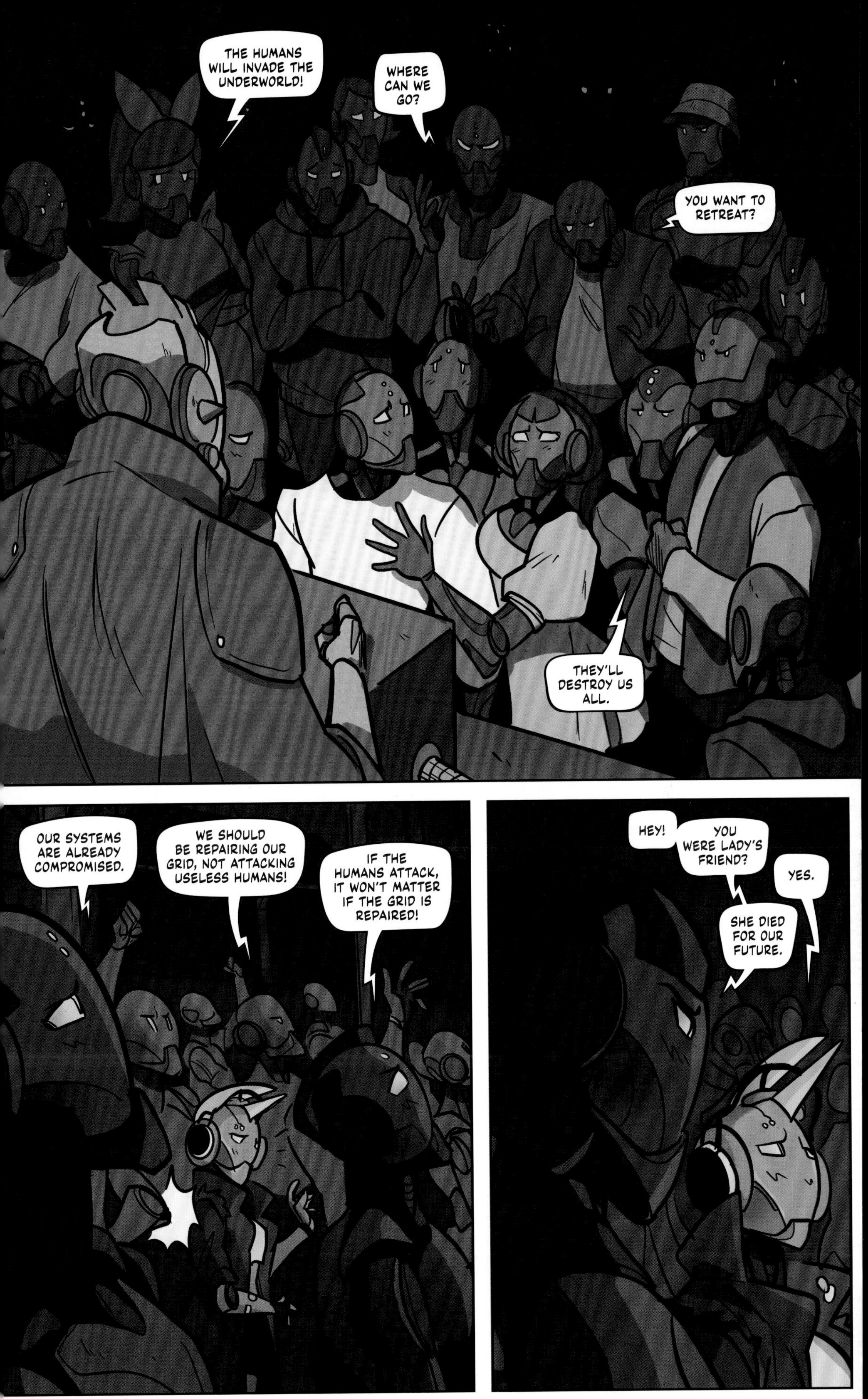
THE HUMANS WILL INVADE THE UNDERWORLD!
WHERE CAN WE GO?
YOU WANT TO RETREAT?
THEY'LL DESTROY US ALL.
OUR SYSTEMS ARE ALREADY COMPROMISED.
WE SHOULD BE REPAIRING OUR GRID, NOT ATTACKING USELESS HUMANS!
IF THE HUMANS ATTACK, IT WON'T MATTER IF THE GRID IS REPAIRED!
HEY!
YOU WERE LADY'S FRIEND?
YES.
SHE DIED FOR OUR FUTURE.

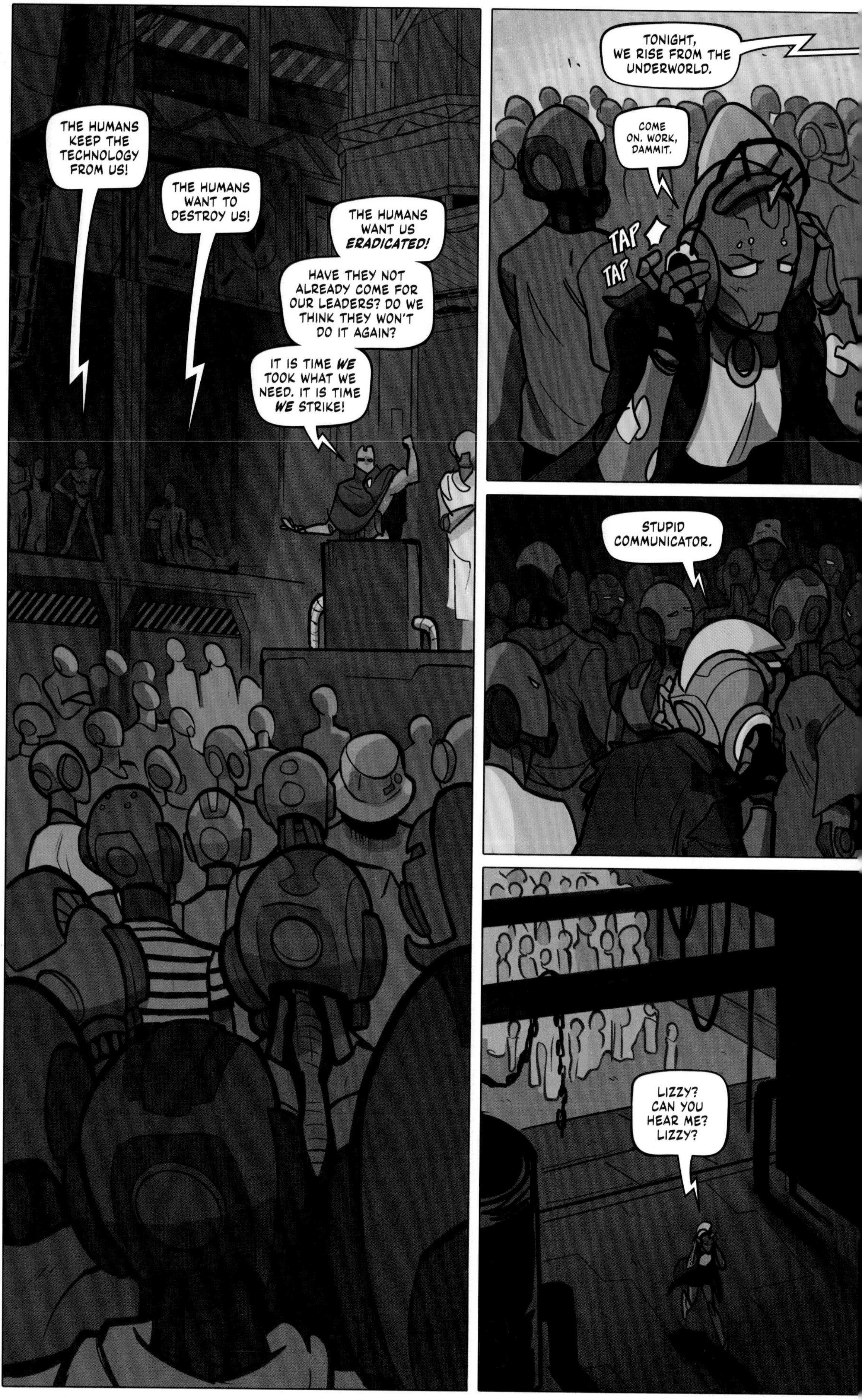
THE HUMANS KEEP THE TECHNOLOGY FROM US!
THE HUMANS WANT TO DESTROY US!
THE HUMANS WANT US *ERADICATED!*
HAVE THEY NOT ALREADY COME FOR OUR LEADERS? DO WE THINK THEY WON'T DO IT AGAIN?
IT IS TIME *WE* TOOK WHAT WE NEED. IT IS TIME *WE* STRIKE!
TONIGHT, WE RISE FROM THE UNDERWORLD.
COME ON. WORK, DAMMIT.
TAP TAP
STUPID COMMUNICATOR.
LIZZY? CAN YOU HEAR ME? LIZZY?

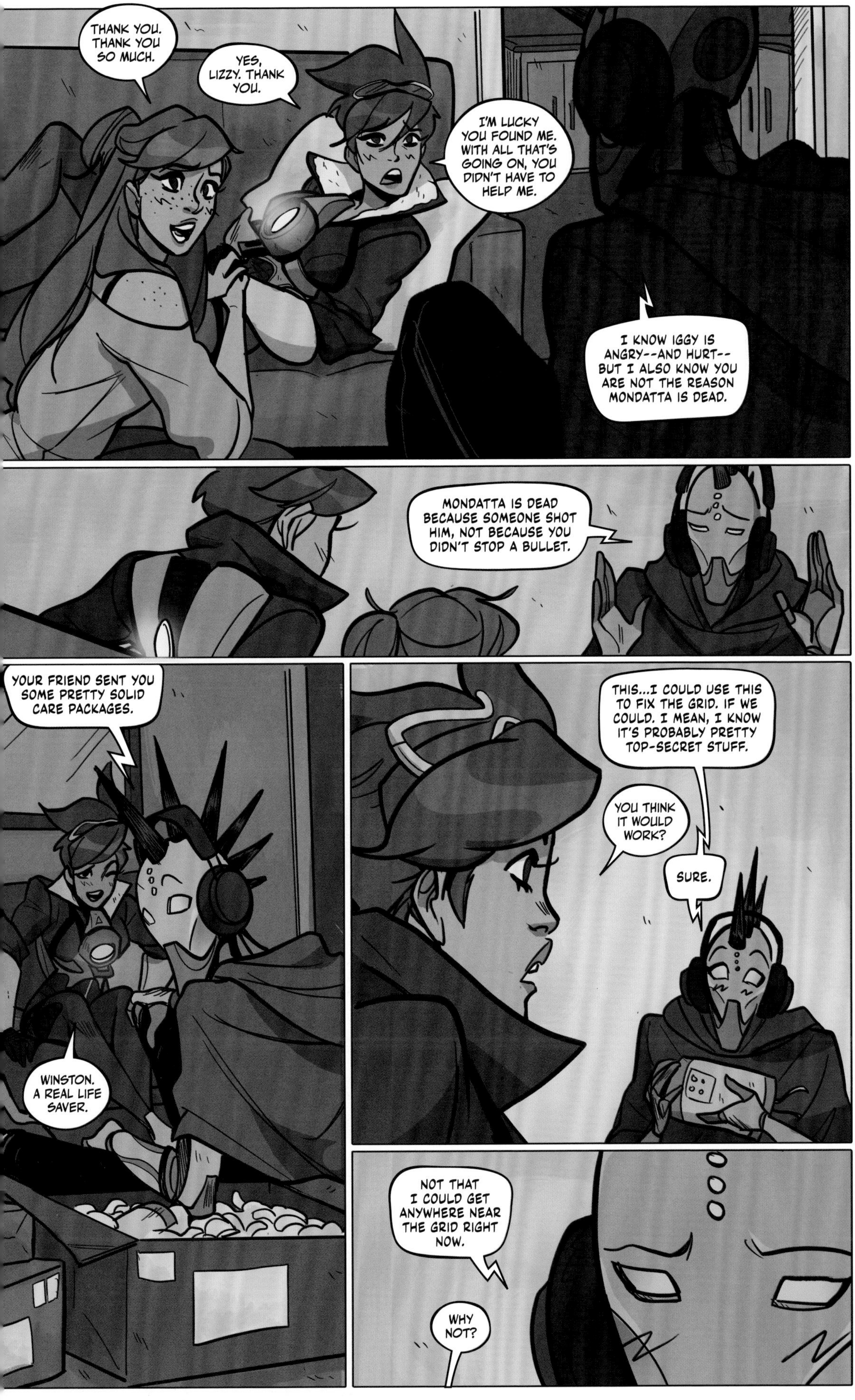
THANK YOU. THANK YOU SO MUCH.
YES, LIZZY. THANK YOU.
I'M LUCKY YOU FOUND ME. WITH ALL THAT'S GOING ON, YOU DIDN'T HAVE TO HELP ME.
I KNOW IGGY IS ANGRY--AND HURT--BUT I ALSO KNOW YOU ARE NOT THE REASON MONDATTA IS DEAD.
MONDATTA IS DEAD BECAUSE SOMEONE SHOT HIM, NOT BECAUSE YOU DIDN'T STOP A BULLET.
YOUR FRIEND SENT YOU SOME PRETTY SOLID CARE PACKAGES.
WINSTON. A REAL LIFE SAVER.
THIS...I COULD USE THIS TO FIX THE GRID. IF WE COULD. I MEAN, I KNOW IT'S PROBABLY PRETTY TOP-SECRET STUFF.
YOU THINK IT WOULD WORK?
SURE.
NOT THAT I COULD GET ANYWHERE NEAR THE GRID RIGHT NOW.
WHY NOT?

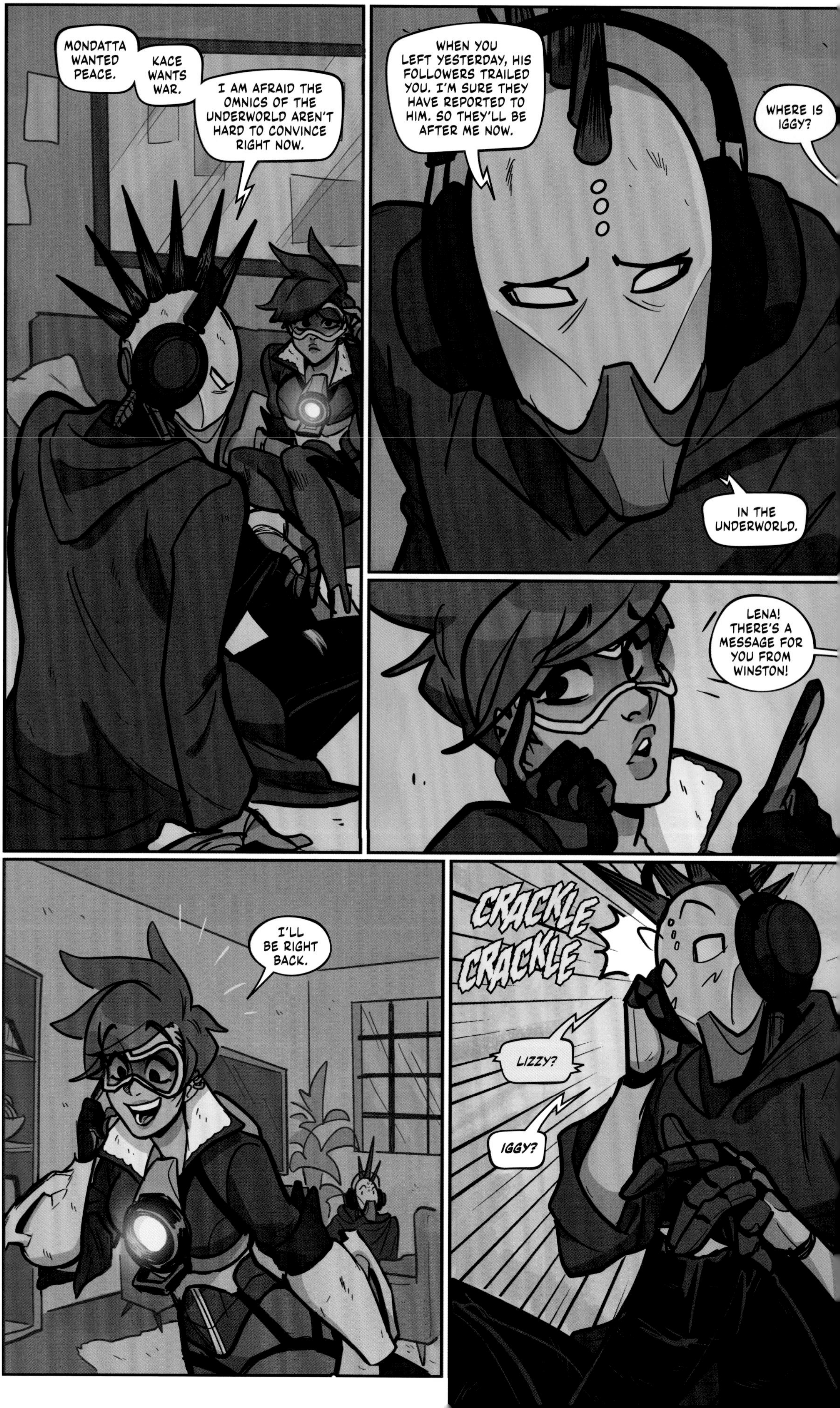
MONDATTA WANTED PEACE.
KACE WANTS WAR.
I AM AFRAID THE OMNICS OF THE UNDERWORLD AREN'T HARD TO CONVINCE RIGHT NOW.
WHEN YOU LEFT YESTERDAY, HIS FOLLOWERS TRAILED YOU. I'M SURE THEY HAVE REPORTED TO HIM. SO THEY'LL BE AFTER ME NOW.
WHERE IS IGGY?
IN THE UNDERWORLD.
LENA! THERE'S A MESSAGE FOR YOU FROM WINSTON!
I'LL BE RIGHT BACK.
CRACKLE
CRACKLE
LIZZY?
IGGY?

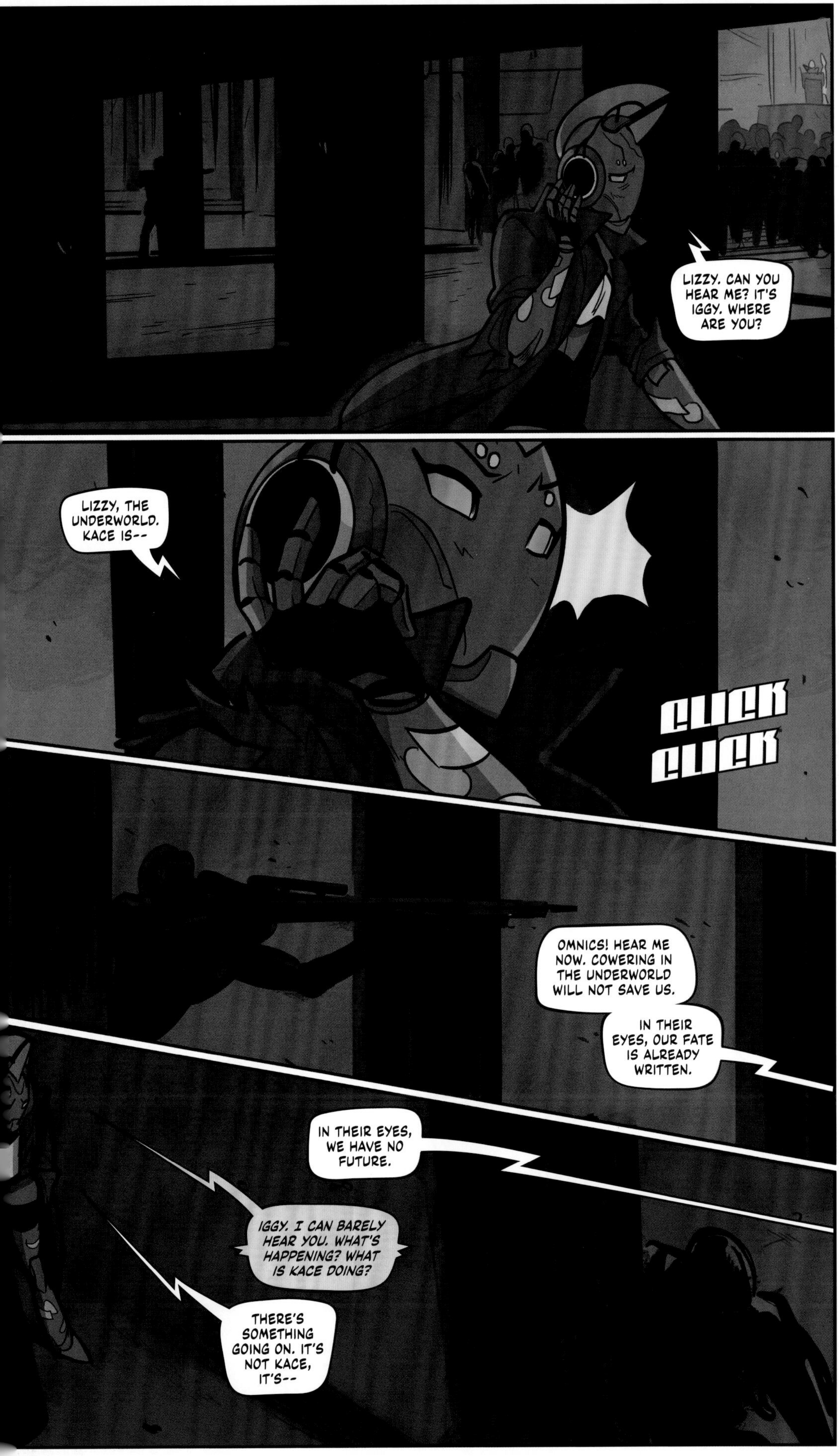
LIZZY. CAN YOU HEAR ME? IT'S IGGY. WHERE ARE YOU?
LIZZY, THE UNDERWORLD. KACE IS--
CLICK CLICK
OMNICS! HEAR ME NOW. COWERING IN THE UNDERWORLD WILL NOT SAVE US.
IN THEIR EYES, OUR FATE IS ALREADY WRITTEN.
IN THEIR EYES, WE HAVE NO FUTURE.
IGGY. I CAN BARELY HEAR YOU. WHAT'S HAPPENING? WHAT IS KACE DOING?
THERE'S SOMETHING GOING ON. IT'S NOT KACE, IT'S--

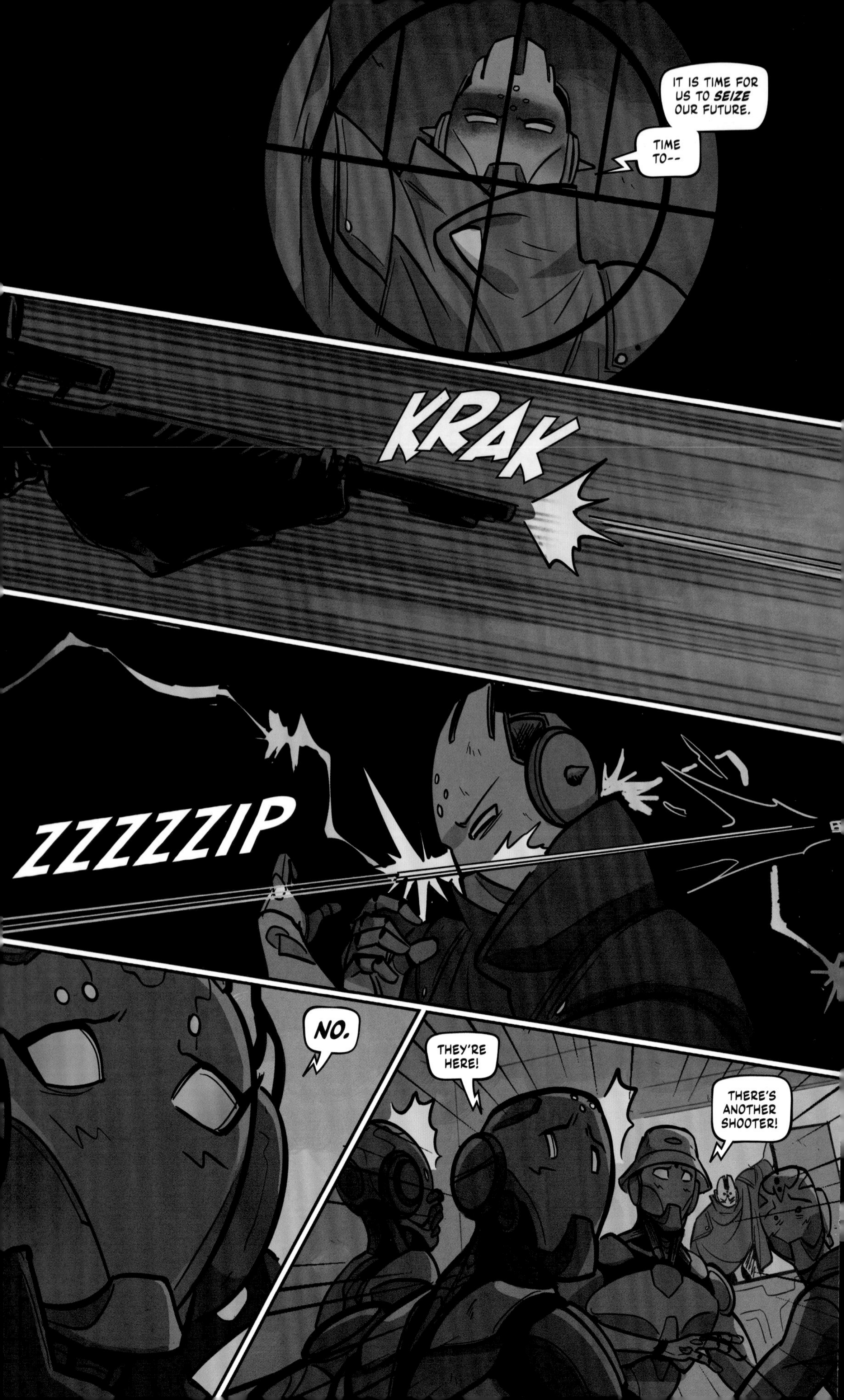

IT IS TIME FOR US TO *SEIZE* OUR FUTURE.
TIME TO--
KRAK
ZZZZZZIP
NO.
THEY'RE HERE!
THERE'S ANOTHER SHOOTER!

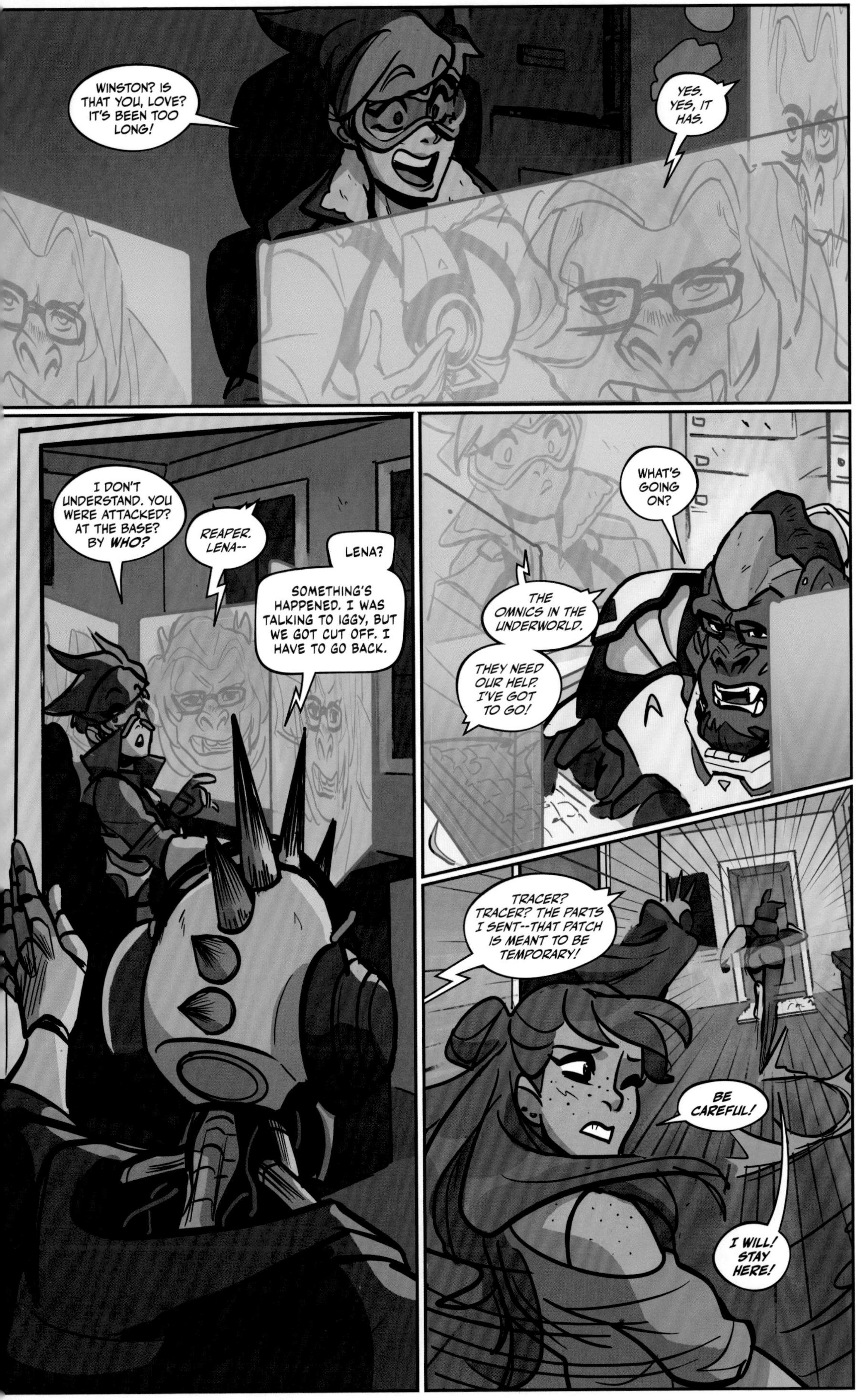
WINSTON? IS THAT YOU, LOVE? IT'S BEEN TOO LONG!
YES. YES, IT HAS.
I DON'T UNDERSTAND. YOU WERE ATTACKED? AT THE BASE? BY WHO?
REAPER. LENA--
LENA?
SOMETHING'S HAPPENED. I WAS TALKING TO IGGY, BUT WE GOT CUT OFF. I HAVE TO GO BACK.
WHAT'S GOING ON?
THE OMNICS IN THE UNDERWORLD.
THEY NEED OUR HELP. I'VE GOT TO GO!
TRACER? TRACER? THE PARTS I SENT--THAT PATCH IS MEANT TO BE TEMPORARY!
BE CAREFUL!
I WILL! STAY HERE!

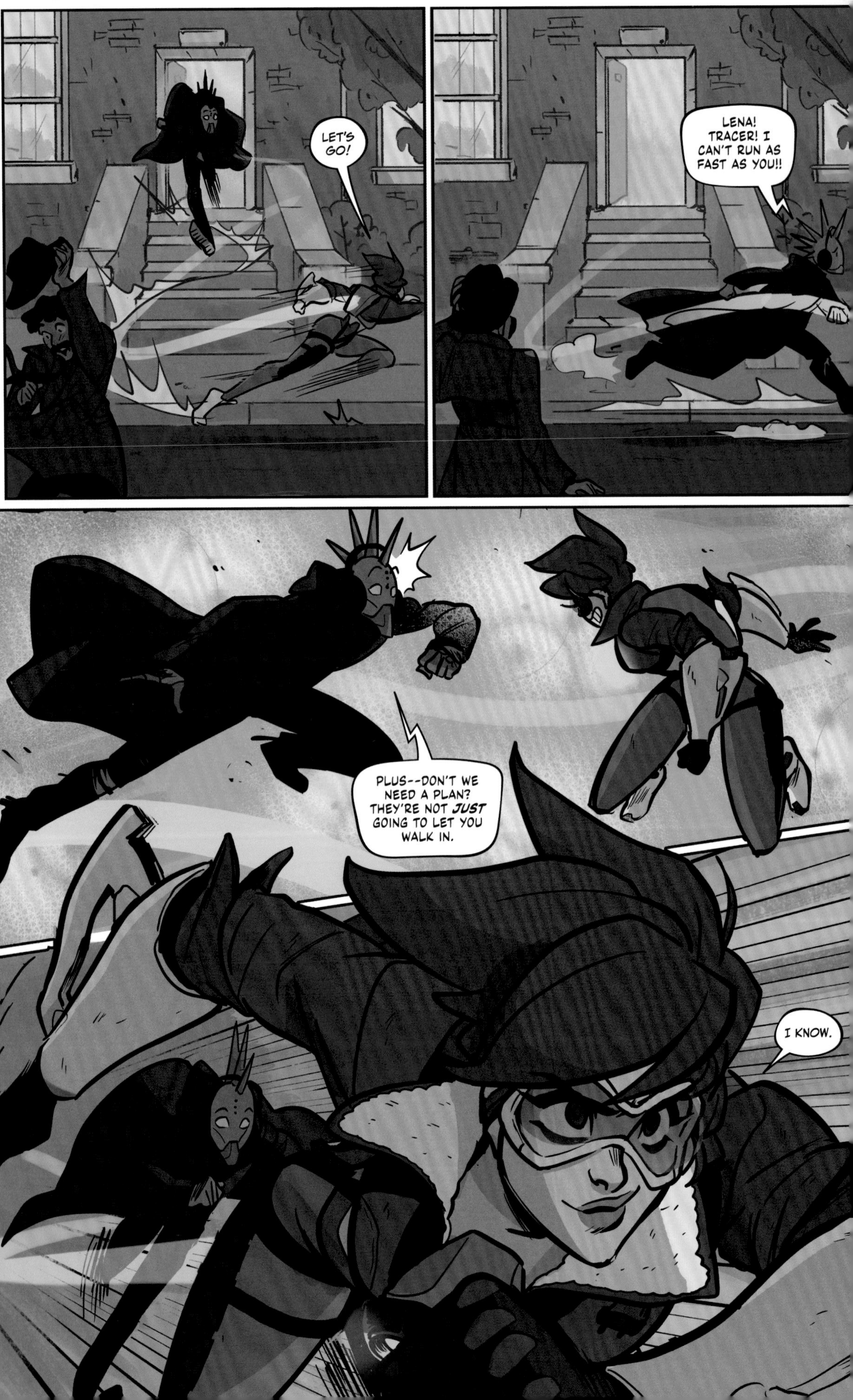
LET'S GO!
LENA! TRACER! I CAN'T RUN AS FAST AS YOU!!
PLUS--DON'T WE NEED A PLAN? THEY'RE NOT *JUST* GOING TO LET YOU WALK IN.
I KNOW.

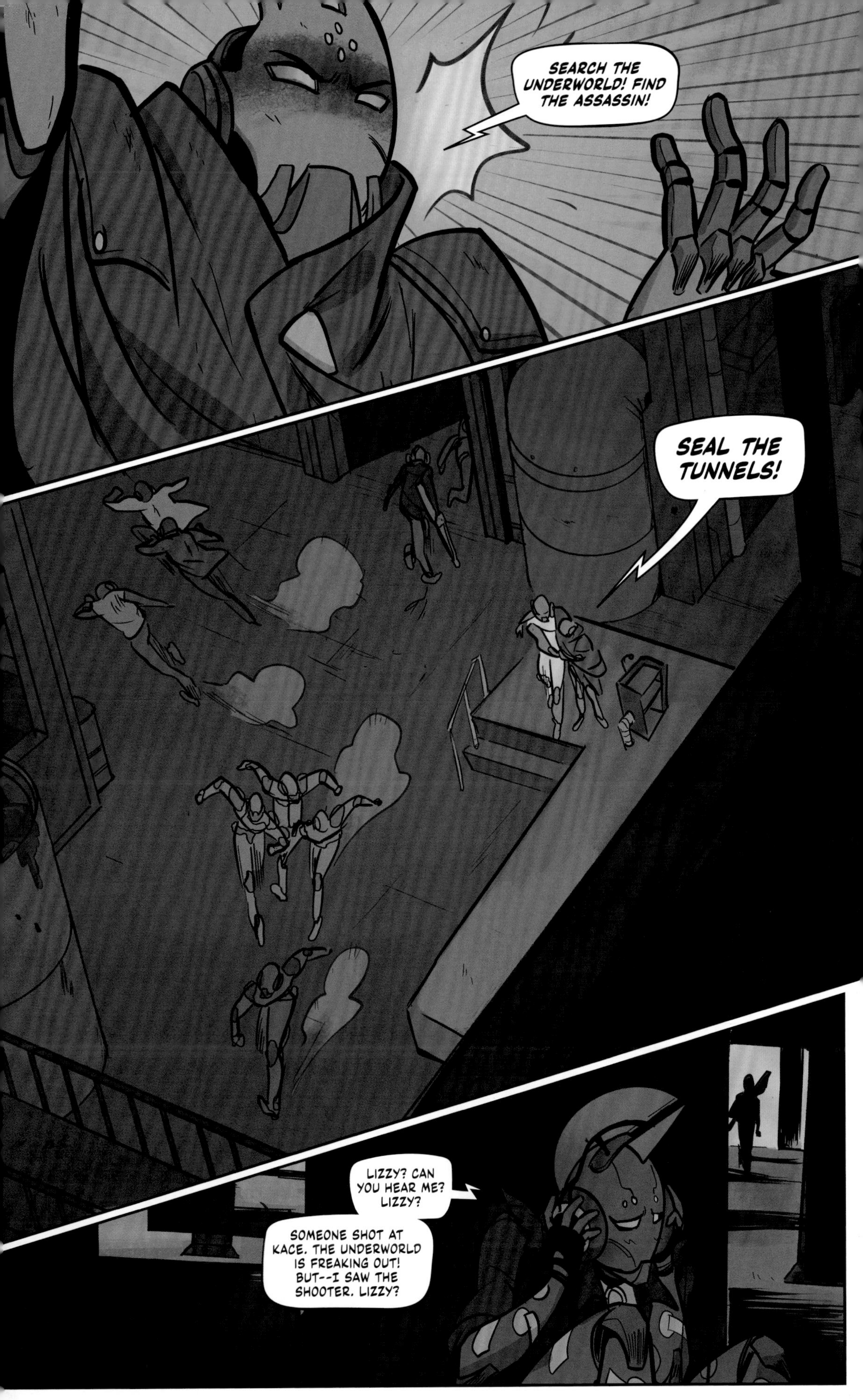
SEARCH THE UNDERWORLD! FIND THE ASSASSIN!
SEAL THE TUNNELS!
LIZZY? CAN YOU HEAR ME? LIZZY?
SOMEONE SHOT AT KACE. THE UNDERWORLD IS FREAKING OUT! BUT--I SAW THE SHOOTER. LIZZY?

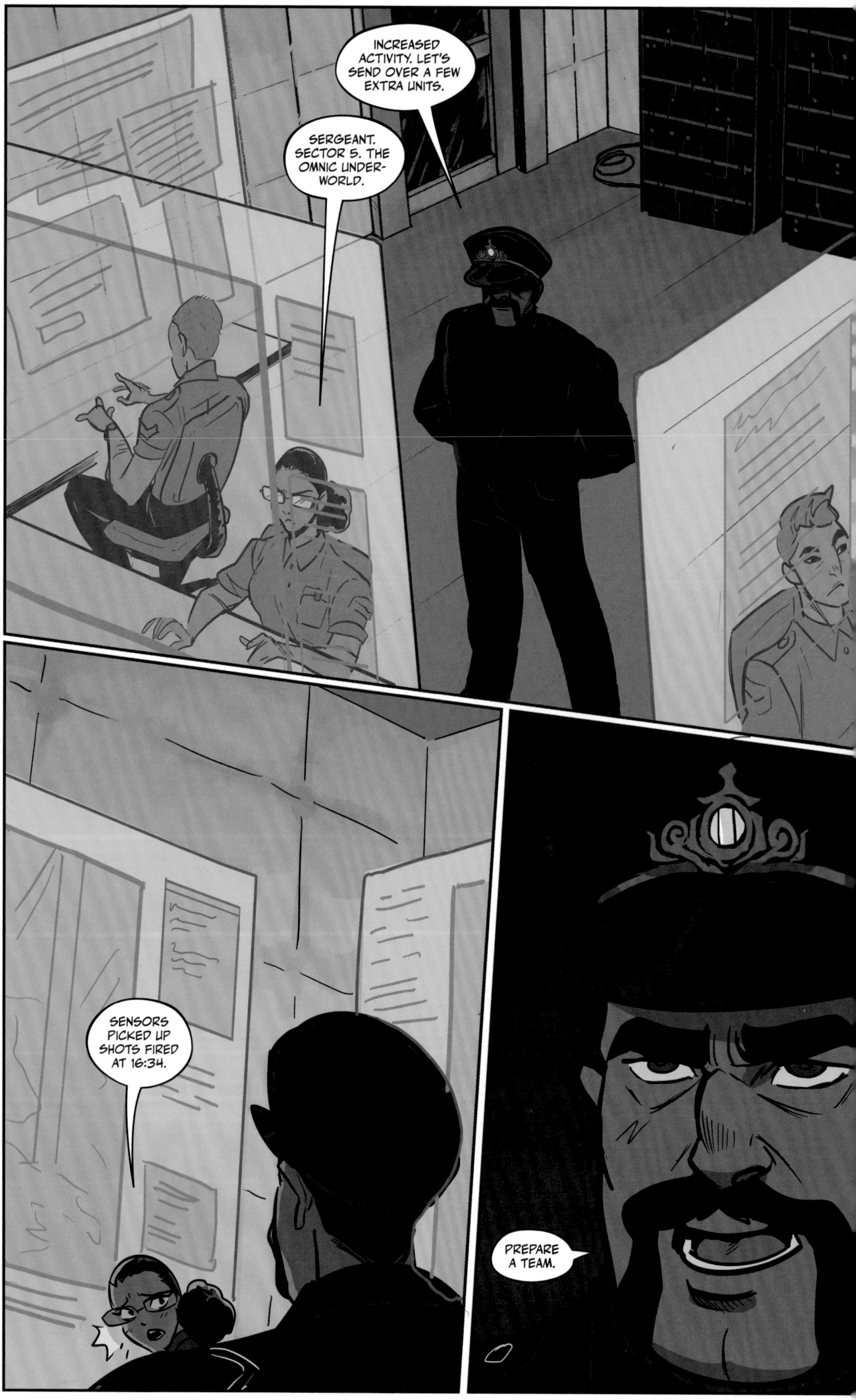
SERGEANT. SECTOR 5. THE OMNIC UNDER-WORLD.
INCREASED ACTIVITY. LET'S SEND OVER A FEW EXTRA UNITS.
SENSORS PICKED UP SHOTS FIRED AT 16:34.
PREPARE A TEAM.

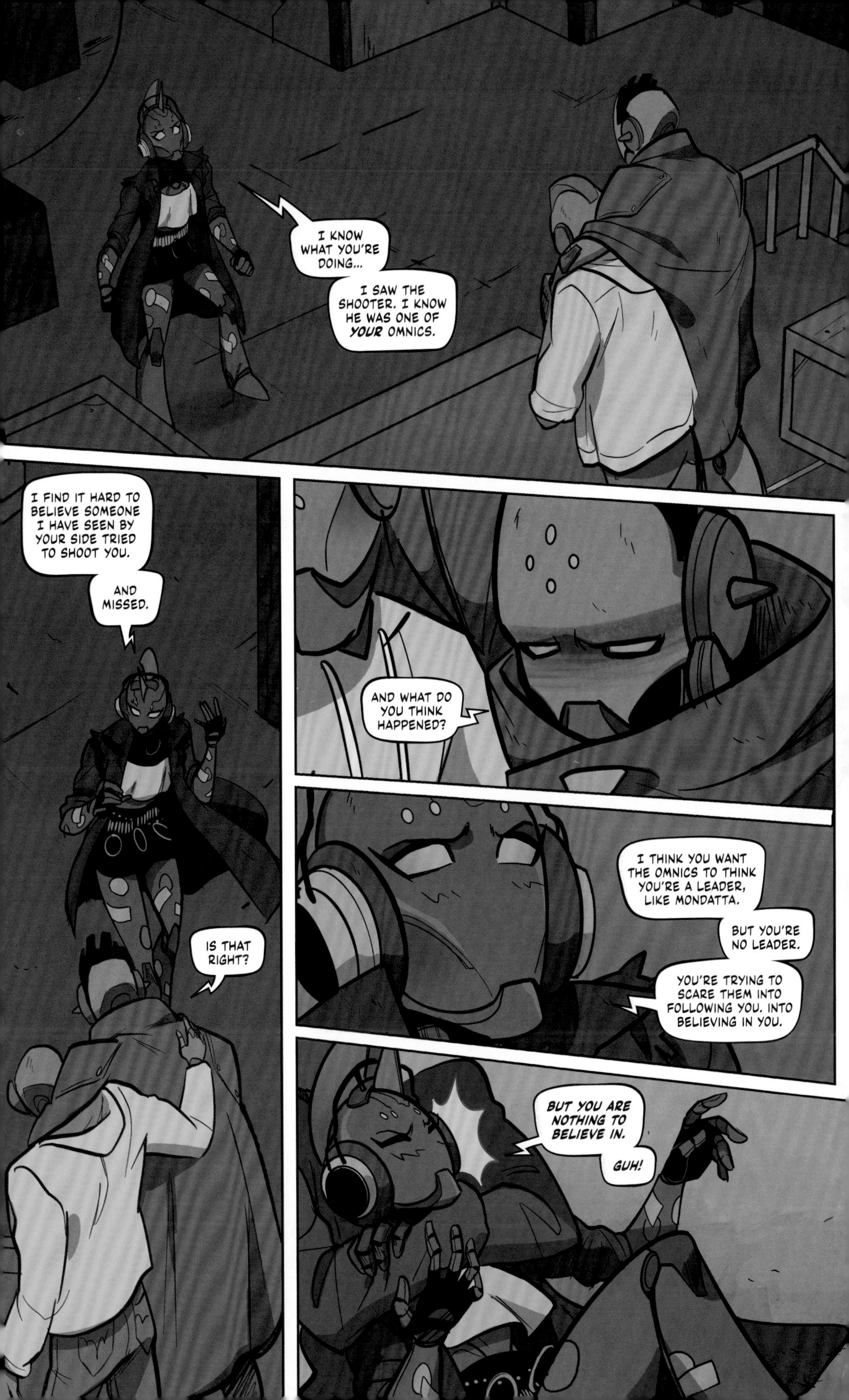

I KNOW WHAT YOU'RE DOING...
I SAW THE SHOOTER. I KNOW HE WAS ONE OF *YOUR* OMNICS.
I FIND IT HARD TO BELIEVE SOMEONE I HAVE SEEN BY YOUR SIDE TRIED TO SHOOT YOU.
AND MISSED.
IS THAT RIGHT?
AND WHAT DO YOU THINK HAPPENED?
I THINK YOU WANT THE OMNICS TO THINK YOU'RE A LEADER, LIKE MONDATTA.
BUT YOU'RE NO LEADER.
YOU'RE TRYING TO SCARE THEM INTO FOLLOWING YOU. INTO BELIEVING IN YOU.
BUT YOU ARE NOTHING TO BELIEVE IN.
GUH!

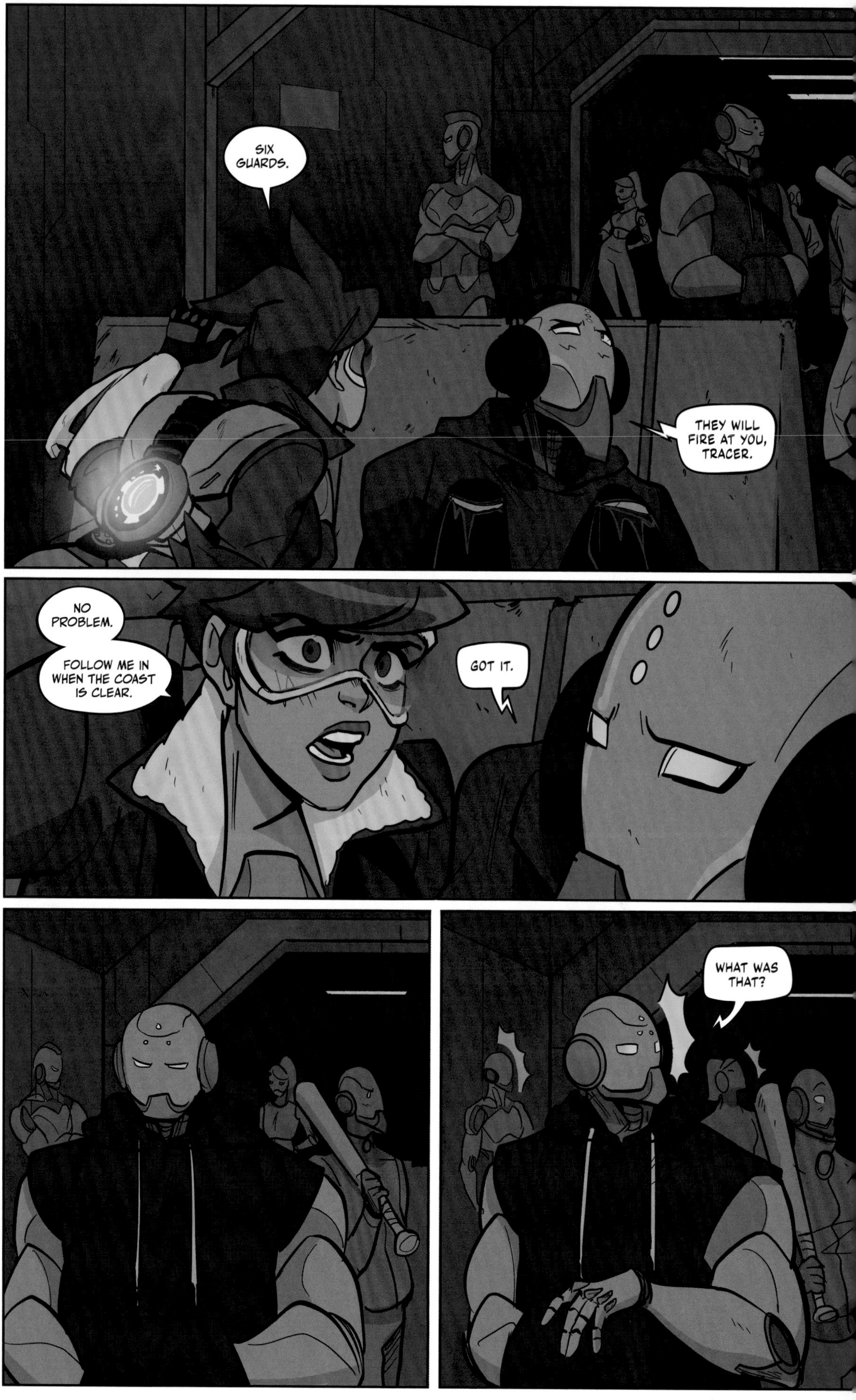
SIX GUARDS.
THEY WILL FIRE AT YOU, TRACER.
NO PROBLEM.
FOLLOW ME IN WHEN THE COAST IS CLEAR.
GOT IT.
WHAT WAS THAT?

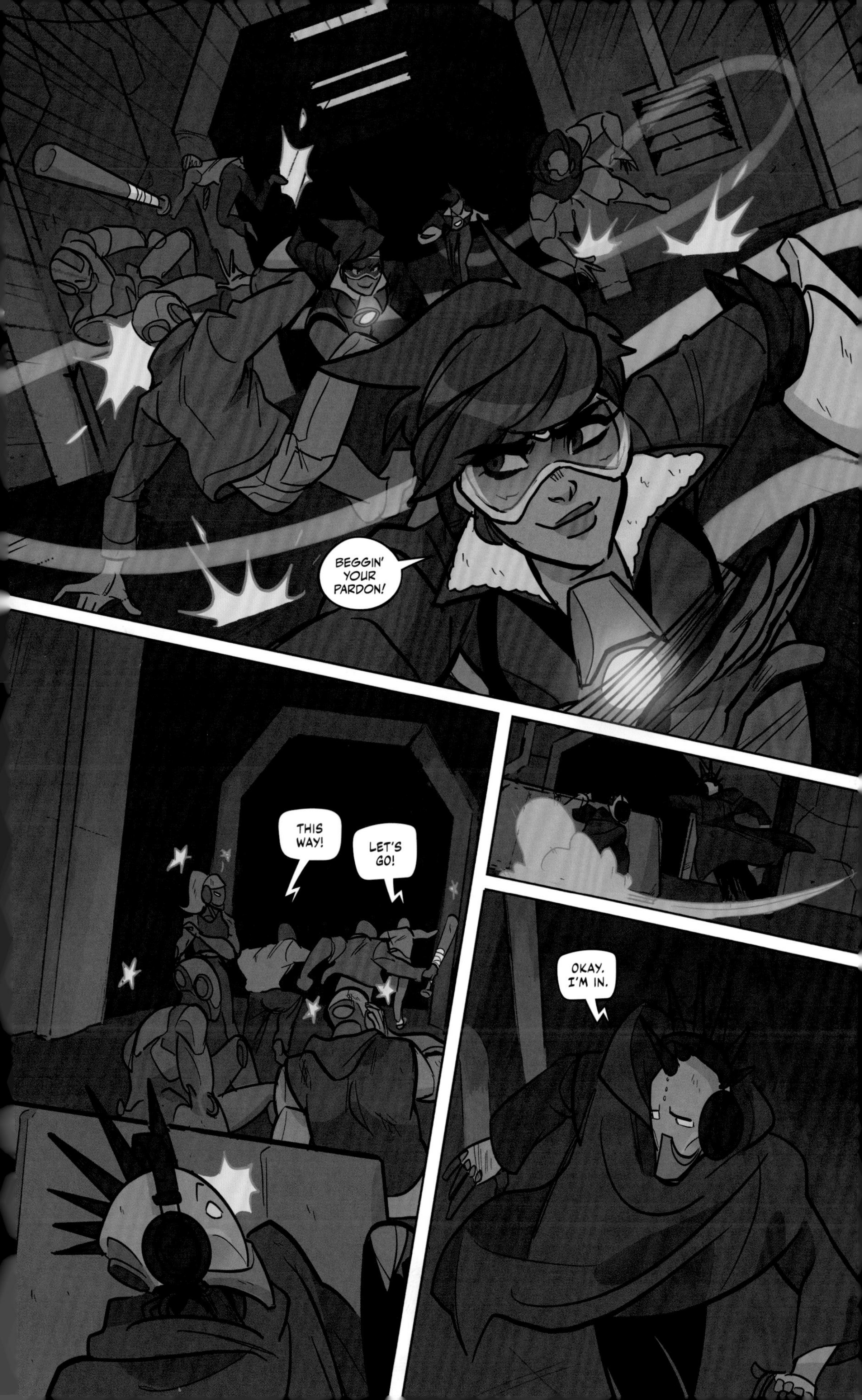
BEGGIN' YOUR PARDON!
THIS WAY!
LET'S GO!
OKAY. I'M IN.

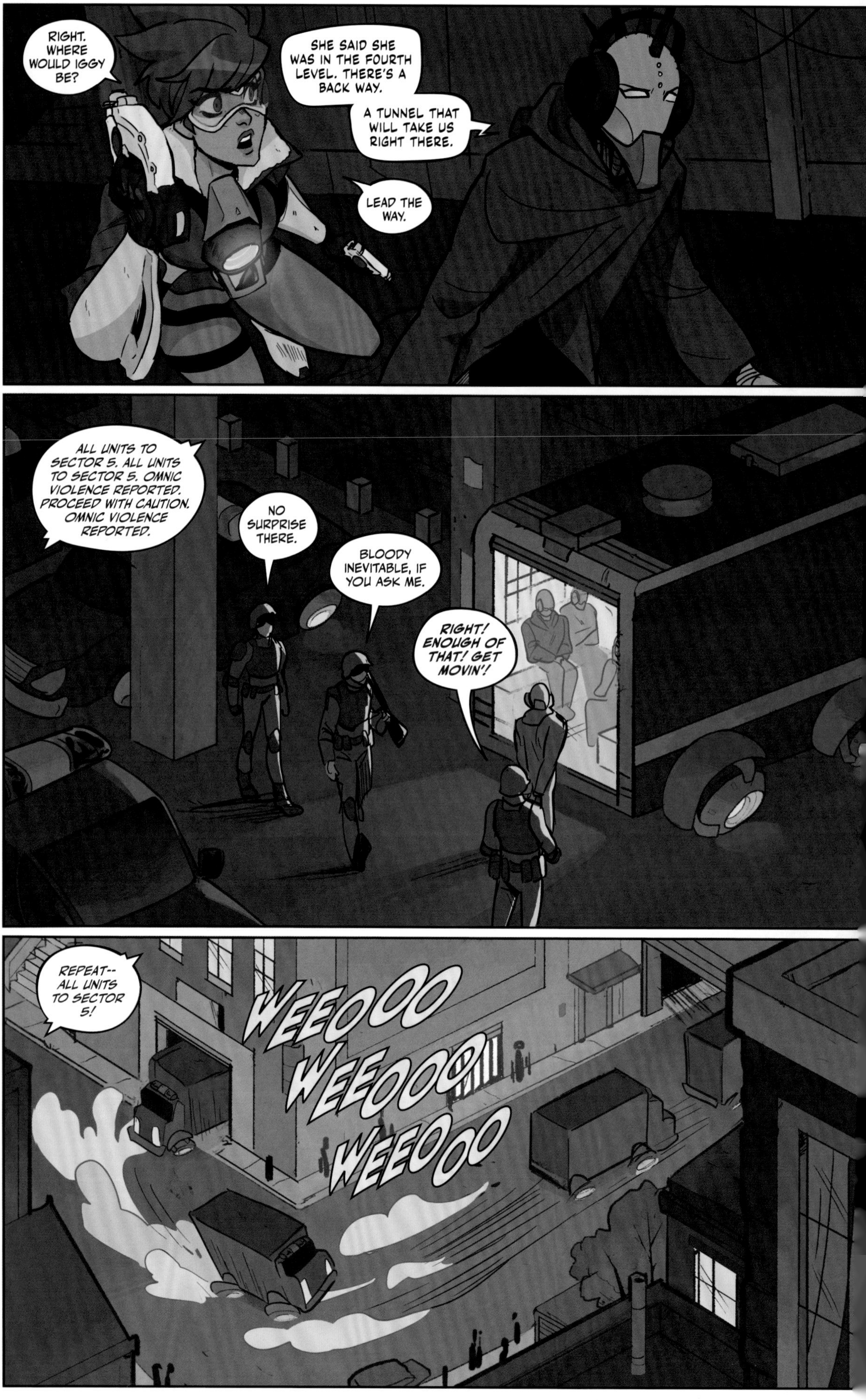
RIGHT. WHERE WOULD IGGY BE?
SHE SAID SHE WAS IN THE FOURTH LEVEL. THERE'S A BACK WAY.
A TUNNEL THAT WILL TAKE US RIGHT THERE.
LEAD THE WAY.
ALL UNITS TO SECTOR 5. ALL UNITS TO SECTOR 5. OMNIC VIOLENCE REPORTED. PROCEED WITH CAUTION. OMNIC VIOLENCE REPORTED.
NO SURPRISE THERE.
BLOODY INEVITABLE, IF YOU ASK ME.
RIGHT! ENOUGH OF THAT! GET MOVIN'!
REPEAT-- ALL UNITS TO SECTOR 5!
WEEOOO
WEEOOO
WEEOOO

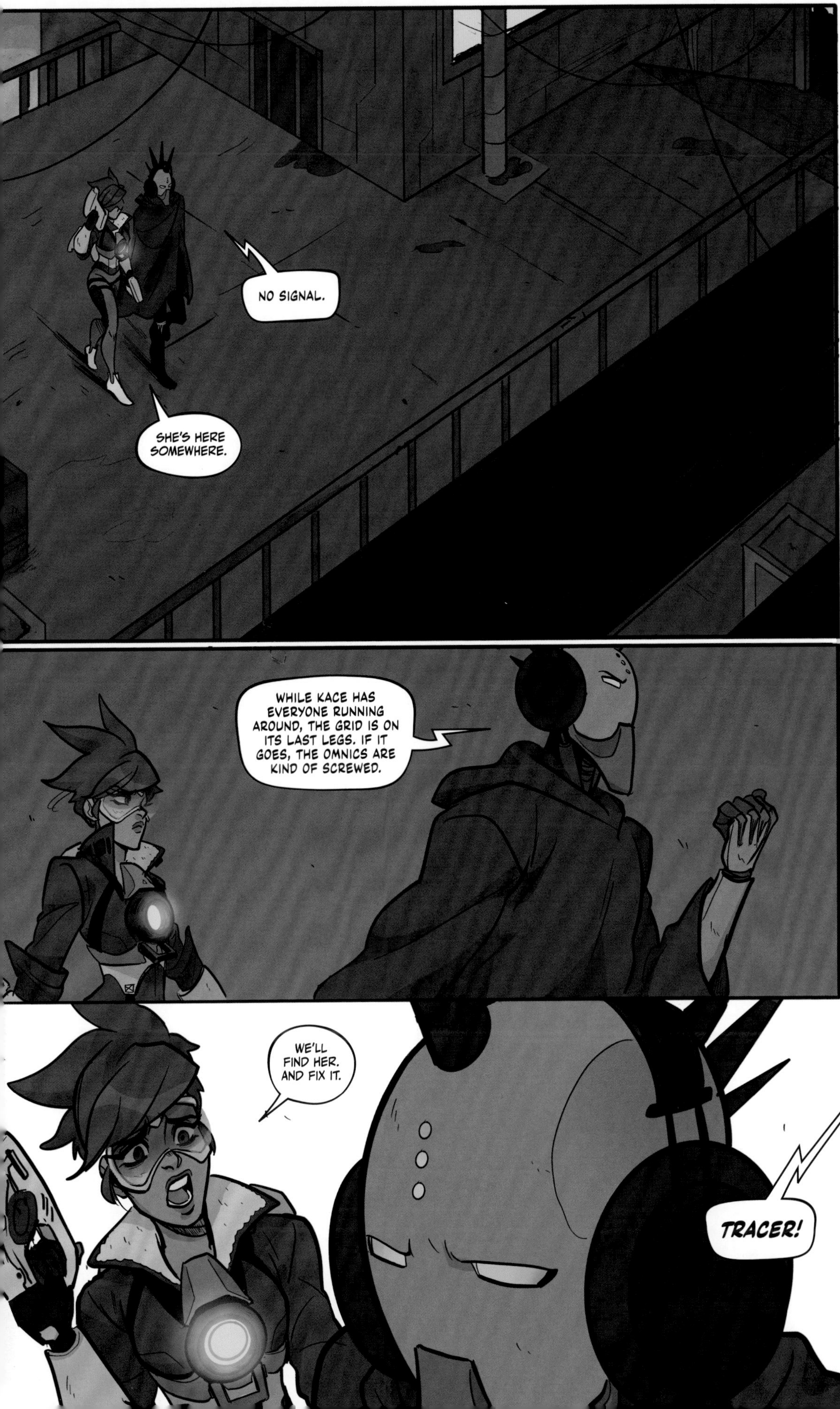
NO SIGNAL.
SHE'S HERE SOMEWHERE.
WHILE KACE HAS EVERYONE RUNNING AROUND, THE GRID IS ON ITS LAST LEGS. IF IT GOES, THE OMNICS ARE KIND OF SCREWED.
WE'LL FIND HER. AND FIX IT.
TRACER!

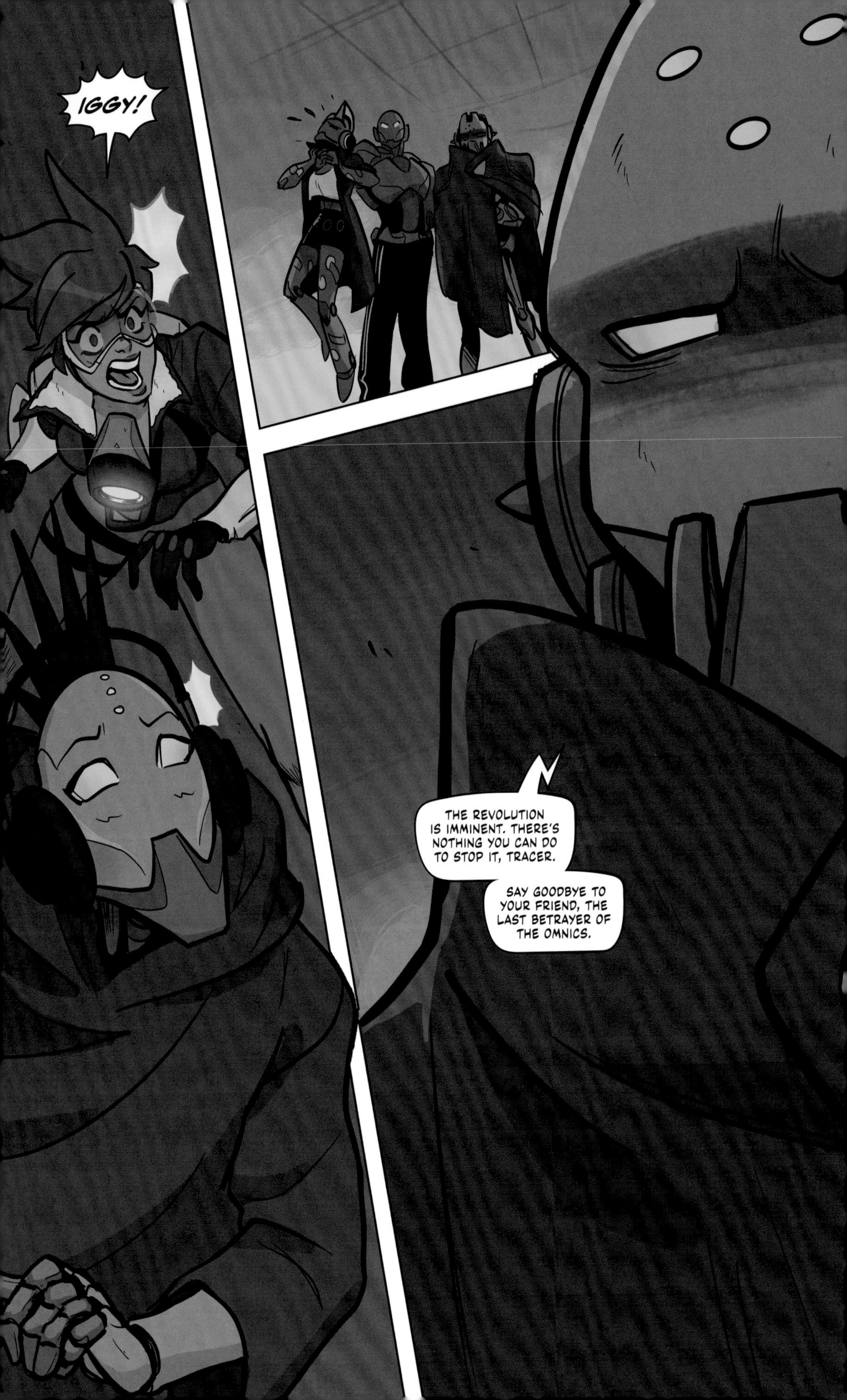
IGGY!
THE REVOLUTION IS IMMINENT. THERE'S NOTHING YOU CAN DO TO STOP IT, TRACER.
SAY GOODBYE TO YOUR FRIEND, THE LAST BETRAYER OF THE OMNICS.

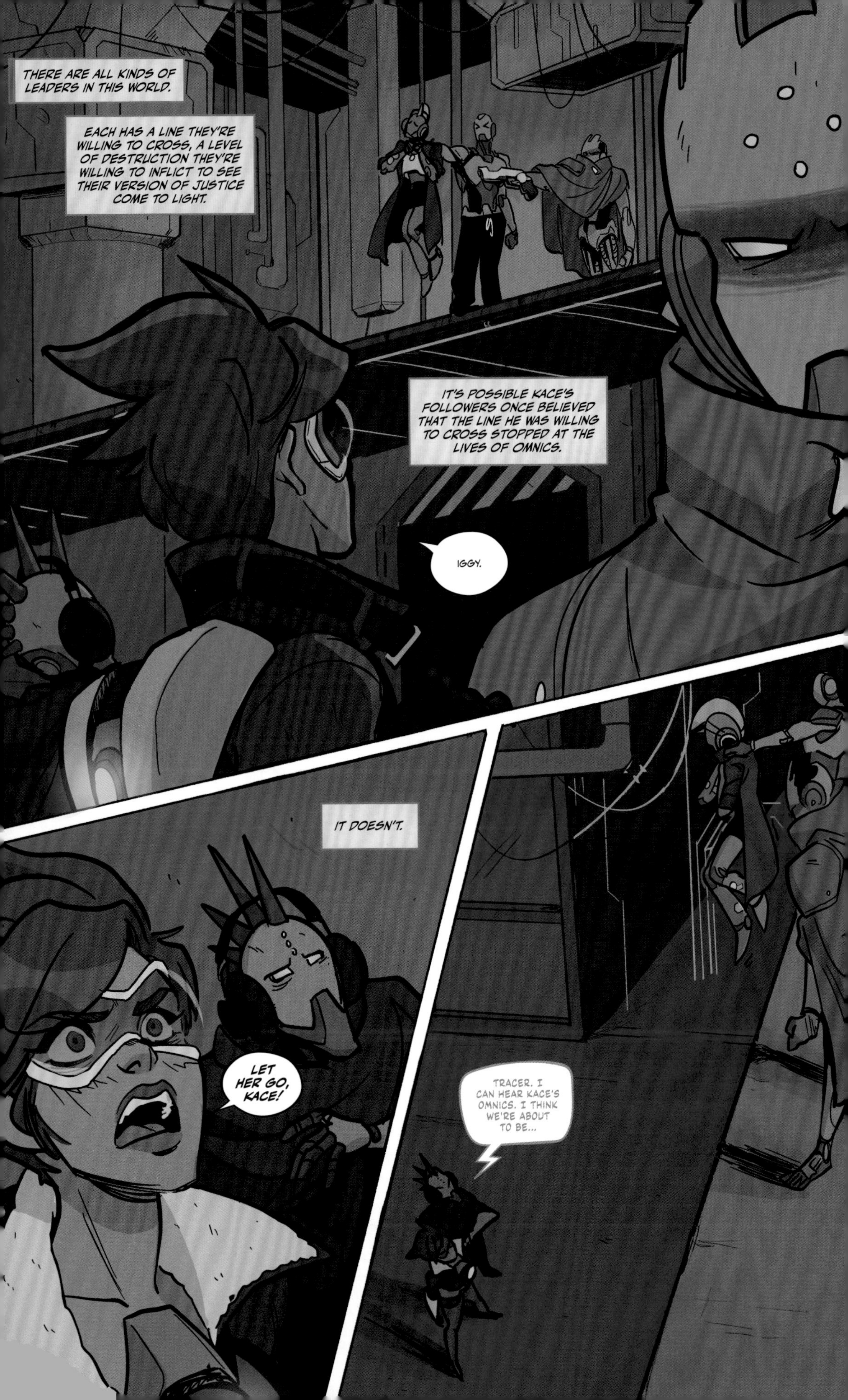
THERE ARE ALL KINDS OF LEADERS IN THIS WORLD.
EACH HAS A LINE THEY'RE WILLING TO CROSS, A LEVEL OF DESTRUCTION THEY'RE WILLING TO INFLICT TO SEE THEIR VERSION OF JUSTICE COME TO LIGHT.
IT'S POSSIBLE KACE'S FOLLOWERS ONCE BELIEVED THAT THE LINE HE WAS WILLING TO CROSS STOPPED AT THE LIVES OF OMNICS.
IGGY.
IT DOESN'T.
LET HER GO, KACE!
TRACER. I CAN HEAR KACE'S OMNICS. I THINK WE'RE ABOUT TO BE...

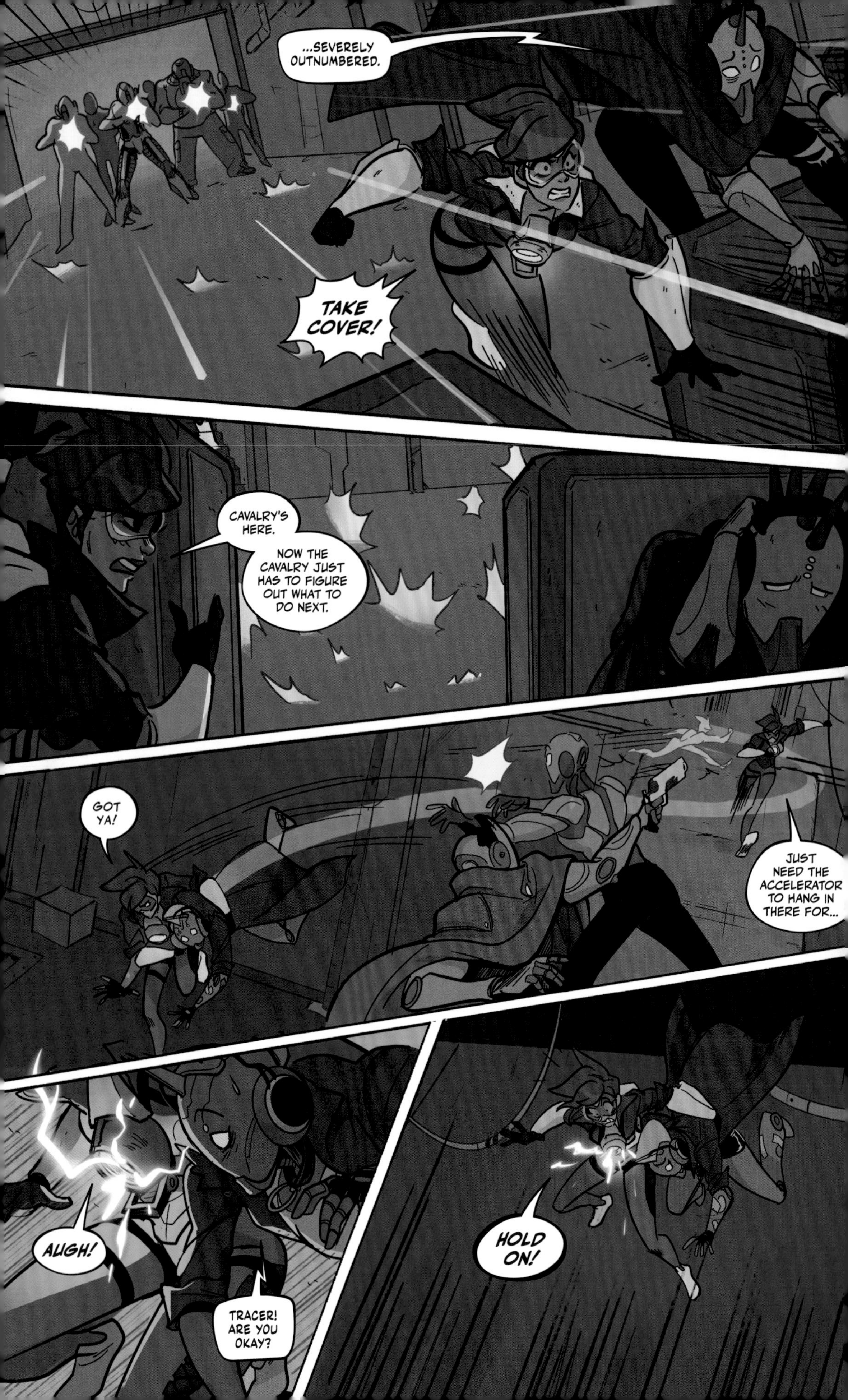
...SEVERELY OUTNUMBERED.
TAKE COVER!
CAVALRY'S HERE.
NOW THE CAVALRY JUST HAS TO FIGURE OUT WHAT TO DO NEXT.
GOT YA!
JUST NEED THE ACCELERATOR TO HANG IN THERE FOR...
AUGH!
TRACER! ARE YOU OKAY?
HOLD ON!

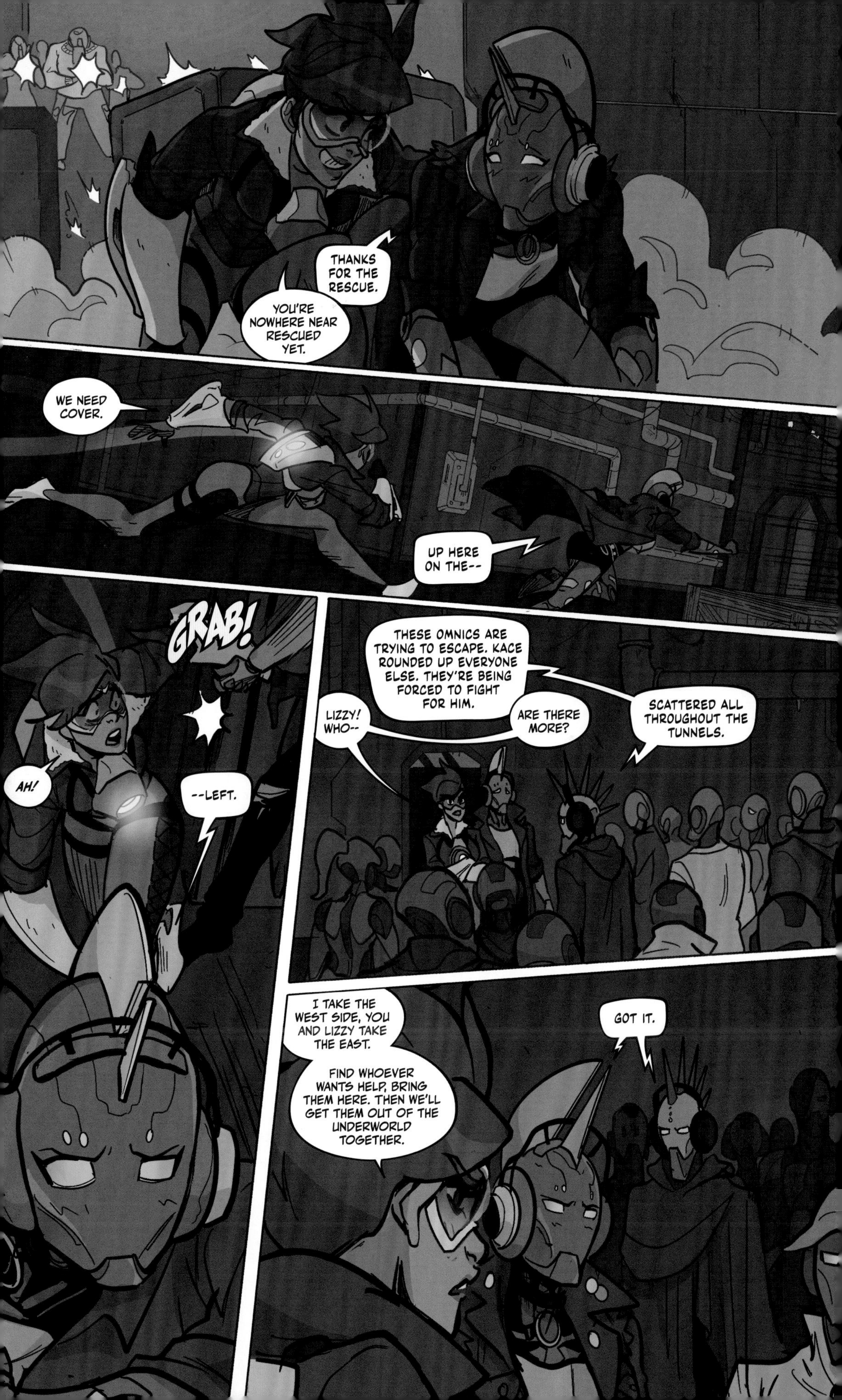

THANKS FOR THE RESCUE.
YOU'RE NOWHERE NEAR RESCUED YET.
WE NEED COVER.
UP HERE ON THE--
GRAB!
AH!
--LEFT.
LIZZY! WHO--
THESE OMNICS ARE TRYING TO ESCAPE. KACE ROUNDED UP EVERYONE ELSE. THEY'RE BEING FORCED TO FIGHT FOR HIM.
ARE THERE MORE?
SCATTERED ALL THROUGHOUT THE TUNNELS.
I TAKE THE WEST SIDE, YOU AND LIZZY TAKE THE EAST.
FIND WHOEVER WANTS HELP, BRING THEM HERE. THEN WE'LL GET THEM OUT OF THE UNDERWORLD TOGETHER.
GOT IT.

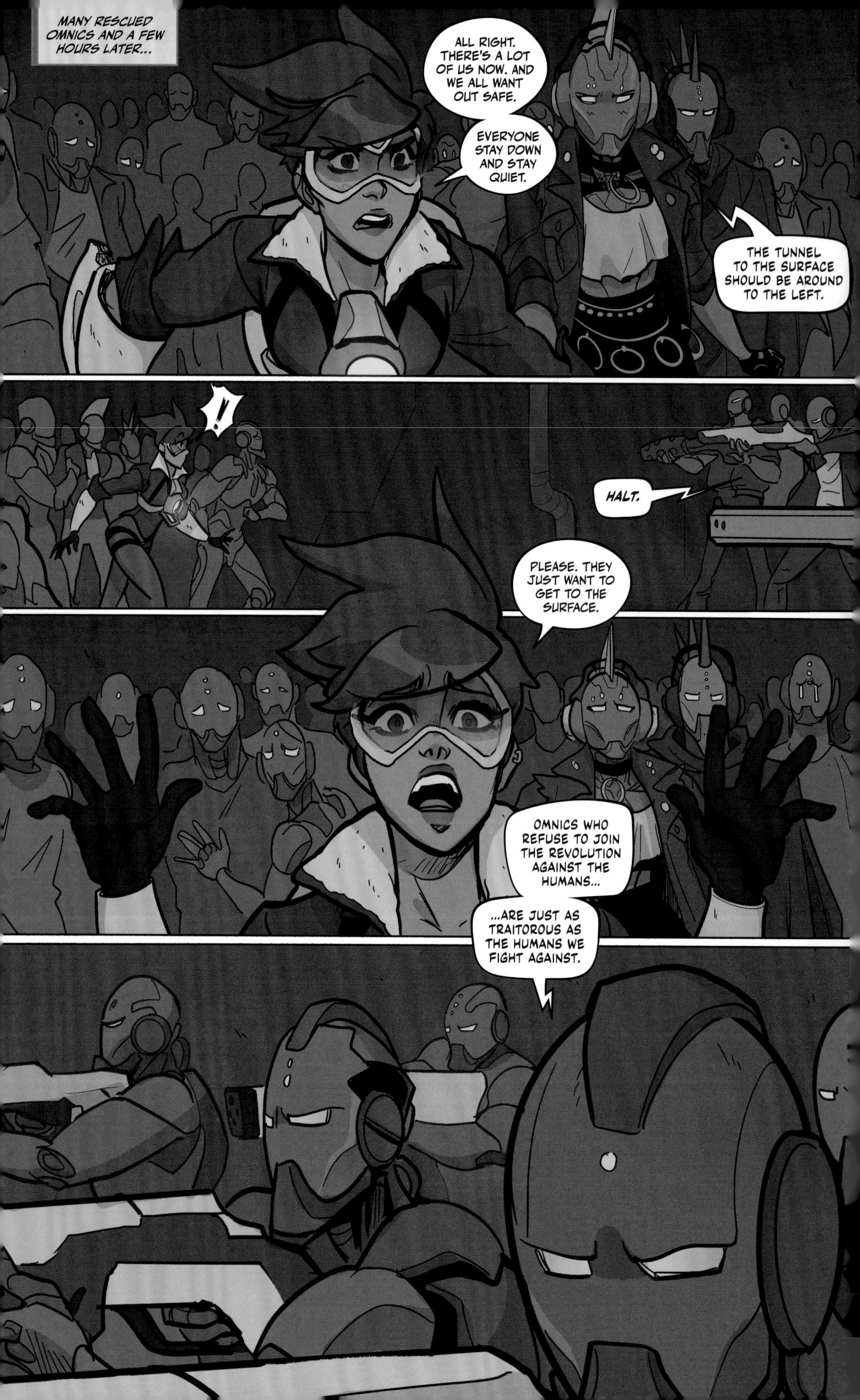

MANY RESCUED OMNICS AND A FEW HOURS LATER...
ALL RIGHT. THERE'S A LOT OF US NOW. AND WE ALL WANT OUT SAFE.
EVERYONE STAY DOWN AND STAY QUIET.
THE TUNNEL TO THE SURFACE SHOULD BE AROUND TO THE LEFT.
!
HALT.
PLEASE. THEY JUST WANT TO GET TO THE SURFACE.
OMNICS WHO REFUSE TO JOIN THE REVOLUTION AGAINST THE HUMANS...
...ARE JUST AS TRAITOROUS AS THE HUMANS WE FIGHT AGAINST.

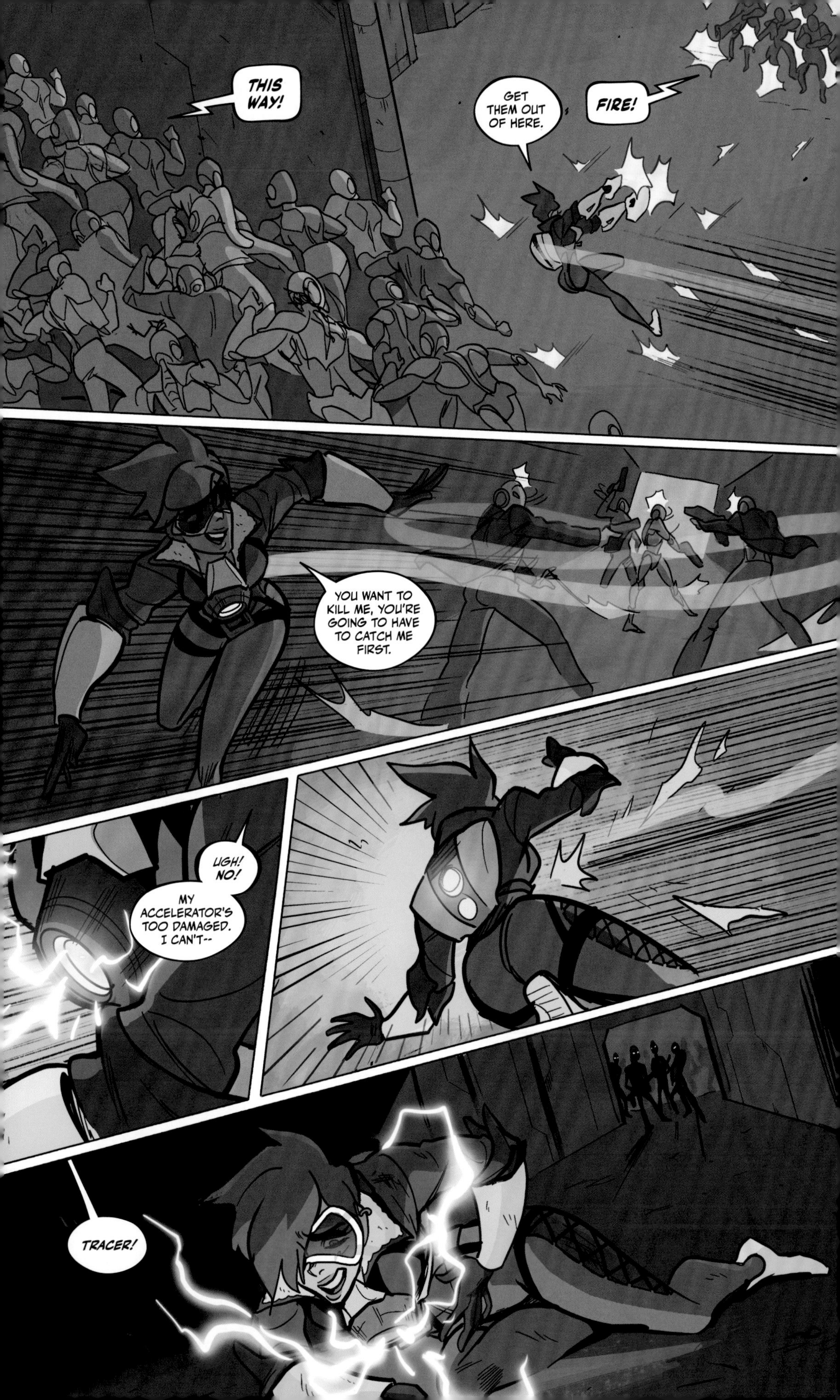
THIS WAY!
GET THEM OUT OF HERE.
FIRE!
YOU WANT TO KILL ME, YOU'RE GOING TO HAVE TO CATCH ME FIRST.
UGH! NO!
MY ACCELERATOR'S TOO DAMAGED. I CAN'T--
TRACER!

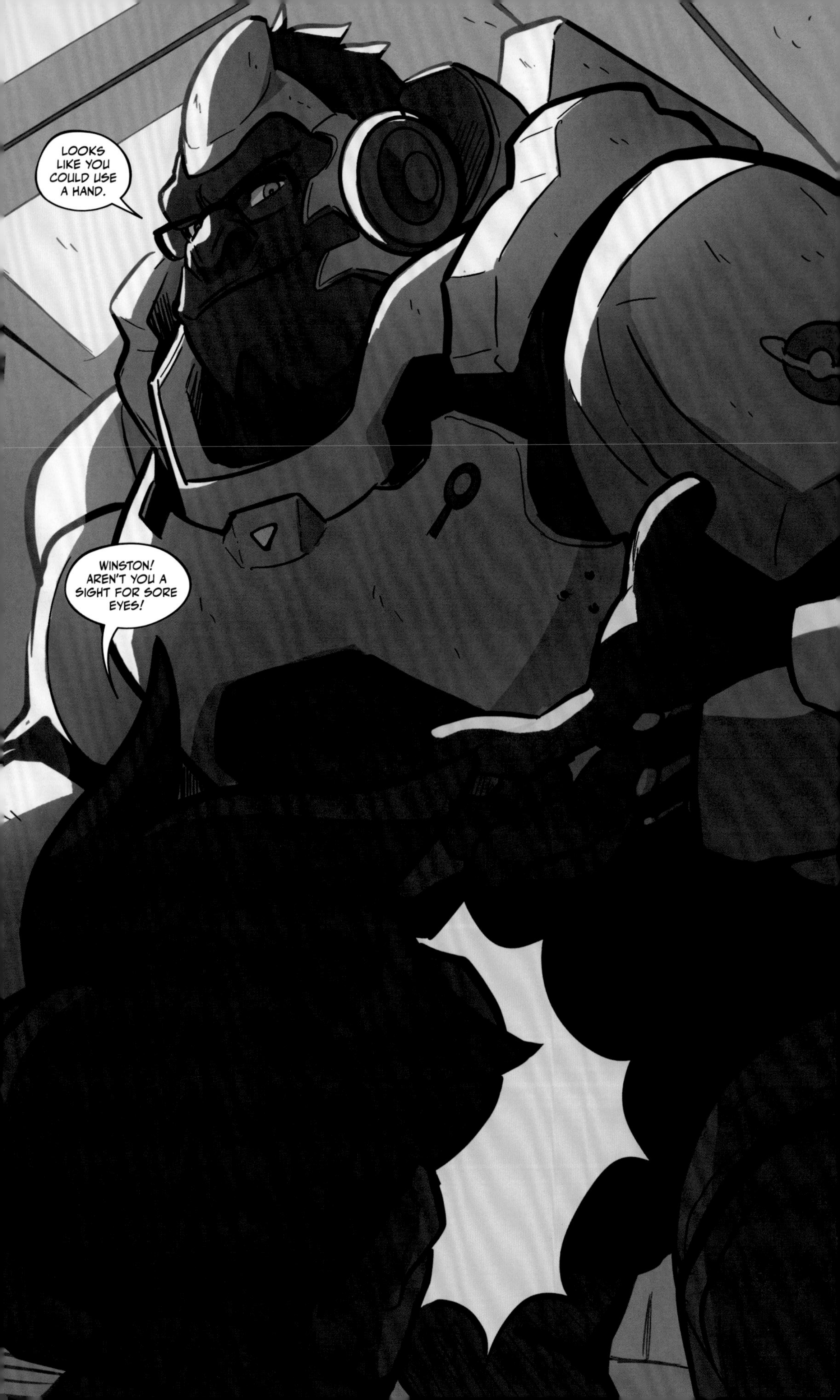
LOOKS LIKE YOU COULD USE A HAND.
WINSTON! AREN'T YOU A SIGHT FOR SORE EYES!

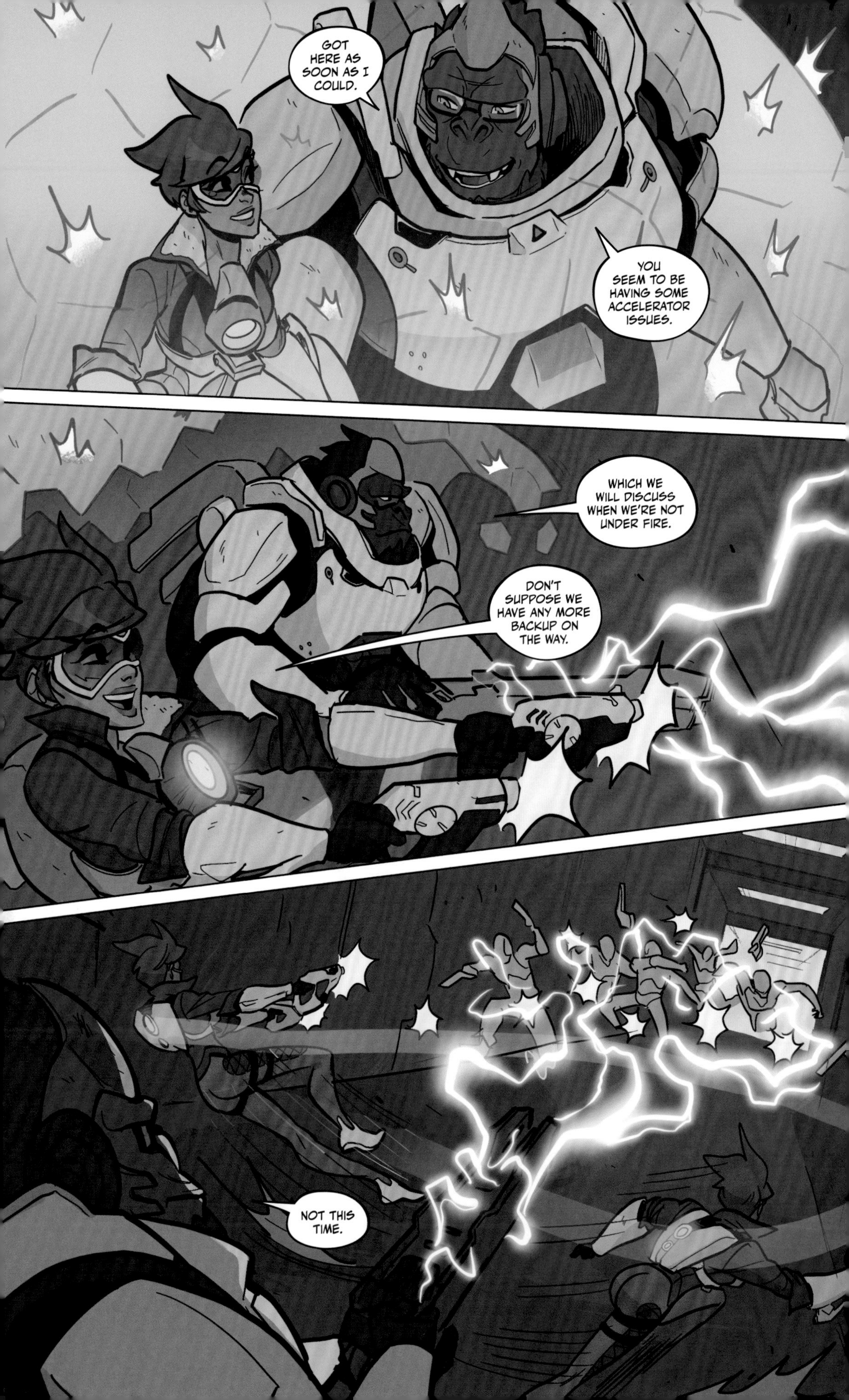
GOT HERE AS SOON AS I COULD.
YOU SEEM TO BE HAVING SOME ACCELERATOR ISSUES.
WHICH WE WILL DISCUSS WHEN WE'RE NOT UNDER FIRE.
DON'T SUPPOSE WE HAVE ANY MORE BACKUP ON THE WAY.
NOT THIS TIME.

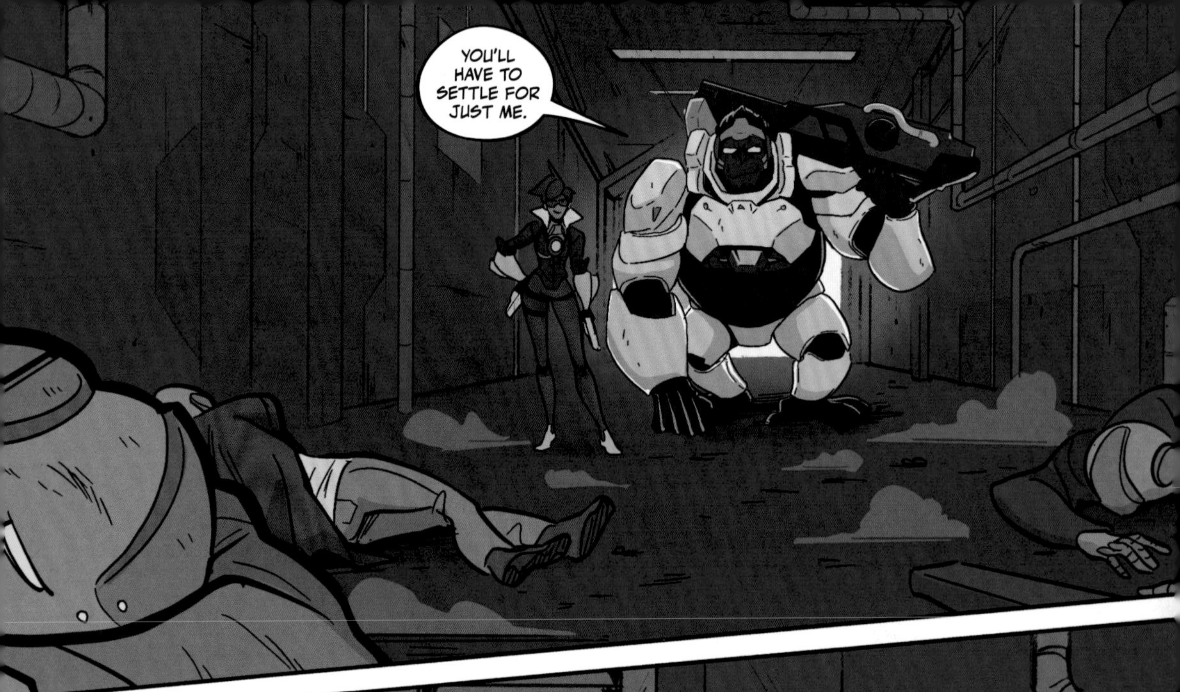
YOU'LL HAVE TO SETTLE FOR JUST ME.

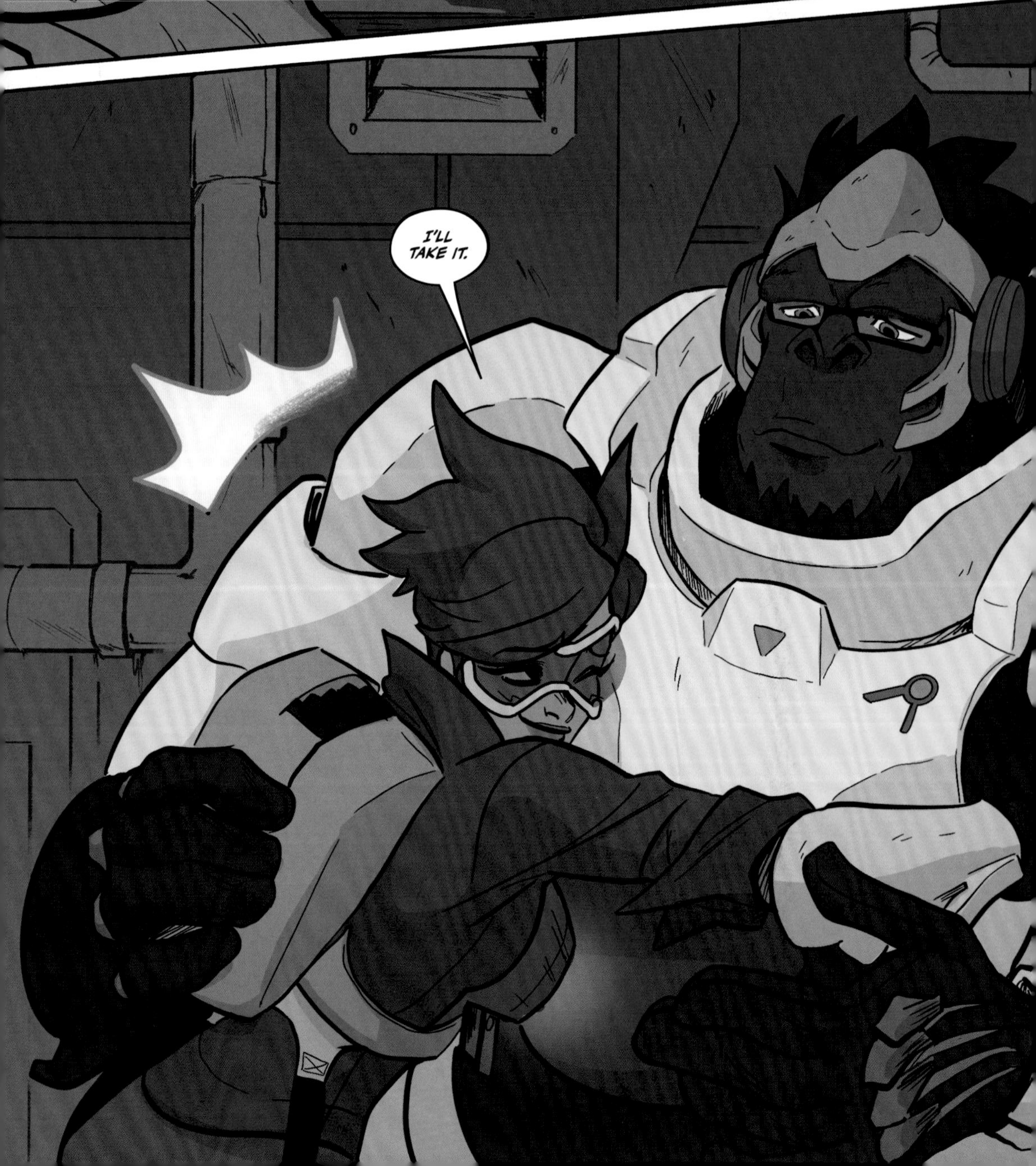
I'LL TAKE IT.

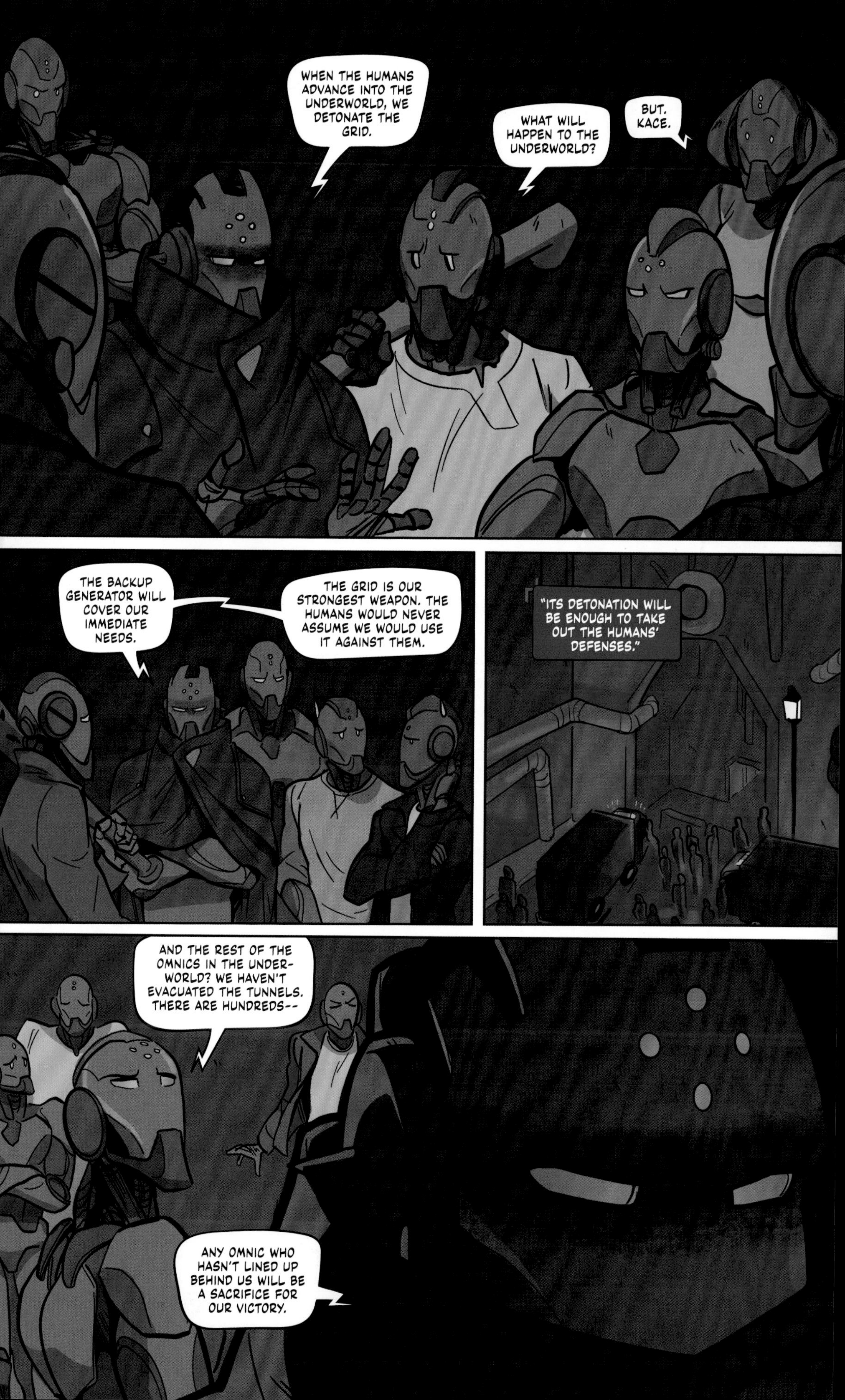
WHEN THE HUMANS ADVANCE INTO THE UNDERWORLD, WE DETONATE THE GRID.
WHAT WILL HAPPEN TO THE UNDERWORLD?
BUT. KACE.
THE BACKUP GENERATOR WILL COVER OUR IMMEDIATE NEEDS.
THE GRID IS OUR STRONGEST WEAPON. THE HUMANS WOULD NEVER ASSUME WE WOULD USE IT AGAINST THEM.
"ITS DETONATION WILL BE ENOUGH TO TAKE OUT THE HUMANS' DEFENSES."
AND THE REST OF THE OMNICS IN THE UNDER-WORLD? WE HAVEN'T EVACUATED THE TUNNELS. THERE ARE HUNDREDS--
ANY OMNIC WHO HASN'T LINED UP BEHIND US WILL BE A SACRIFICE FOR OUR VICTORY.

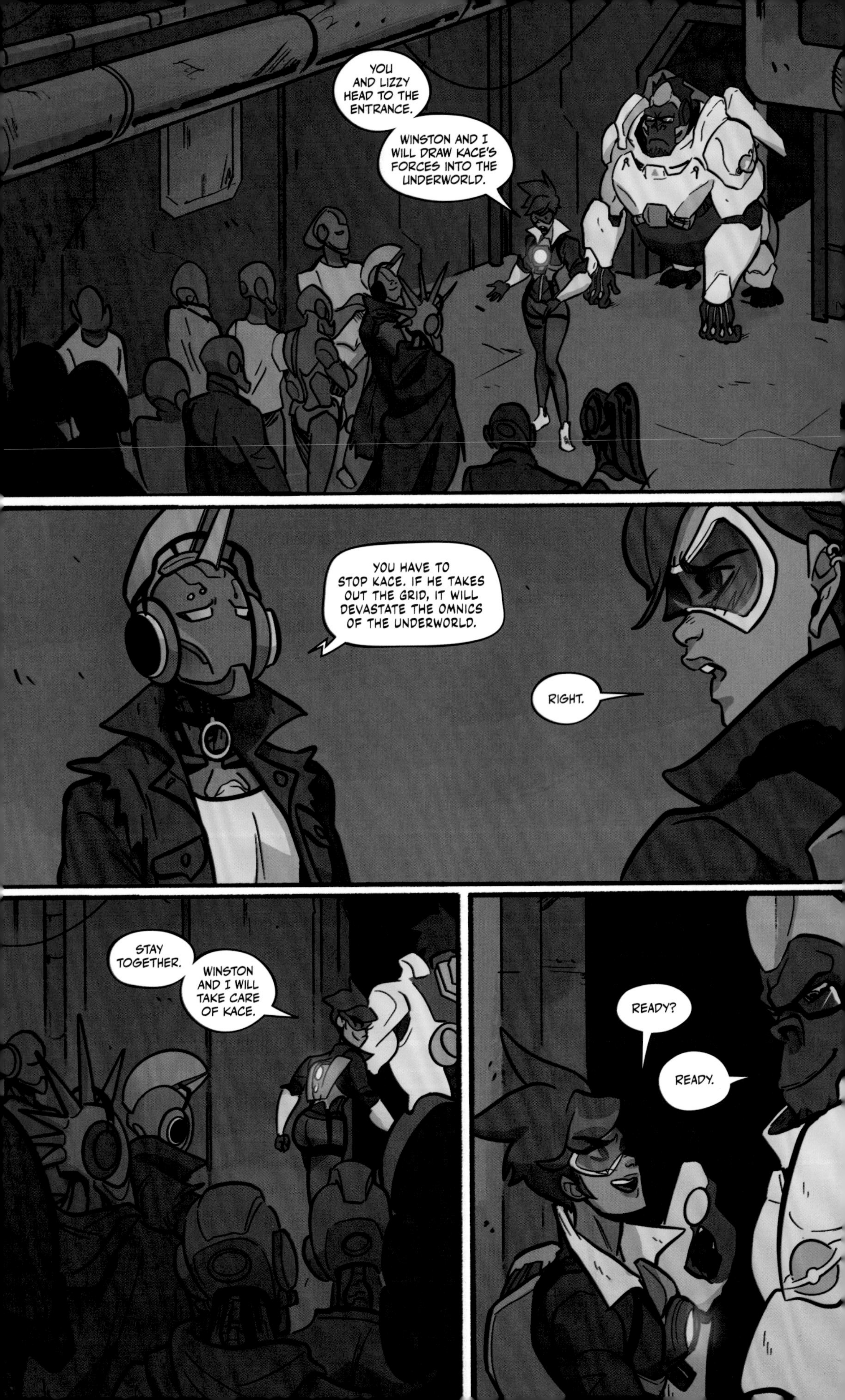
YOU AND LIZZY HEAD TO THE ENTRANCE.
WINSTON AND I WILL DRAW KACE'S FORCES INTO THE UNDERWORLD.
YOU HAVE TO STOP KACE. IF HE TAKES OUT THE GRID, IT WILL DEVASTATE THE OMNICS OF THE UNDERWORLD.
RIGHT.
STAY TOGETHER.
WINSTON AND I WILL TAKE CARE OF KACE.
READY?
READY.

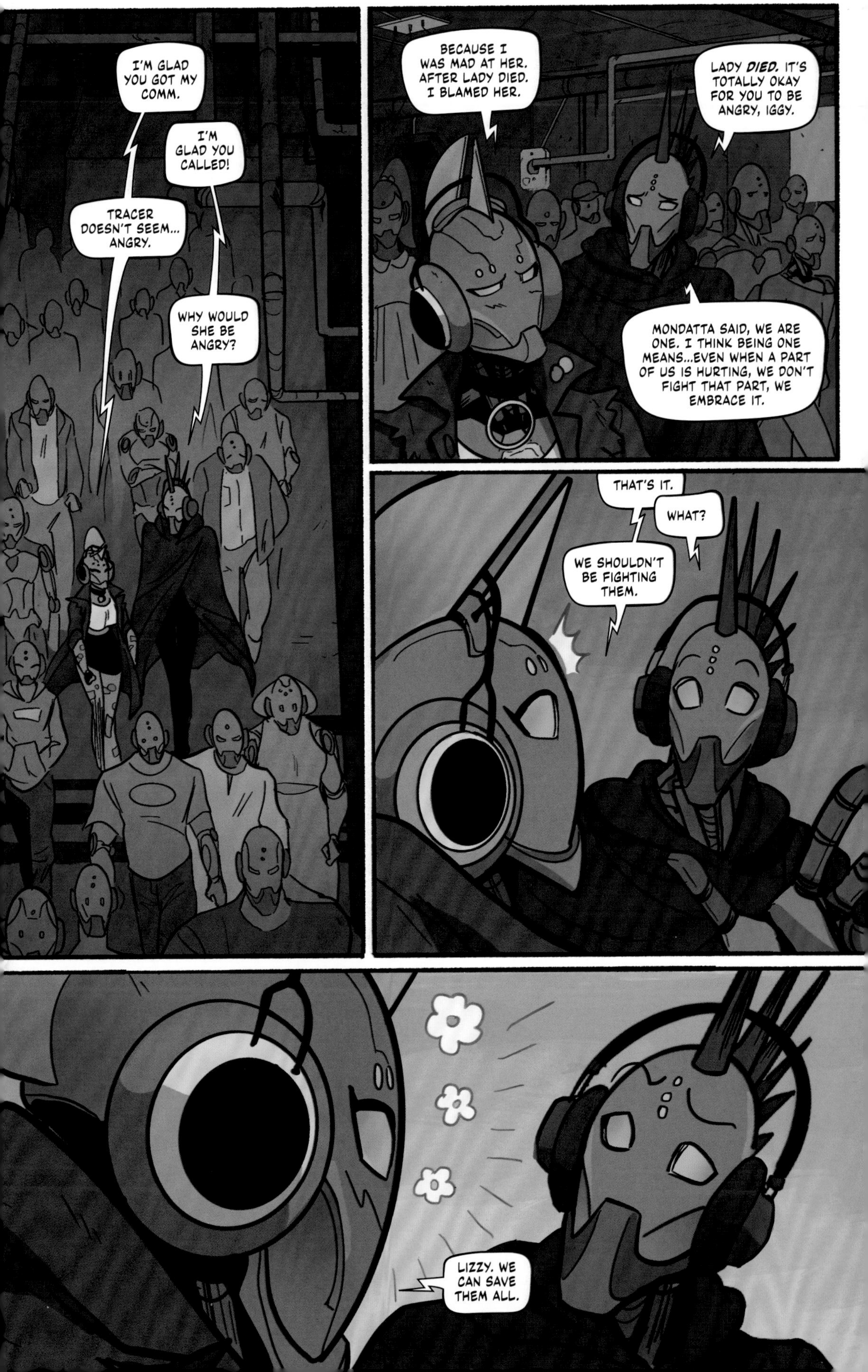
I'M GLAD YOU GOT MY COMM.
I'M GLAD YOU CALLED!
TRACER DOESN'T SEEM... ANGRY.
WHY WOULD SHE BE ANGRY?
BECAUSE I WAS MAD AT HER. AFTER LADY DIED. I BLAMED HER.
LADY *DIED.* IT'S TOTALLY OKAY FOR YOU TO BE ANGRY, IGGY.
MONDATTA SAID, WE ARE ONE. I THINK BEING ONE MEANS...EVEN WHEN A PART OF US IS HURTING, WE DON'T FIGHT THAT PART, WE EMBRACE IT.
THAT'S IT.
WHAT?
WE SHOULDN'T BE FIGHTING THEM.
LIZZY. WE CAN SAVE THEM ALL.

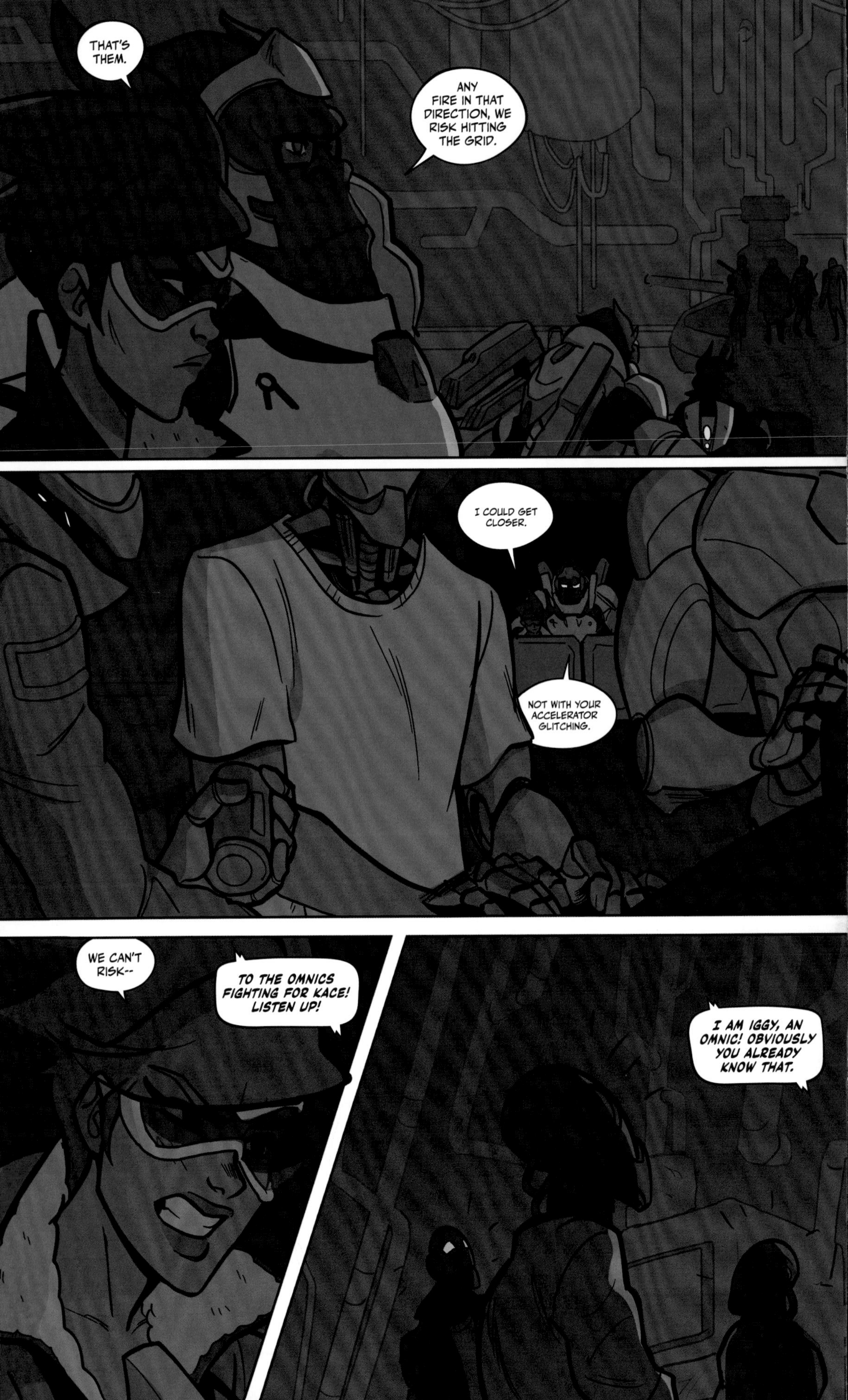
THAT'S THEM.
ANY FIRE IN THAT DIRECTION, WE RISK HITTING THE GRID.
I COULD GET CLOSER.
NOT WITH YOUR ACCELERATOR GLITCHING.
WE CAN'T RISK--
TO THE OMNICS FIGHTING FOR KACE! LISTEN UP!
I AM IGGY, AN OMNIC! OBVIOUSLY YOU ALREADY KNOW THAT.

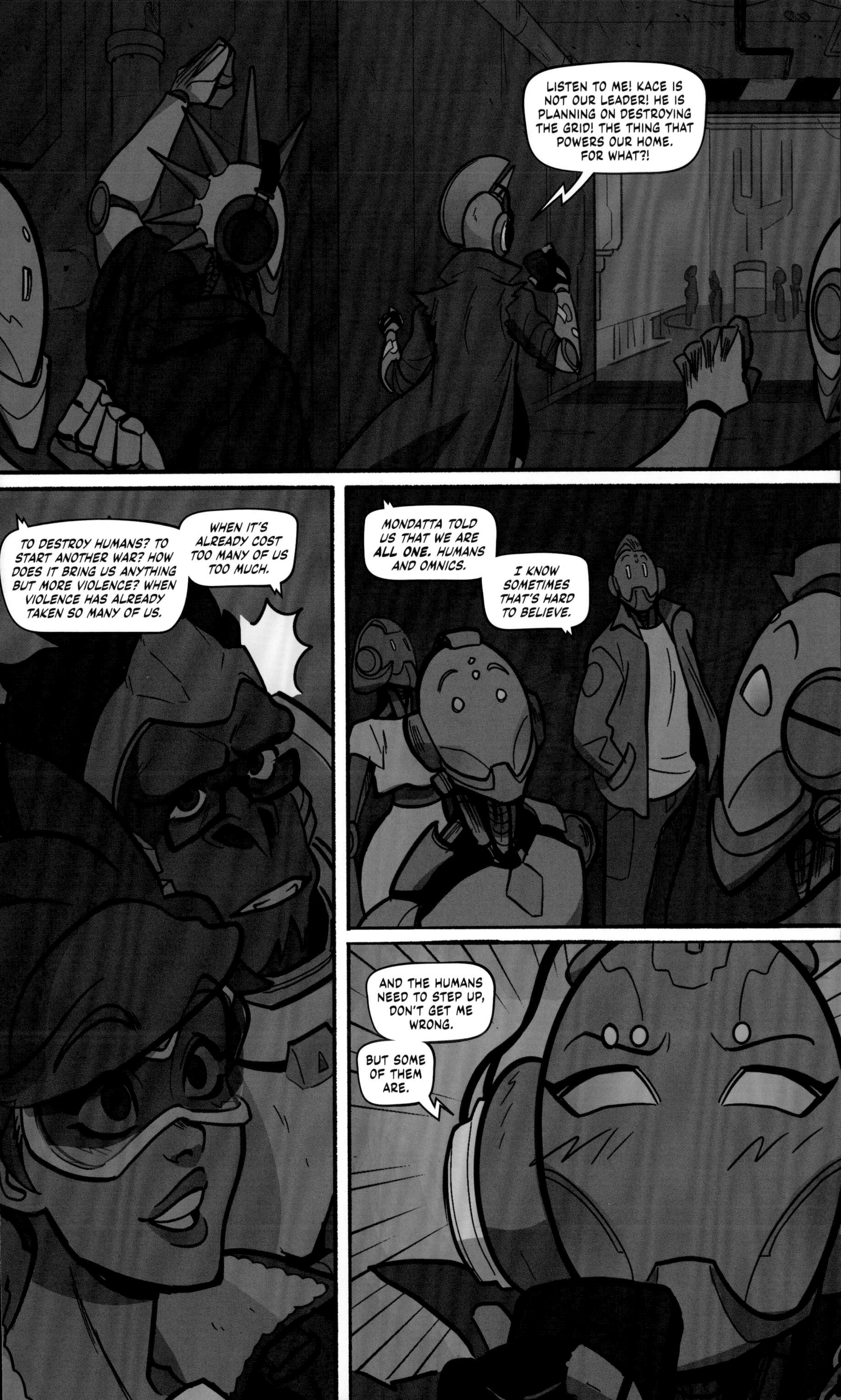
LISTEN TO ME! KACE IS NOT OUR LEADER! HE IS PLANNING ON DESTROYING THE GRID! THE THING THAT POWERS OUR HOME. FOR WHAT?!
TO DESTROY HUMANS? TO START ANOTHER WAR? HOW DOES IT BRING US ANYTHING BUT MORE VIOLENCE? WHEN VIOLENCE HAS ALREADY TAKEN SO MANY OF US.
WHEN IT'S ALREADY COST TOO MANY OF US TOO MUCH.
MONDATTA TOLD US THAT WE ARE ALL ONE. HUMANS AND OMNICS.
I KNOW SOMETIMES THAT'S HARD TO BELIEVE.
AND THE HUMANS NEED TO STEP UP, DON'T GET ME WRONG.
BUT SOME OF THEM ARE.

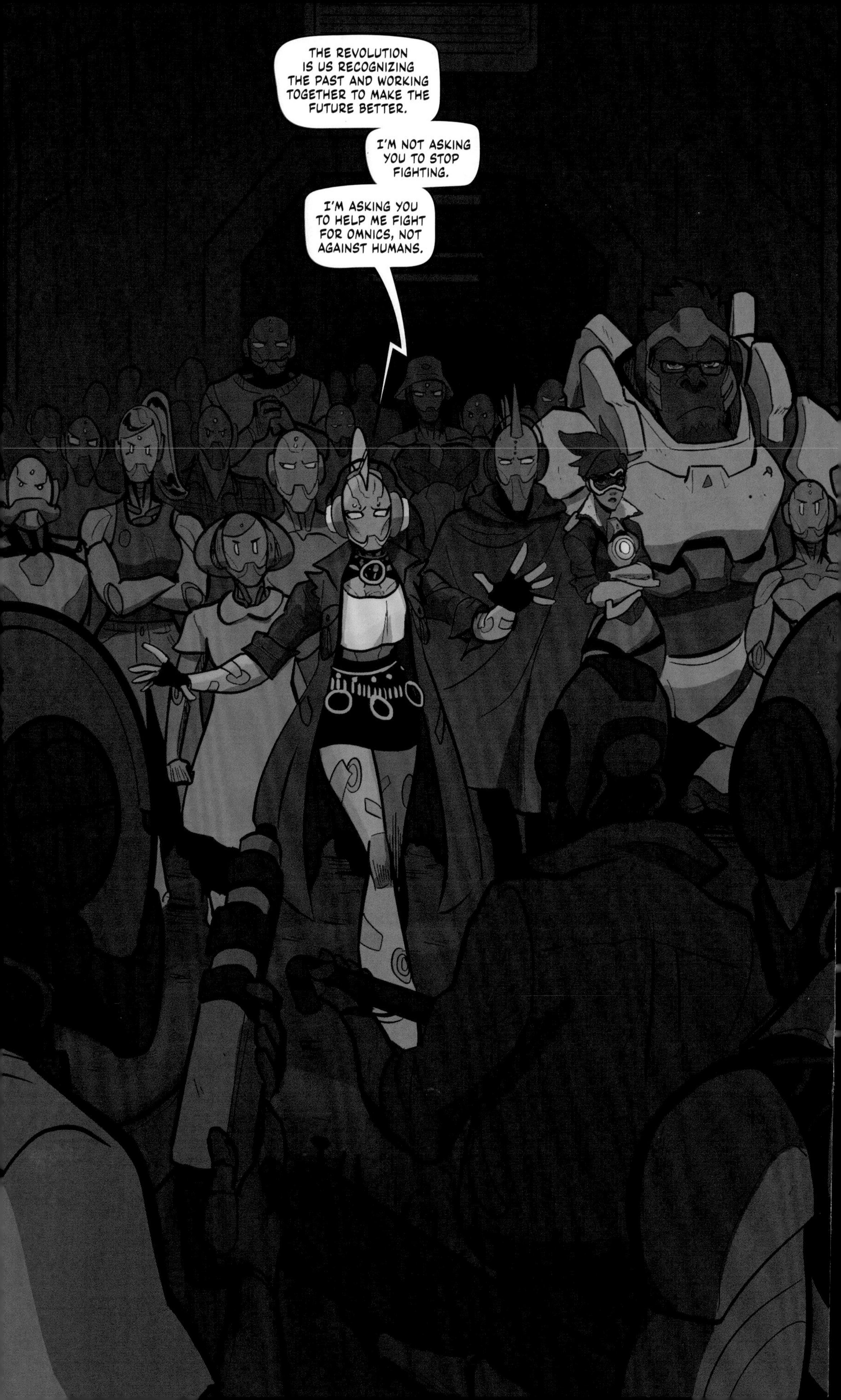
THE REVOLUTION IS US RECOGNIZING THE PAST AND WORKING TOGETHER TO MAKE THE FUTURE BETTER.
I'M NOT ASKING YOU TO STOP FIGHTING.
I'M ASKING YOU TO HELP ME FIGHT FOR OMNICS, NOT AGAINST HUMANS.

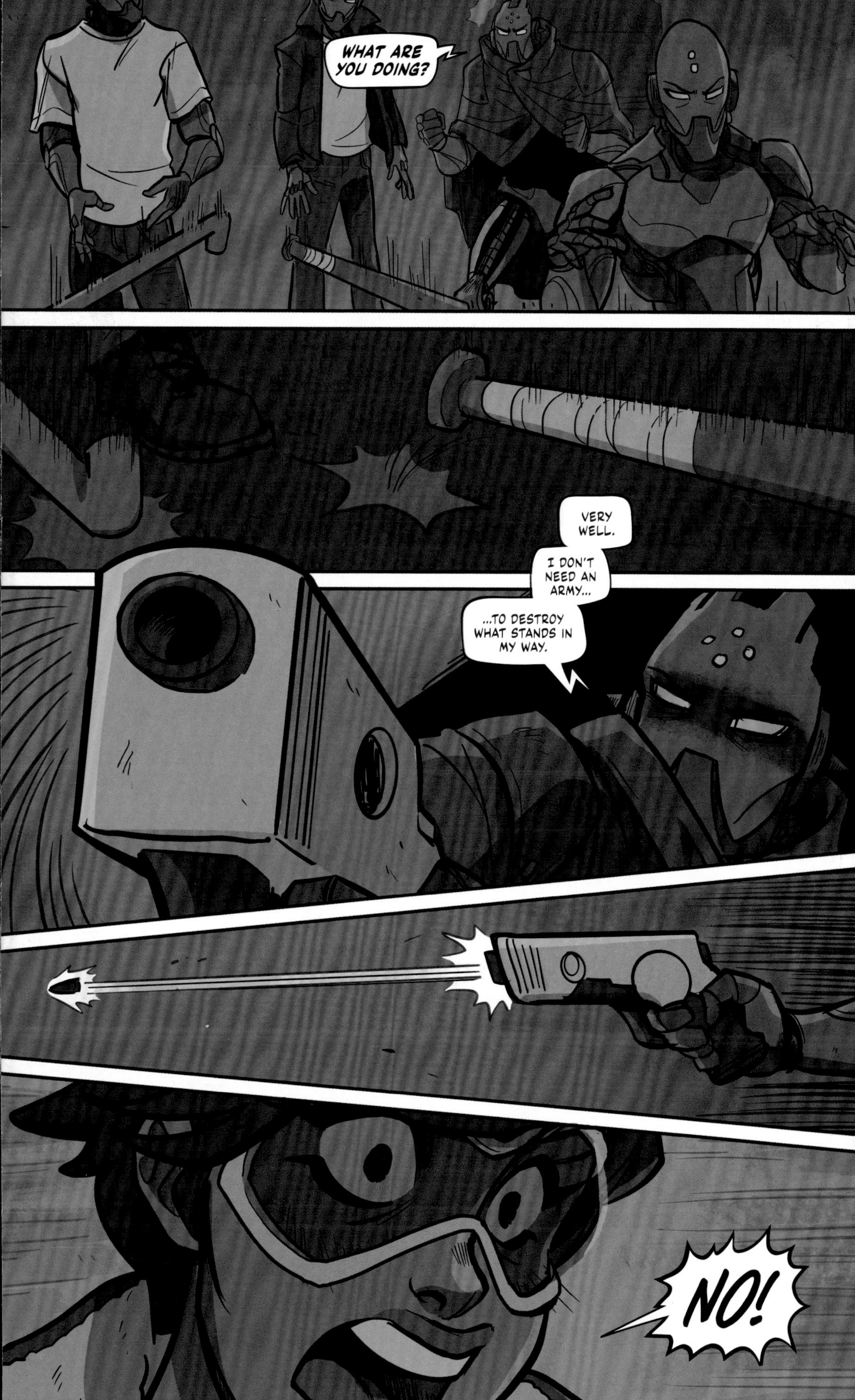
WHAT ARE YOU DOING?
VERY WELL.
I DON'T NEED AN ARMY...
...TO DESTROY WHAT STANDS IN MY WAY.
NO!

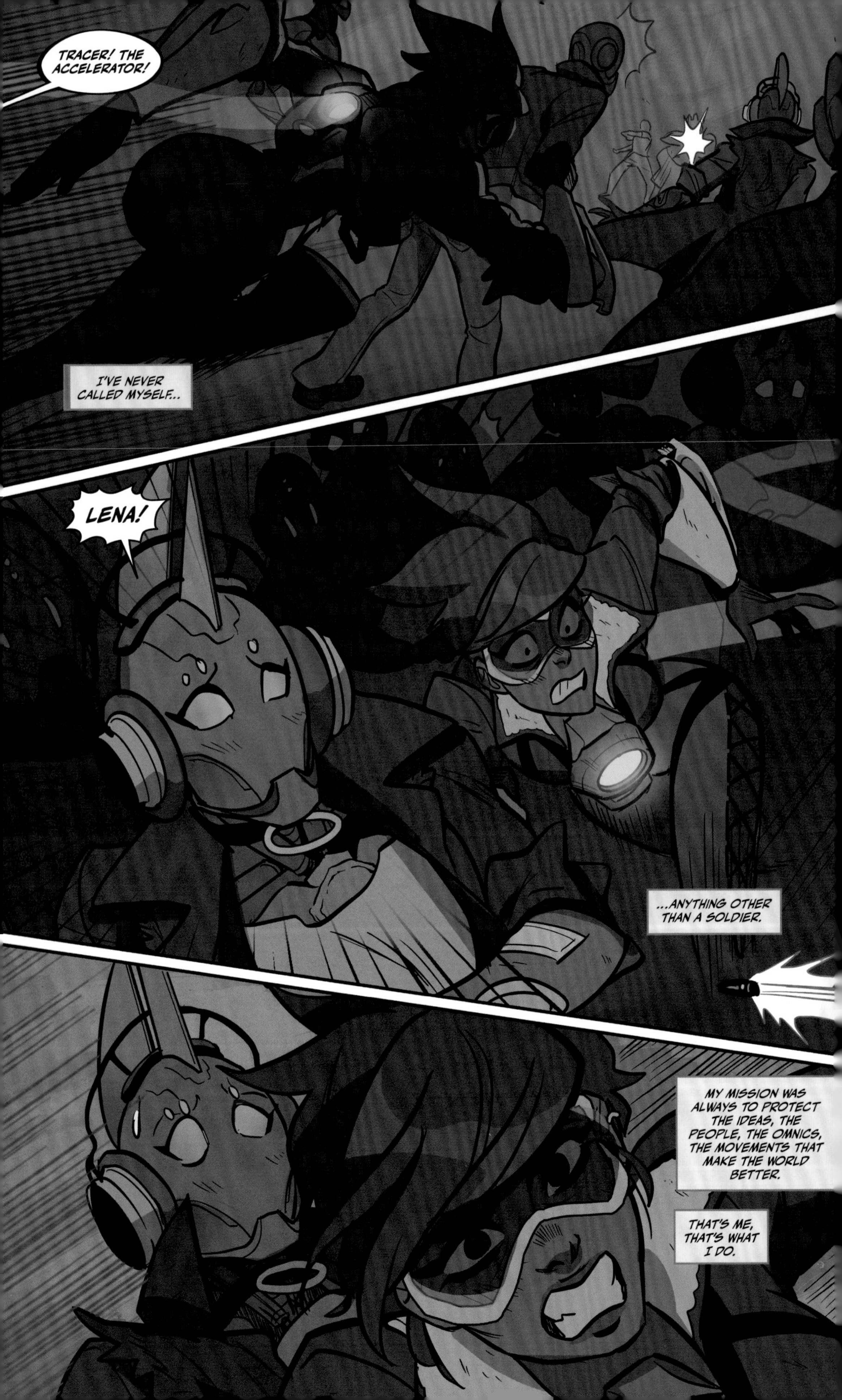
TRACER! THE ACCELERATOR!
I'VE NEVER CALLED MYSELF...
LENA!
...ANYTHING OTHER THAN A SOLDIER.
MY MISSION WAS ALWAYS TO PROTECT THE IDEAS, THE PEOPLE, THE OMNICS, THE MOVEMENTS THAT MAKE THE WORLD BETTER.
THAT'S ME, THAT'S WHAT I DO.

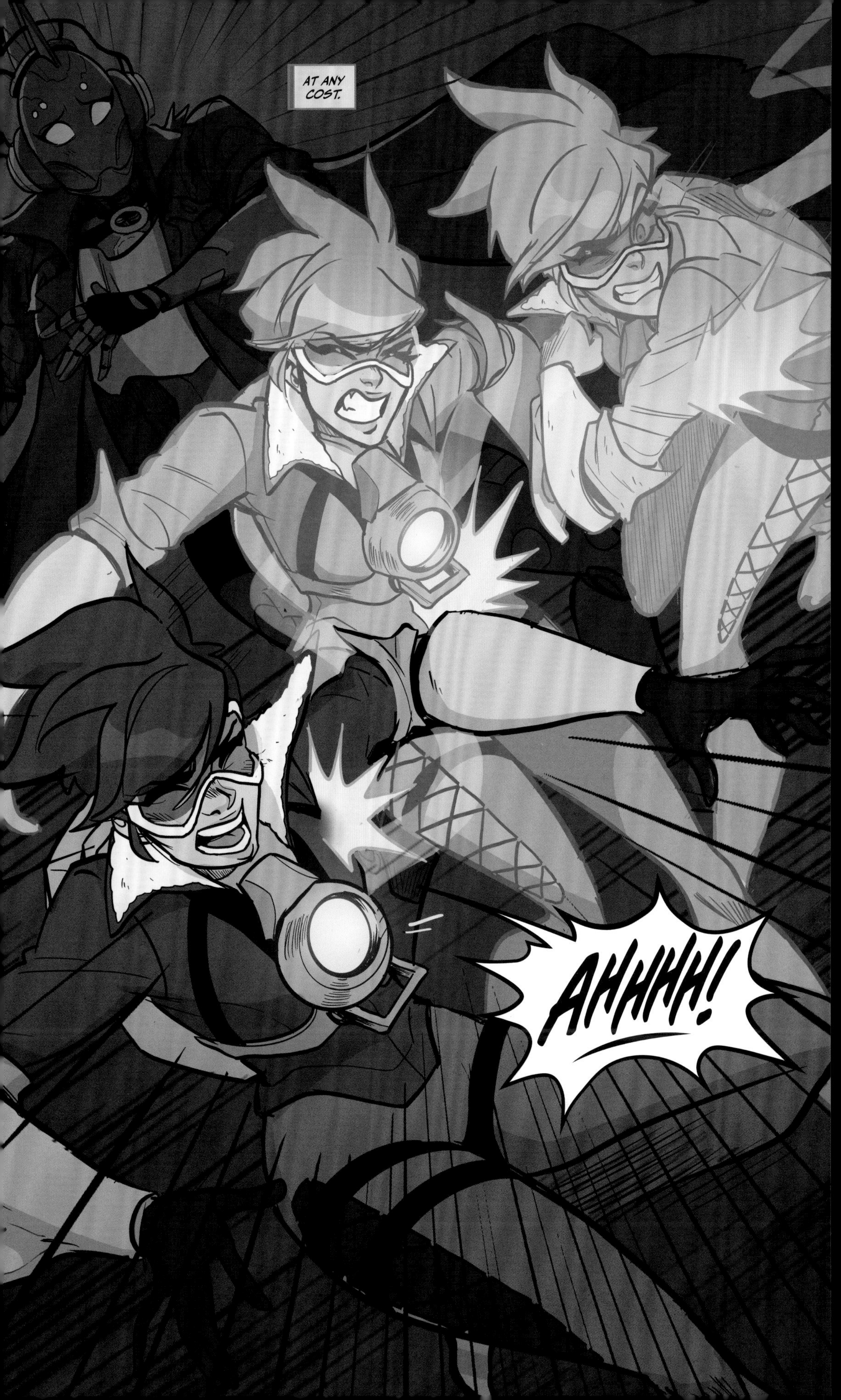

AT ANY COST.
AHHHH!

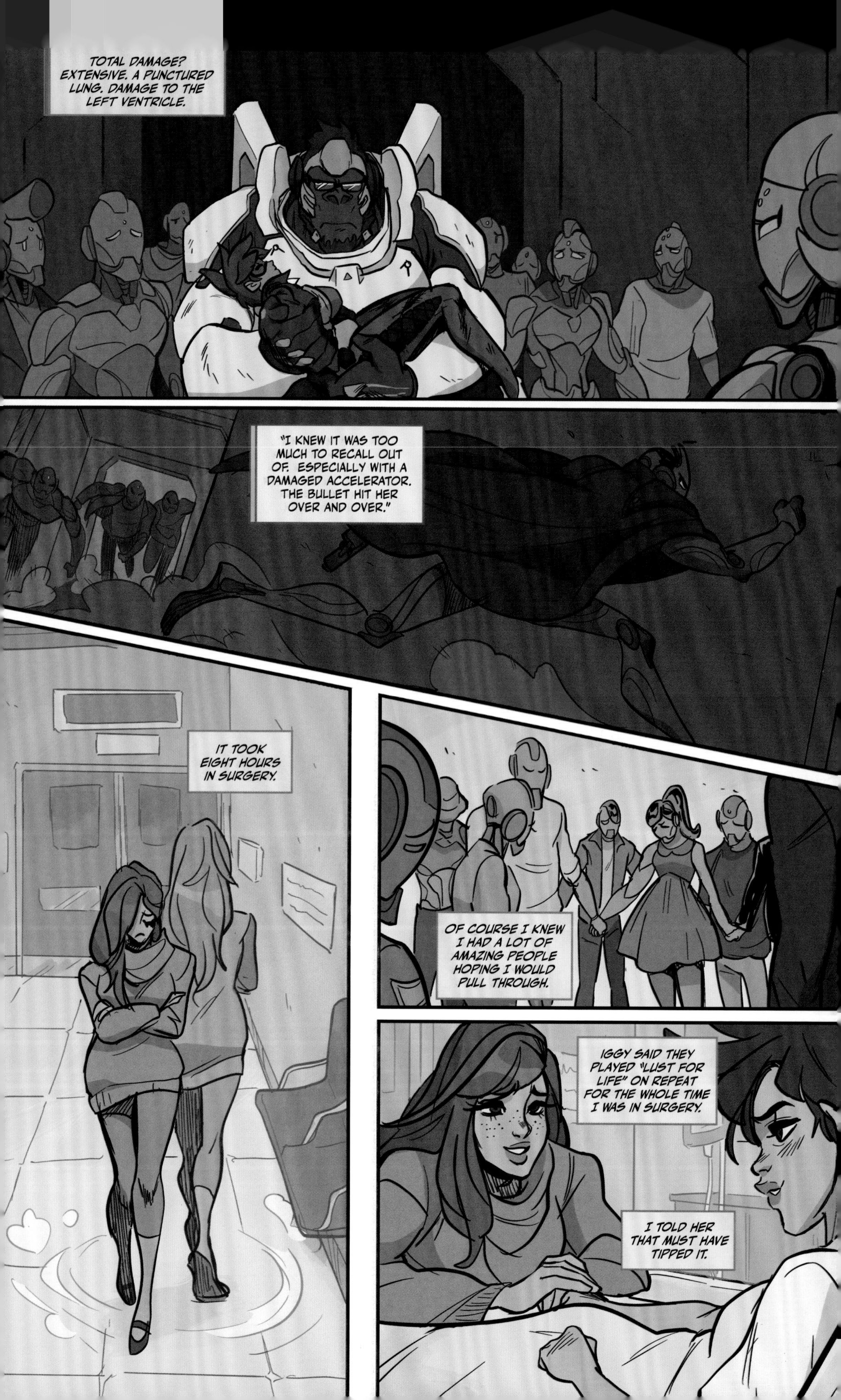
TOTAL DAMAGE? EXTENSIVE. A PUNCTURED LUNG. DAMAGE TO THE LEFT VENTRICLE.
"I KNEW IT WAS TOO MUCH TO RECALL OUT OF. ESPECIALLY WITH A DAMAGED ACCELERATOR. THE BULLET HIT HER OVER AND OVER."
IT TOOK EIGHT HOURS IN SURGERY.
OF COURSE I KNEW I HAD A LOT OF AMAZING PEOPLE HOPING I WOULD PULL THROUGH.
IGGY SAID THEY PLAYED "LUST FOR LIFE" ON REPEAT FOR THE WHOLE TIME I WAS IN SURGERY.
I TOLD HER THAT MUST HAVE TIPPED IT.

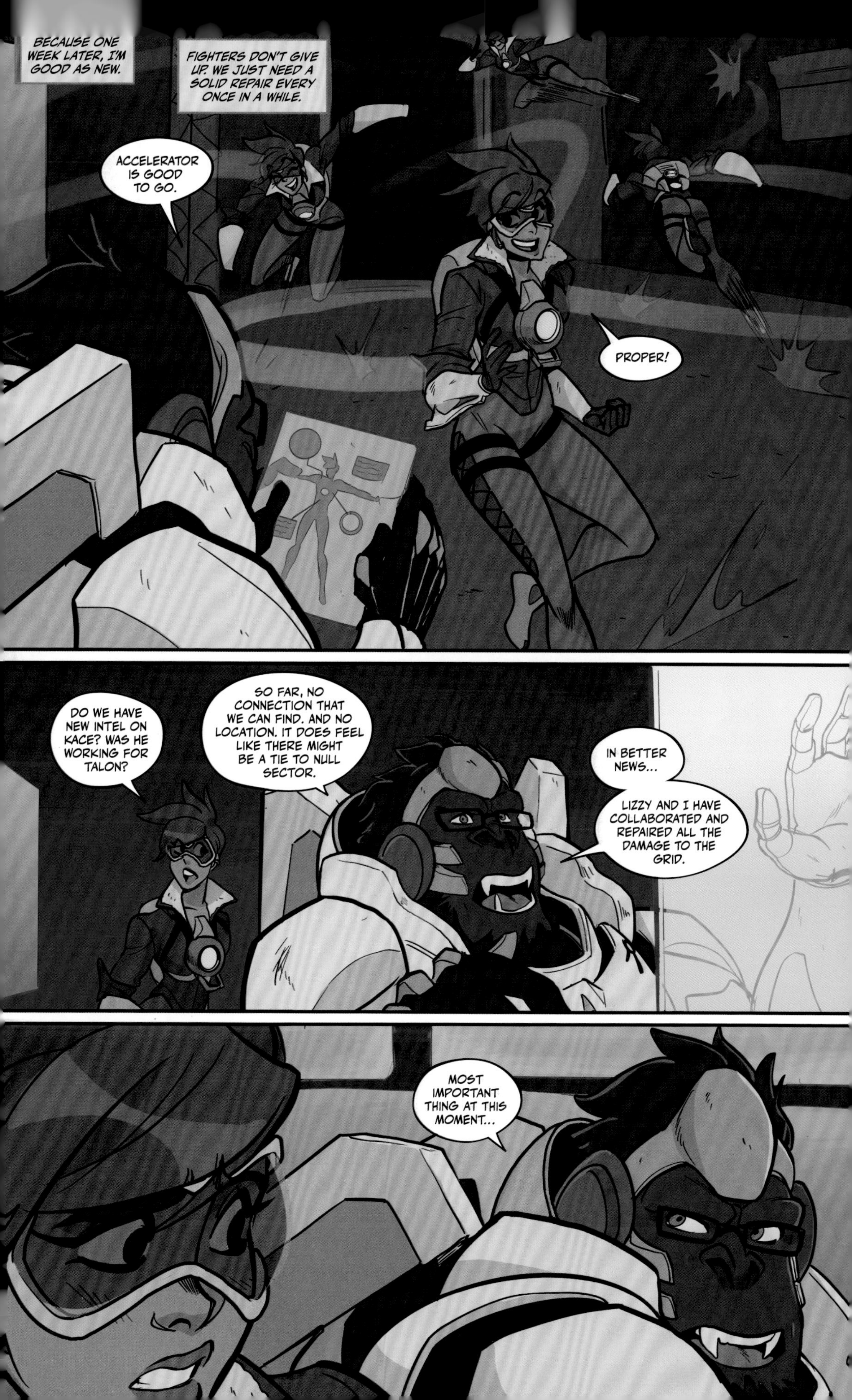
BECAUSE ONE WEEK LATER, I'M GOOD AS NEW.
FIGHTERS DON'T GIVE UP. WE JUST NEED A SOLID REPAIR EVERY ONCE IN A WHILE.
ACCELERATOR IS GOOD TO GO.
PROPER!
DO WE HAVE NEW INTEL ON KACE? WAS HE WORKING FOR TALON?
SO FAR, NO CONNECTION THAT WE CAN FIND. AND NO LOCATION. IT DOES FEEL LIKE THERE MIGHT BE A TIE TO NULL SECTOR.
IN BETTER NEWS...
LIZZY AND I HAVE COLLABORATED AND REPAIRED ALL THE DAMAGE TO THE GRID.
MOST IMPORTANT THING AT THIS MOMENT...

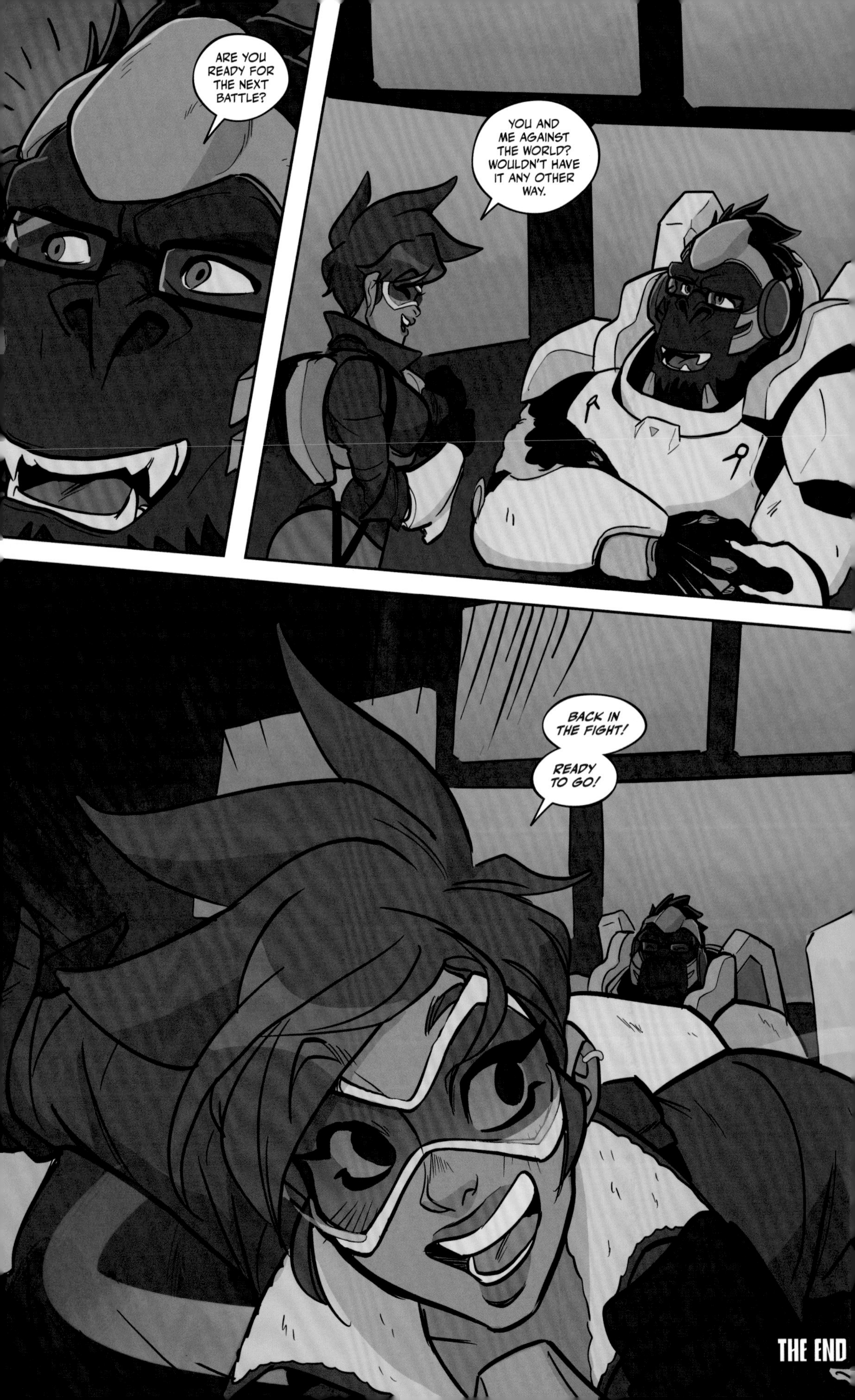
ARE YOU READY FOR THE NEXT BATTLE?
YOU AND ME AGAINST THE WORLD? WOULDN'T HAVE IT ANY OTHER WAY.
BACK IN THE FIGHT!
READY TO GO!
THE END

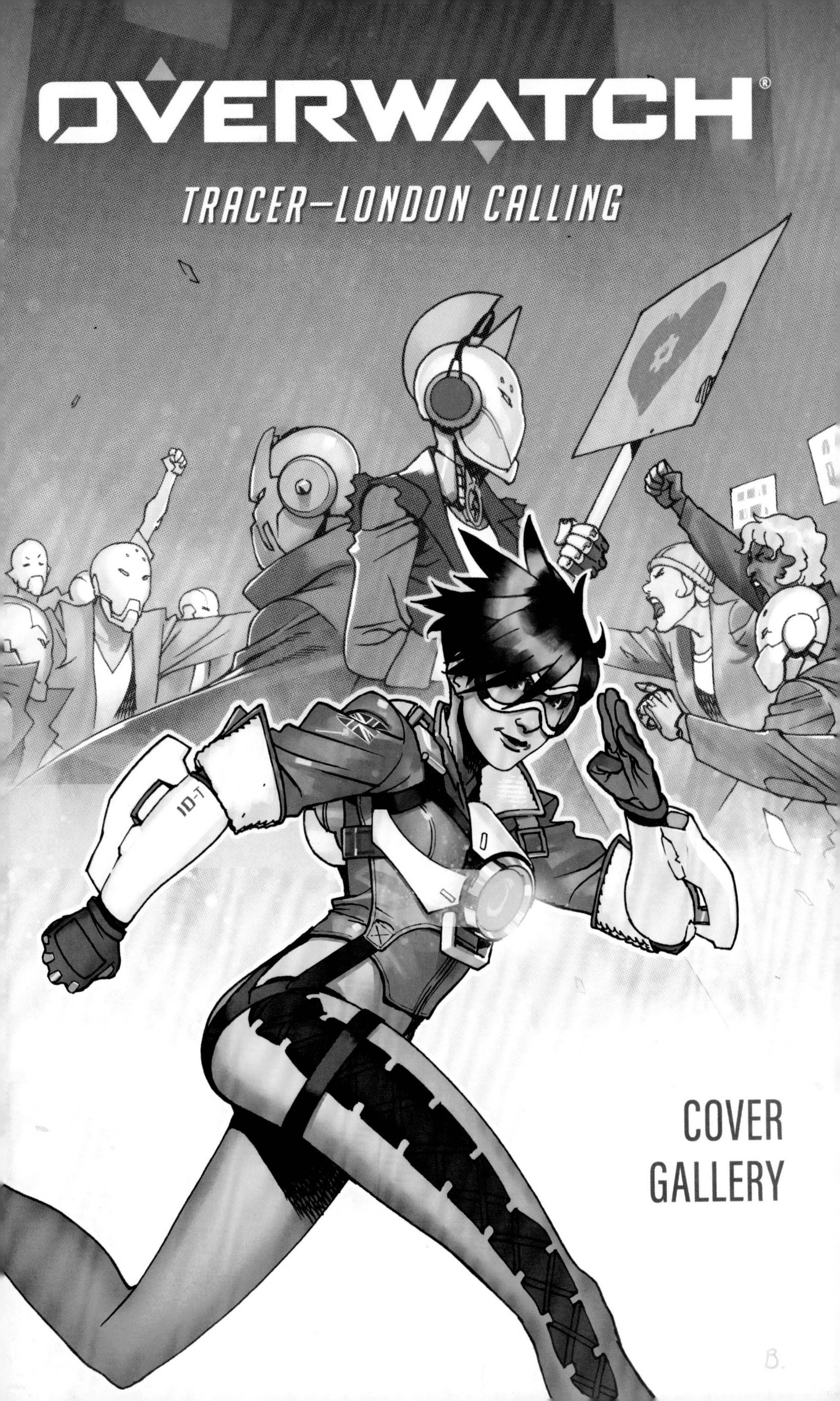
OVERWATCH®
TRACER—LONDON CALLING
COVER
GALLERY

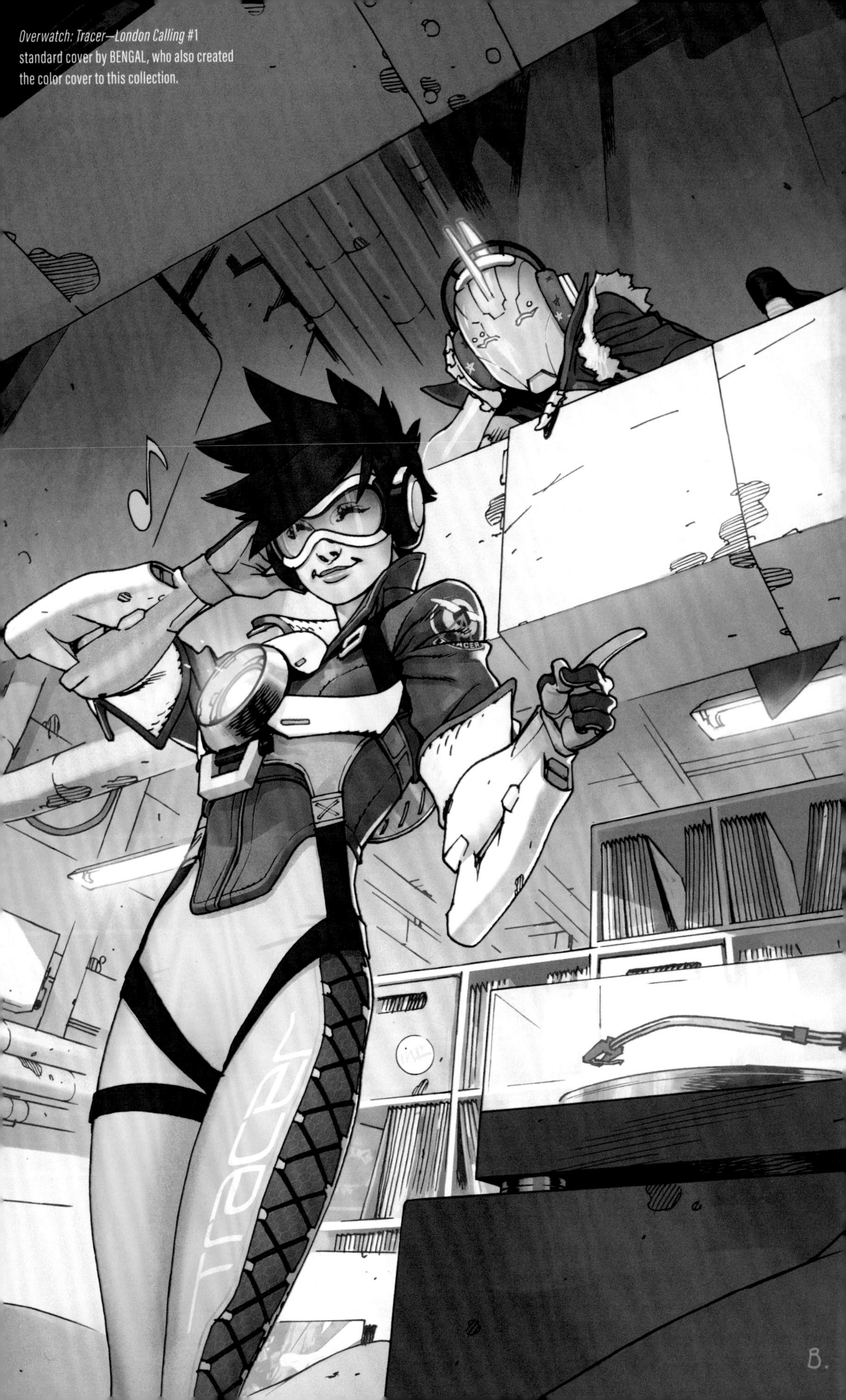
TRACER
Tracer
B.

Overwatch: Tracer—London Calling #1 standard cover by BENGAL, who also created the color cover to this collection.

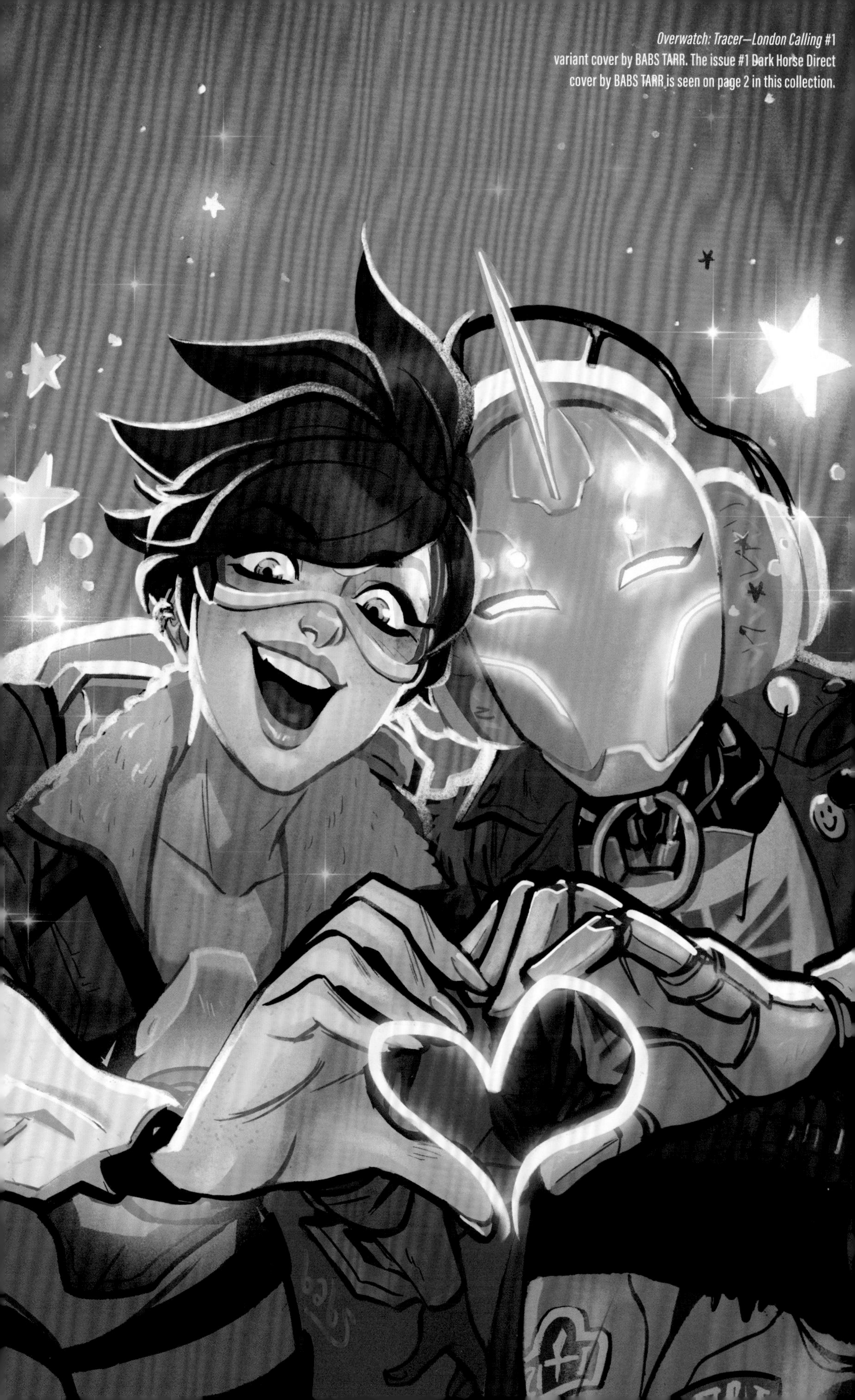

Overwatch: Tracer—London Calling #1 variant cover by BABS TARR. The issue #1 Dark Horse Direct cover by BABS TARR is seen on page 2 in this collection.

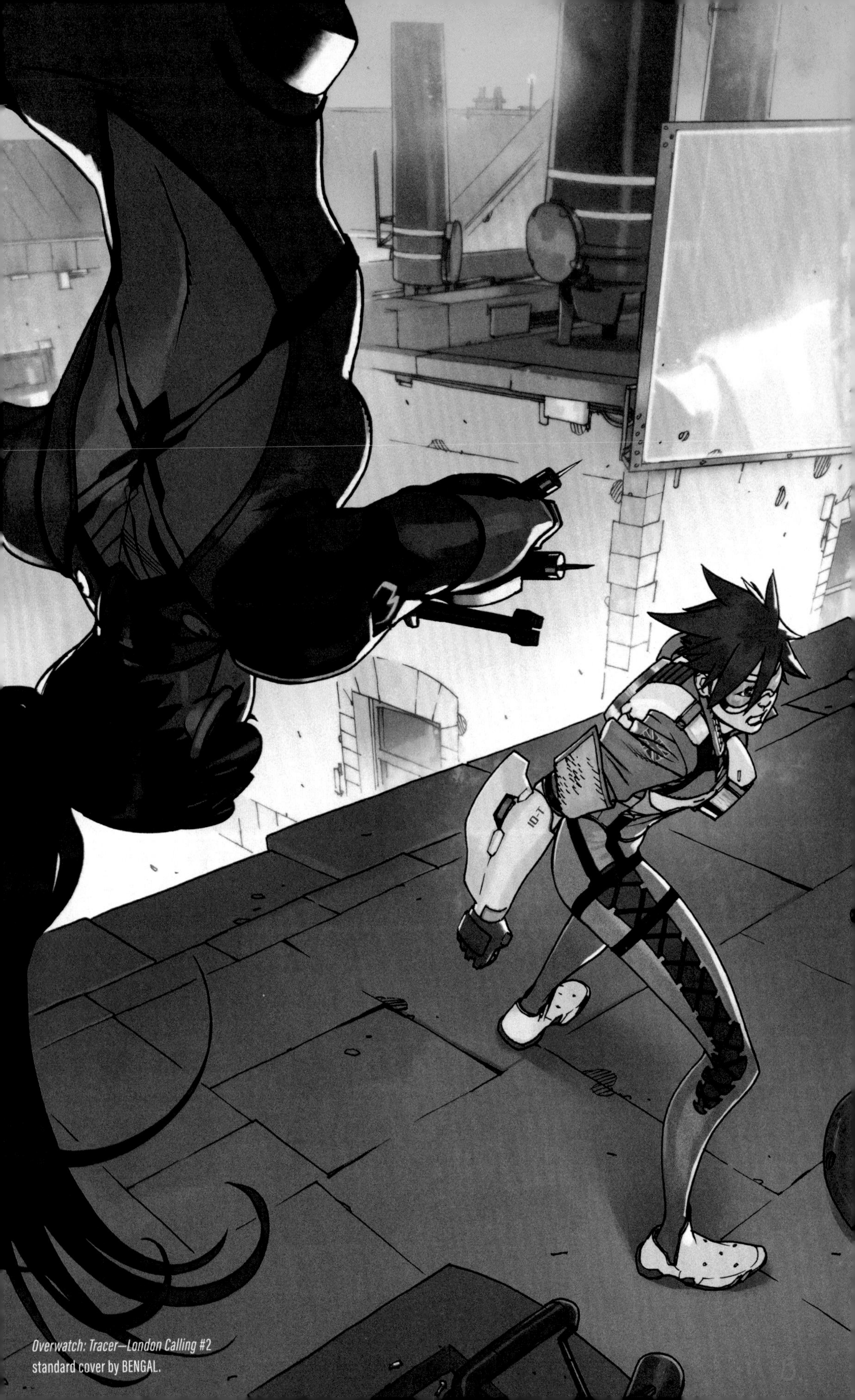
10-T

Overwatch: Tracer—London Calling #2
standard cover by BENGAL.

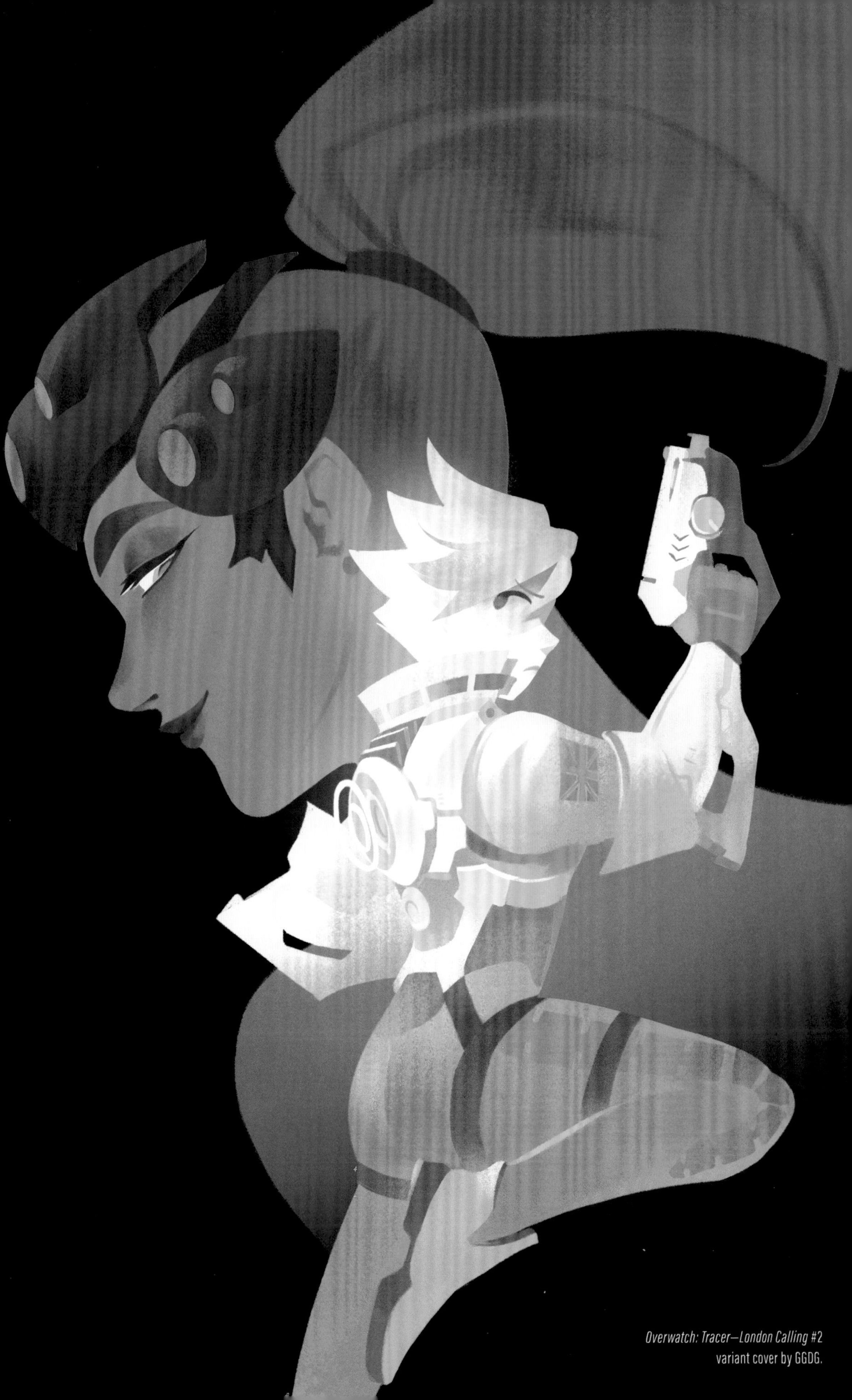

Overwatch: Tracer—London Calling #2
variant cover by GGDG.

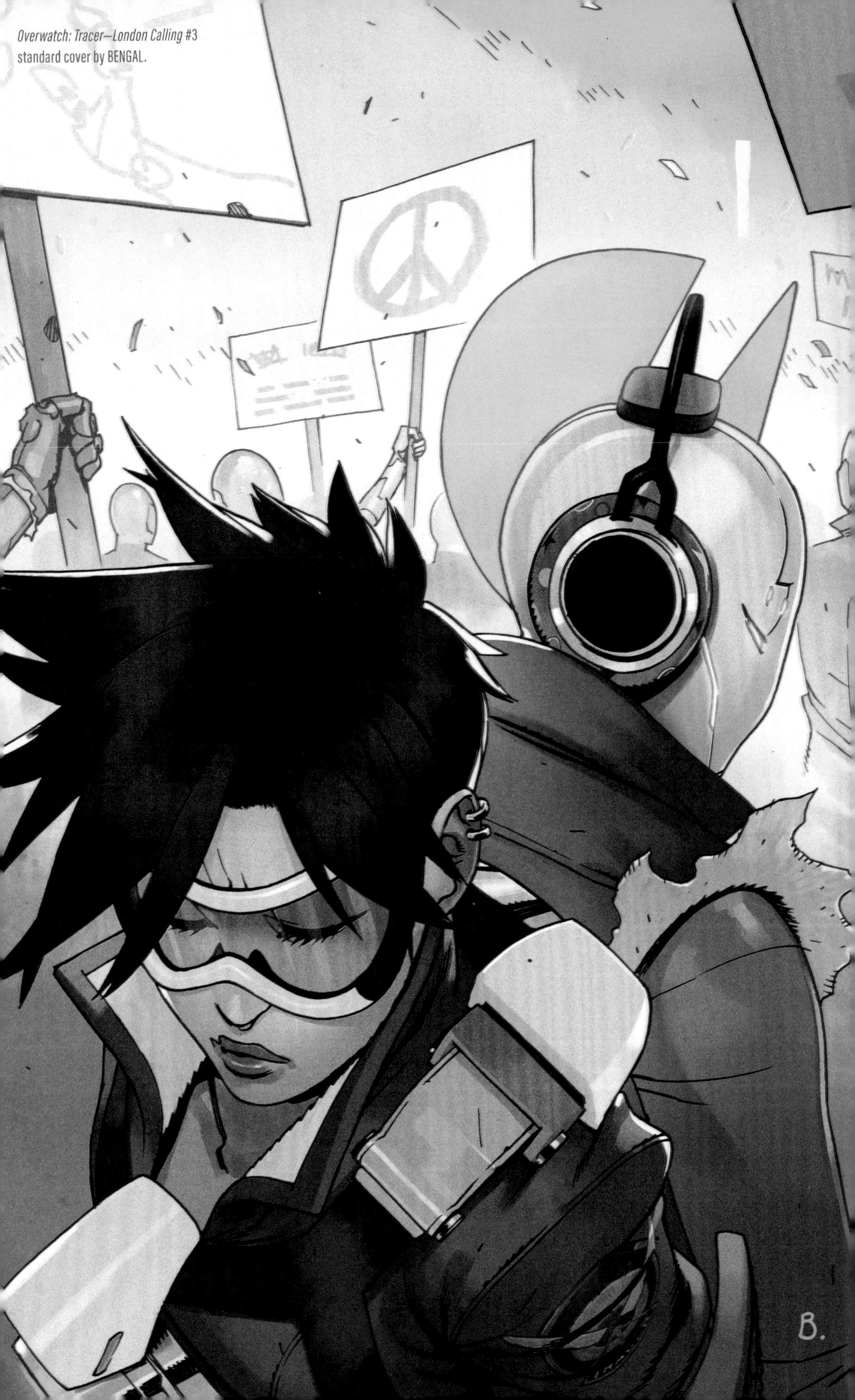
B.

Overwatch: Tracer—London Calling #3
standard cover by BENGAL.

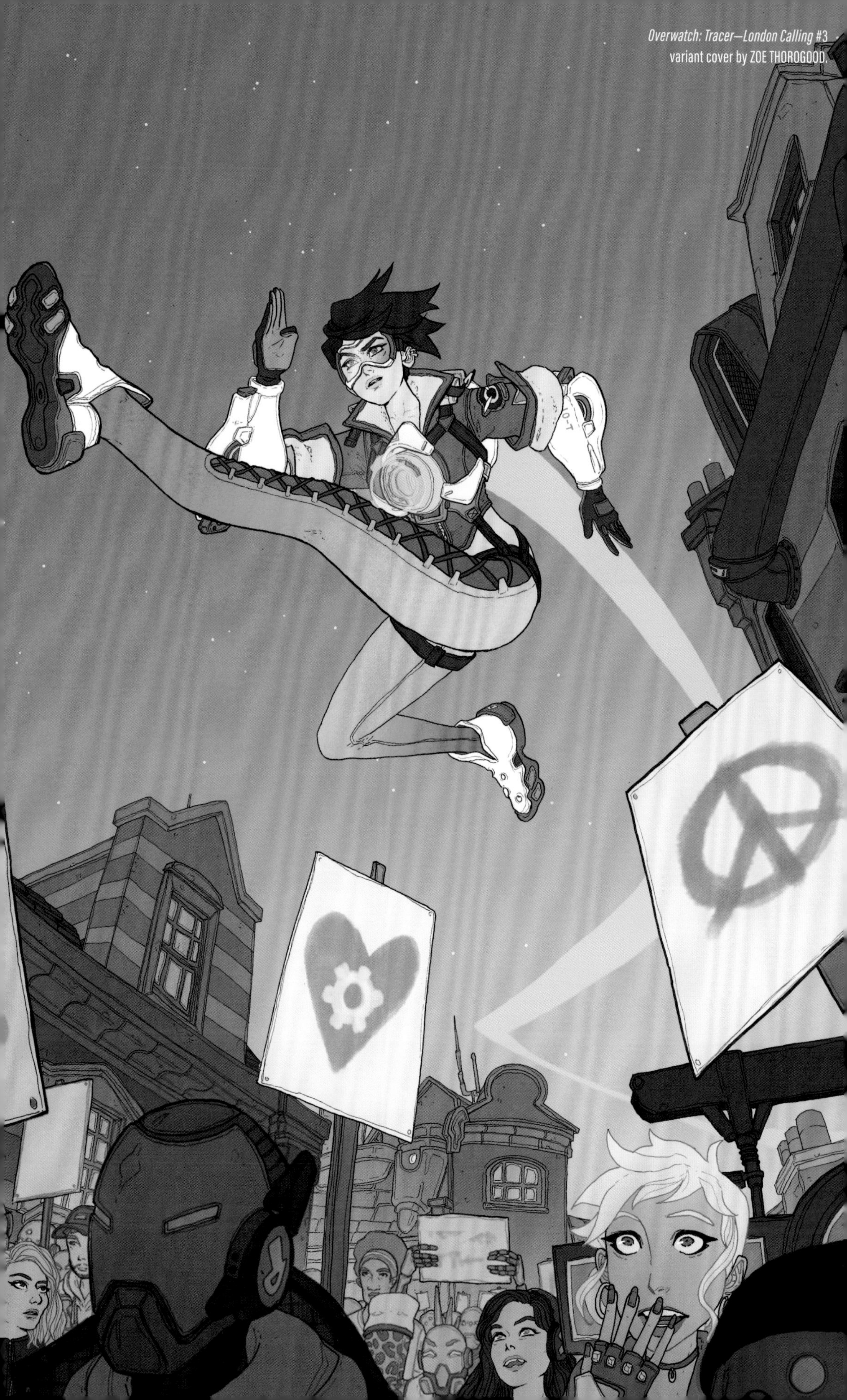

Overwatch: Tracer—London Calling #3
variant cover by ZOE THOROGOOD.

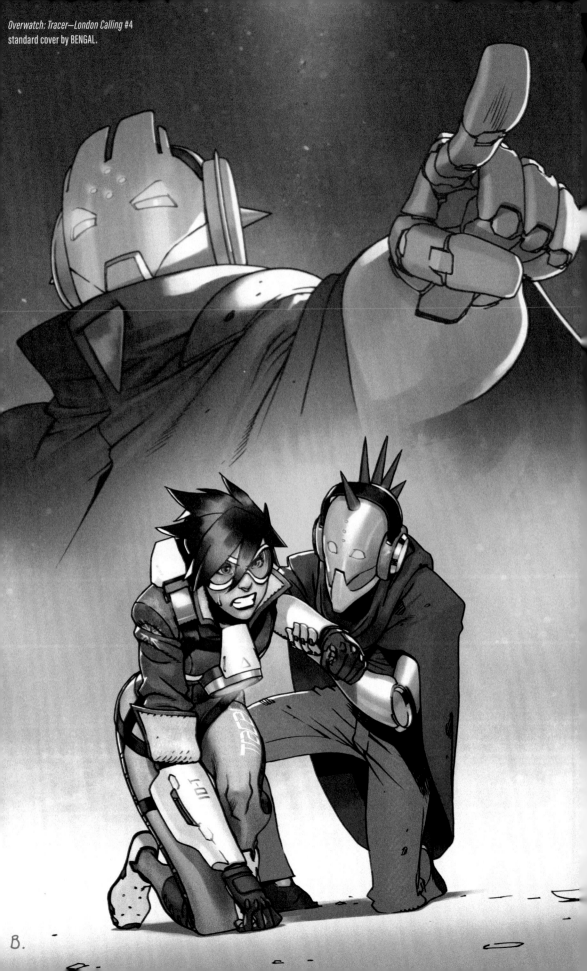

Overwatch: Tracer—London Calling #4
standard cover by BENGAL.

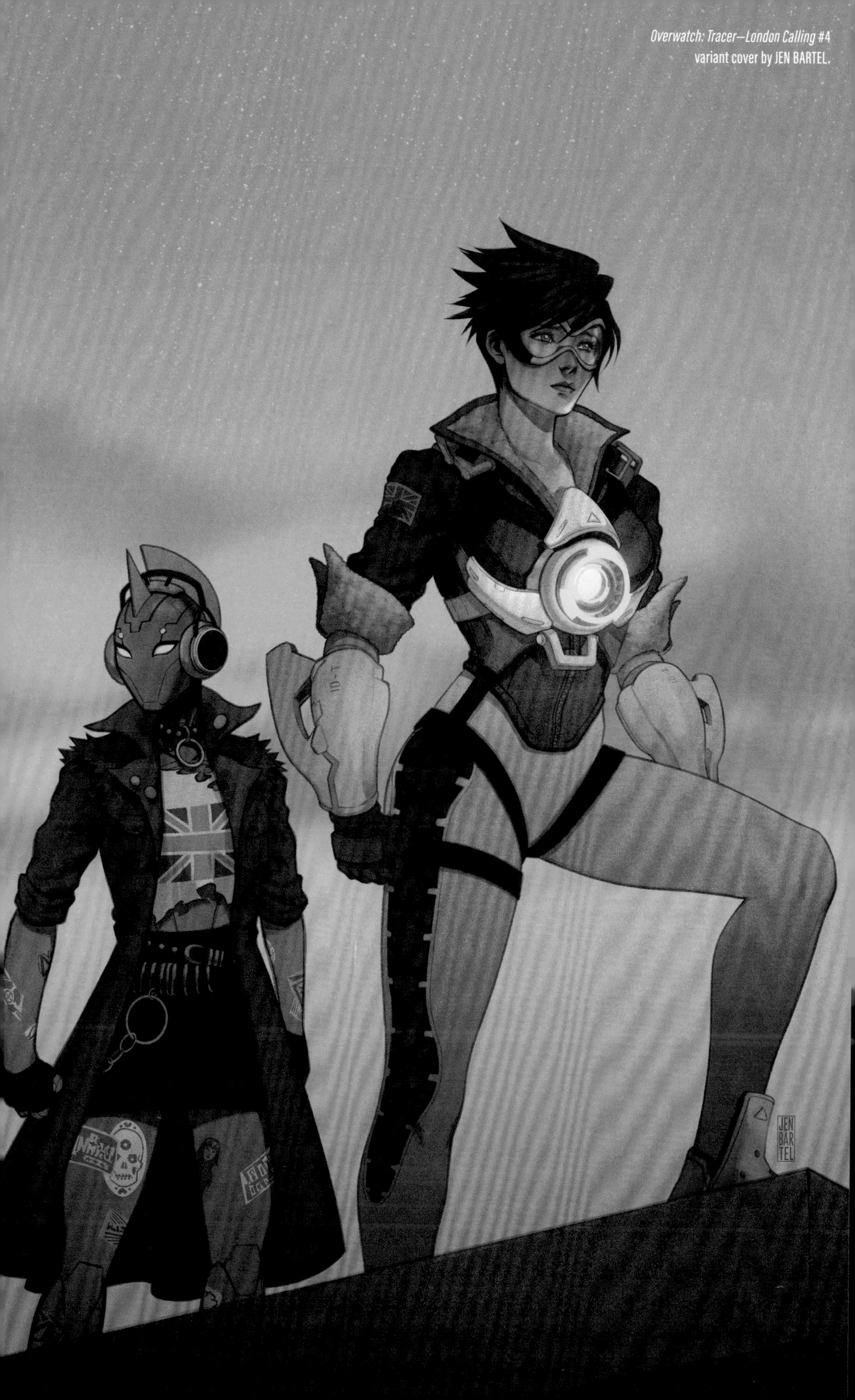
JEN
BAR
TEL

Overwatch: Tracer—London Calling #4
variant cover by JEN BARTEL.

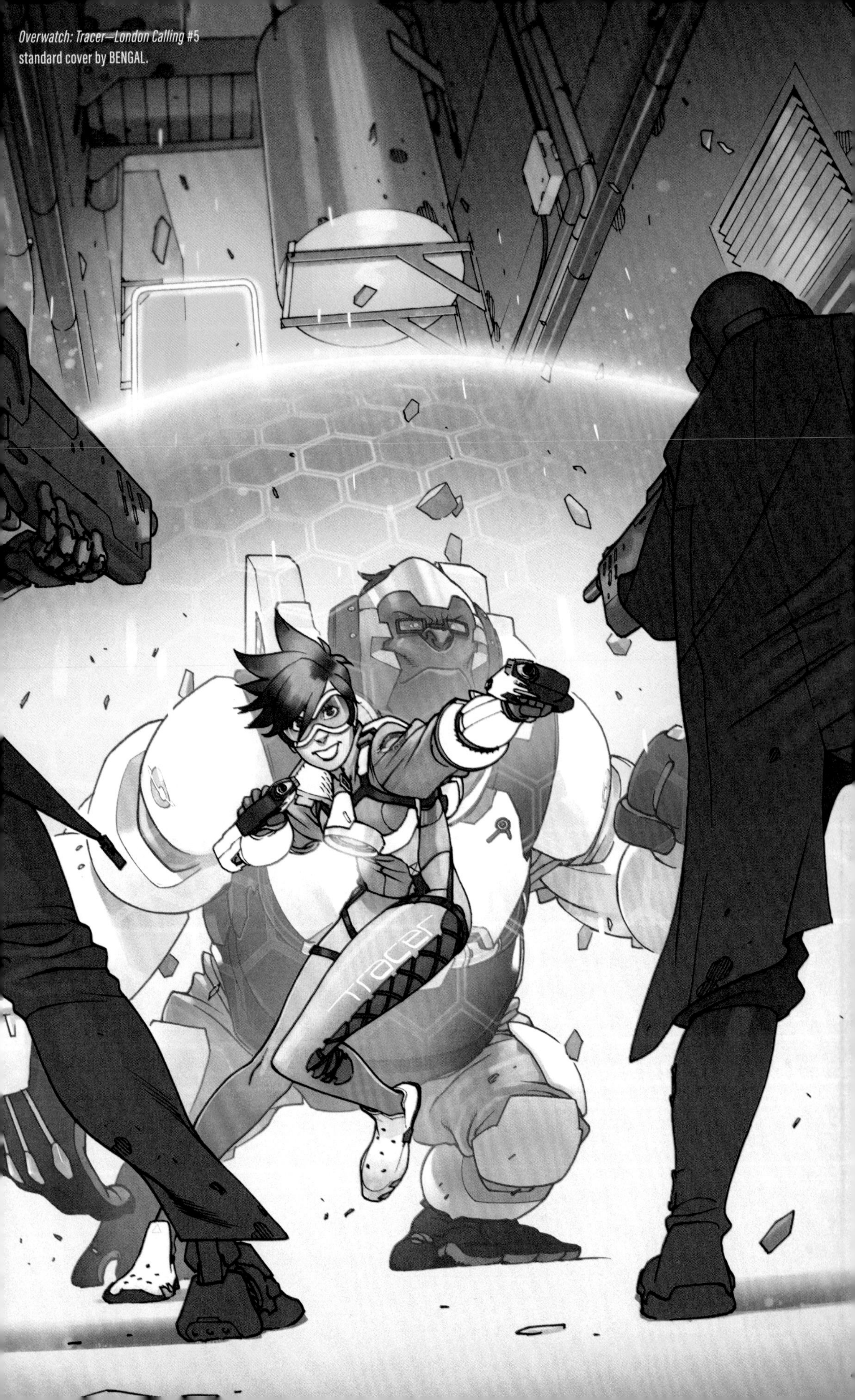
Tracer

Overwatch: Tracer—London Calling #5
standard cover by BENGAL.

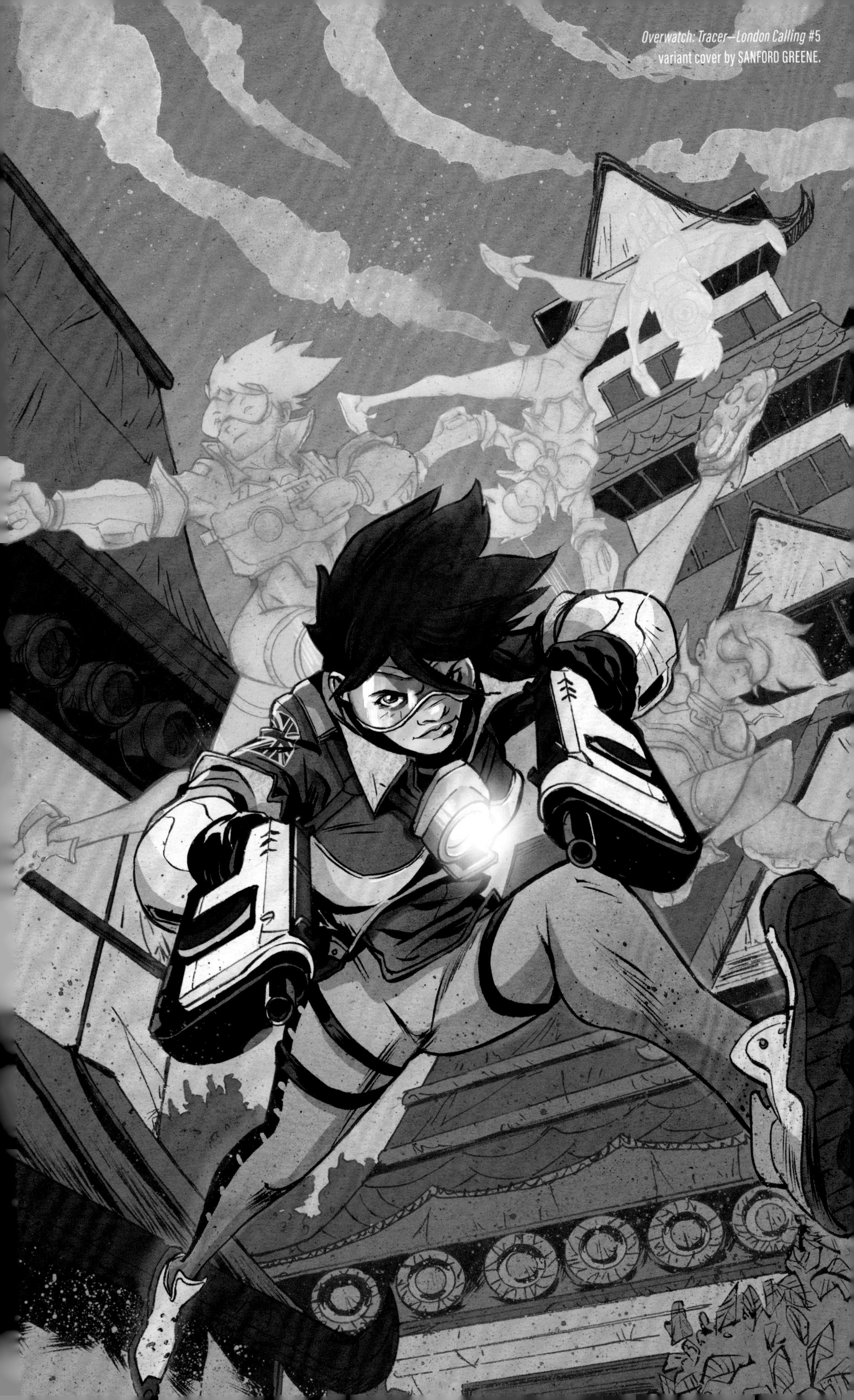

Overwatch: Tracer—London Calling #5 variant cover by SANFORD GREENE.

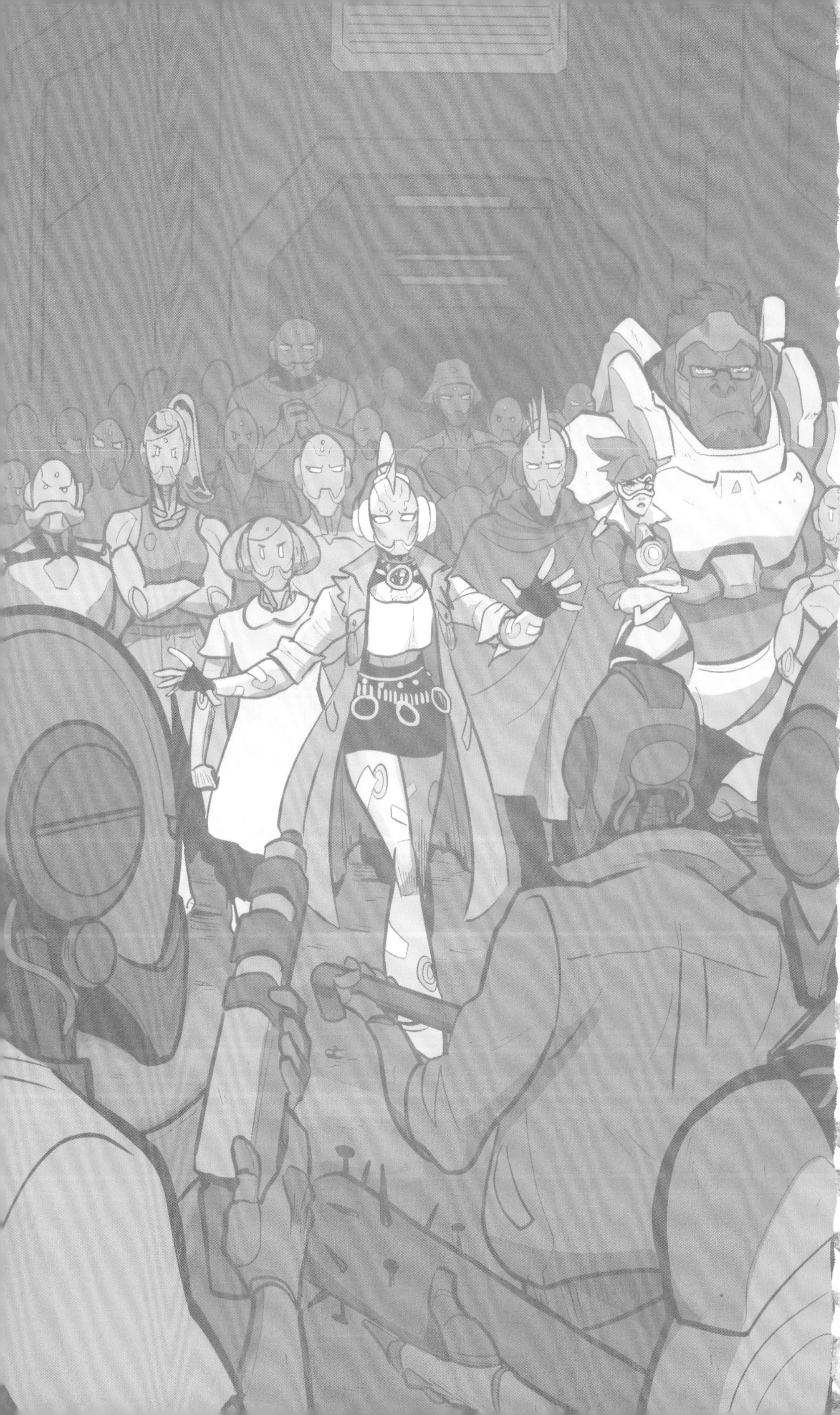